I0812835

IMAGES
of America

CUYAHOGA FALLS
OHIO

IMAGES
of America

CUYAHOGA FALLS
OHIO

Marilyn and Scott Seguin

ARCADIA
PUBLISHING

ISBN 978-0-7385-0721-7

Published by Arcadia Publishing
Charleston, South Carolina

Printed in the United States of America

Library of Congress Catalog Card Number: 00-103151

For all general information contact Arcadia Publishing:
Telephone 843-853-2070
Fax 843-853-0044
E-mail sales@arcadiapublishing.com
For customer service and orders:
Toll-Free 1-888-313-2665

Visit us on the Internet at www.arcadiapublishing.com

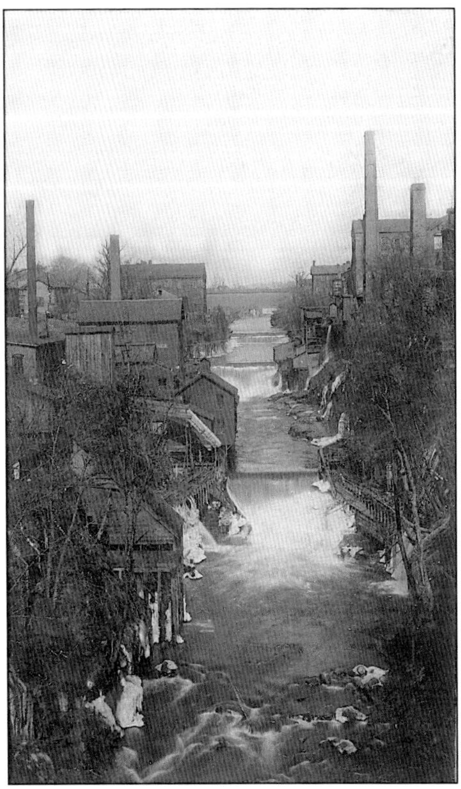

"It is hoped . . . that this magnificent stream will be vocal with the hum of busy wheels, where for many ages have been heard only the song of the waters . . ." Thomas Fairchild, speaking of the Cuyahoga River in a centennial address given in Cuyahoga Falls on July 4, 1876.

Contents

ACKNOWLEDGMENTS

This book is not a definitive history of Cuyahoga Falls, but rather a showcase of the image collection of the Cuyahoga Falls Historical Society. The contents are arranged topically by chapter and somewhat chronologically within each chapter. Spellings of names of people seen in the composites are taken from the backs of the images.

We would not have been able to put this book together without the enthusiastic cooperation of Cuyahoga Falls Historical Society museum curator, Liz Cross, and her assistants Lou Atleson, Babette Robinson, and Alice Royer. The museum is located at 2751 Hudson Drive and is open every Monday from 9:30 A.M. to 12:30 P.M. Thanks also to the Historical Society Board and its trustees for their support and encouragement of this project from the very beginning: Bob Kerr, Dick Horn, Mim Peters, Alma Canfield, Dave Brown, Marion Casto, John Bender, Jim Mortenson, and Eileen Tench..

We are grateful to the staff of Taylor Memorial Public Library for their research assistance; special thanks to Virginia Bloetscher, archivist of the local history room (now retired), and noted local history author. Sincere appreciation to Carl Ehmann, photographer and local historian, who provided copies of images as well as many details about the history of our town. For providing information and/or photographs about days past, we also thank Mary Caruso Sullivan, Pete Mellinger, Earl and Alice Royer, and Dale Platt. Any inaccuracies are our own. Finally, we wish to thank Roland Seguin and Katy Seguin for their support during this project.

Marilyn Weymouth Seguin and Scott Seguin
Cuyahoga Falls, 2000

INTRODUCTION

Cuyahoga Falls was first settled in 1812 on land carved out of four townships—Stow, Northhampton, Tallmadge and Portage. Names of early settlers included Newberry, Wetmore, Sill, Richardson, and Stow. The village of Cuyahoga Falls began as a small settlement about 2 miles square. The village was originally named Manchester, but since there were many other towns of the same name, early citizens realized that they needed their own identity. The Cuyahoga River and its great falls were the lifeblood of the village, so the new name given to the town was Cuyahoga Falls. By 1851, when new township lines were drawn, Cuyahoga Falls was able to manage its own affairs.

The steady growth of the town can be largely attributed to the magnificent river that is its namesake. The rapid descent of the river was a great asset for the early inhabitants of the village. As early as 1837, three dams converted the water force of the Cuyahoga River into power. Soon, the hum of busy wheels could be heard along the river banks as the water provided a steady source of power to the many industries built there. The force generated by the falling of the river was estimated at 3,460 horsepower; the natural power that this river generated made Cuyahoga Falls one of the fastest growing cities in the United States. By 1840, Cuyahoga Falls had a greater variety of manufacturing plants than any other settlement in Ohio.

The river also provided early citizens of Cuyahoga Falls with a place for recreation. Parks such as High Bridge Glens, and Riverview, with their many adventurous hiking trails, picnic grounds, and dance pavilions, made Cuyahoga Falls one of the most popular cities for people to visit during the late 1800s and early 1900s. Tourists came in droves to enjoy the song of the waters of the Cuyahoga River.

The Cuyahoga ("crooked river") was in part bent by the early citizens of Cuyahoga Falls to their own ends. They dammed it to harness water power for industry, sculpted its shores to provide hiking trails for recreation, leveled it to form a canal, and tried to siphon off its power to build a great industrial center. In Cuyahoga Falls today, its power is no longer harnessed, and most of the last vestiges of High Bridge Glens and Riverview Parks were destroyed in the 1913 flood. However, the citizens of Cuyahoga Falls did not turn their backs on the crooked river. Today the Cuyahoga River is the centerpiece of downtown urban renewal, where citizens gather for events at Riverfront Centre. Tourists and travelers enjoy the hiking trails at Gorge Park and the Glens. The Cuyahoga River has come full circle as "the song of the waters" replaces the "hum of busy wheels."

Although the river was an important stimulus in the growth of Cuyahoga Falls, it would not have been possible without the work of its people. Citizens were responsible for the organization of schools, churches, and police and fire departments. Through the work of residents and public servants, Cuyahoga Falls remains a thriving community today, and promises an even brighter future.

One

The Song of the Waters

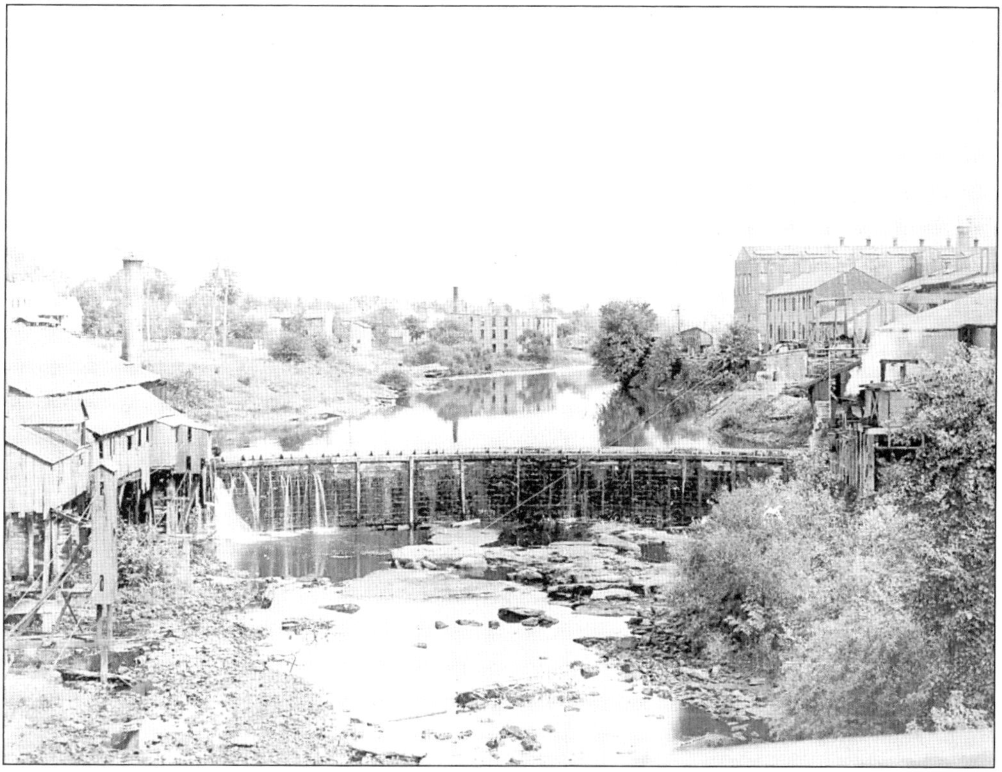

The native Americans called the area Coppacaw, which meant "shedding tears." Later, the rapid descent of the Cuyahoga River from Akron to Cleveland became the source of continuous power for industries on both sides of the river in Cuyahoga Falls. The city is more than 400 feet above Lake Erie, and the falls extend for about 2 miles, making a descent of about 220 feet. In the nineteenth century, some predicted that Cuyahoga Falls was destined to be to the West what Lowell, Massachusetts was to the East. In 1830, Henry Newberry ran an ad in newspapers in the East attempting to lure industrialists to the region. The ad copy claimed ". . . settlers [of Cuyahoga Falls] will at once enjoy the advantages of schools, and as good a society as is to be found in the country. . ." By 1840, Cuyahoga Falls had a great diversity of manufacturing facilities—more than any other Ohio settlement.

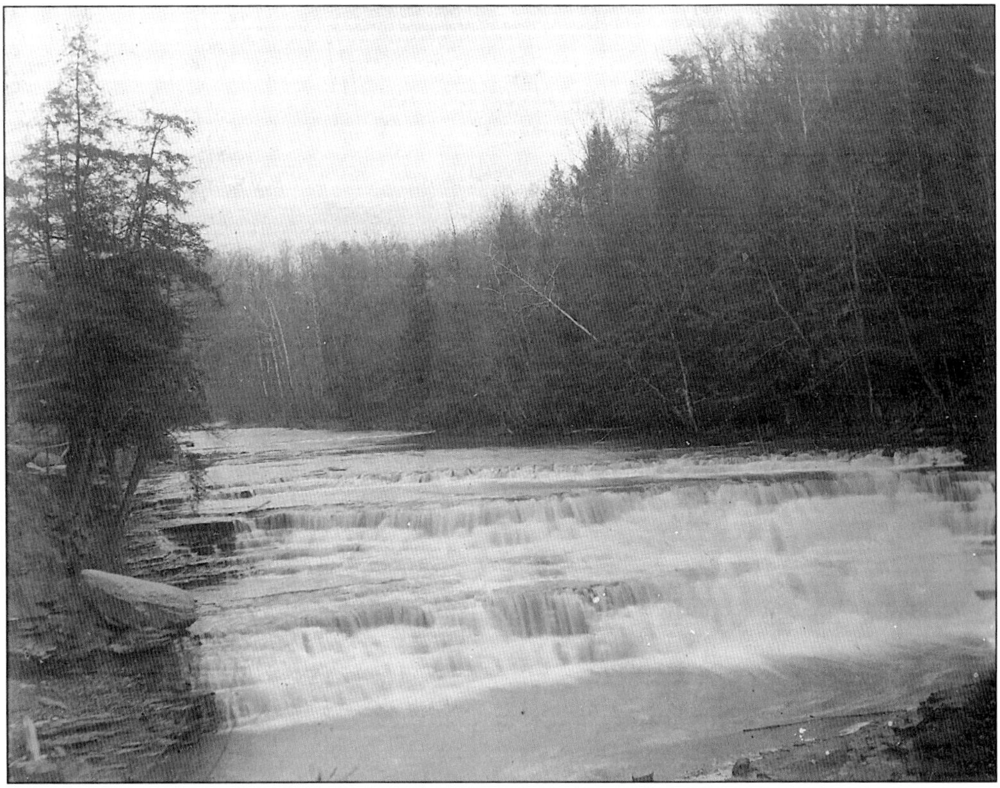

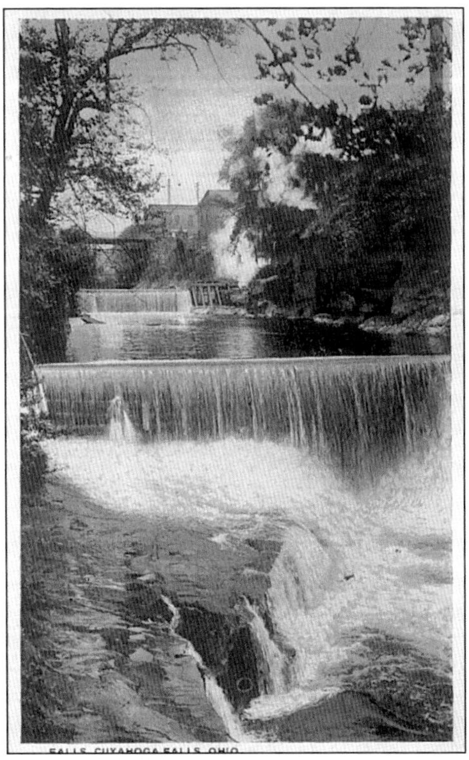

Cuyahoga Falls was named for the many waterfalls that descend through the region. Originally, the village was named Manchester; however, as there were already so many towns with this name in the area, the postmaster general requested that the name be changed. The Ohio Edison dam now covers the waterfalls in this picture.

In the nineteenth century, several dams were constructed on the Cuyahoga River to provide power for industry. Kelsey and Wilcox constructed the first dam in 1812 at the present site of Bailey Road. In 1825, William Wetmore constructed a dam north of the Portage Street Bridge, which flooded the old dam; thus the town began to expand towards the south.

In 1880, L.W. Loomis and Harvey Parks developed a portion of the river gorge known as "the glens" into a recreational park called High Bridge Glens. At the height of the park's popularity, trolleys brought 60 loads of tourists to Cuyahoga Falls daily to enjoy the park's natural beauty and the entertainment provided.

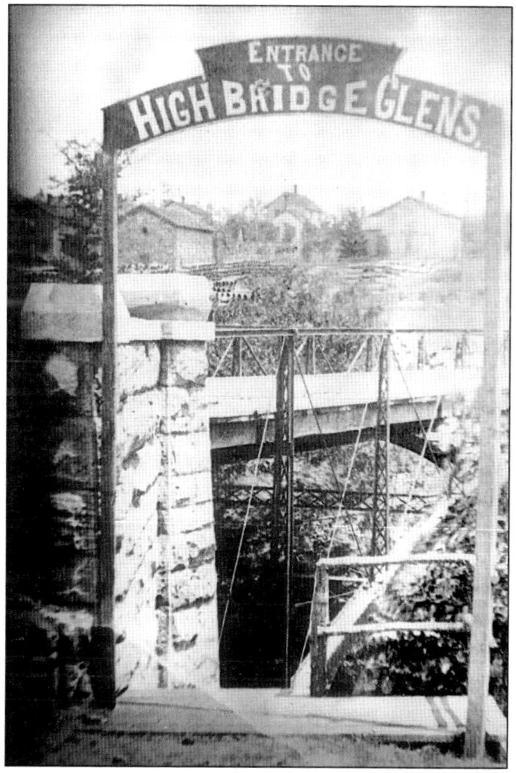

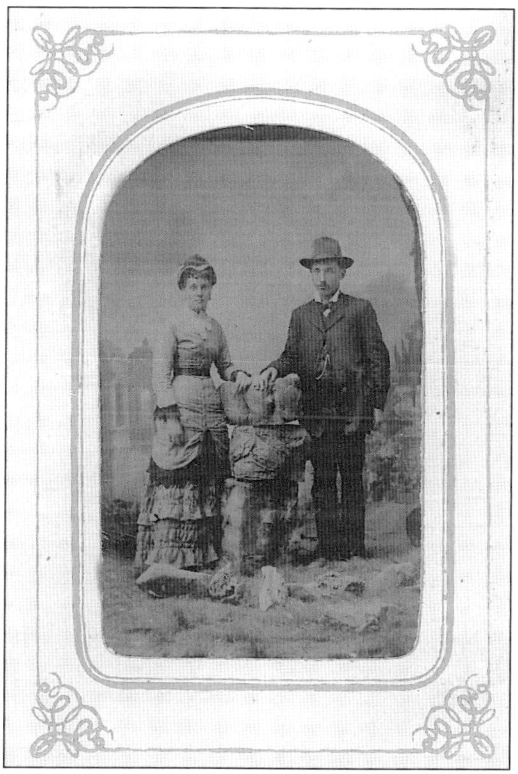

Visitors to the High Bridge Glens could enjoy the natural beauty of the Cuyahoga River gorge by hiking along the trails, or they could enjoy the croquet fields, dance hall, and skating rink. The park also featured a restaurant, natural caves for exploration, and a thrilling new ride called a roller coaster. This photo was taken in 1882 as a souvenir of the couple's visit to High Bridge Glens.

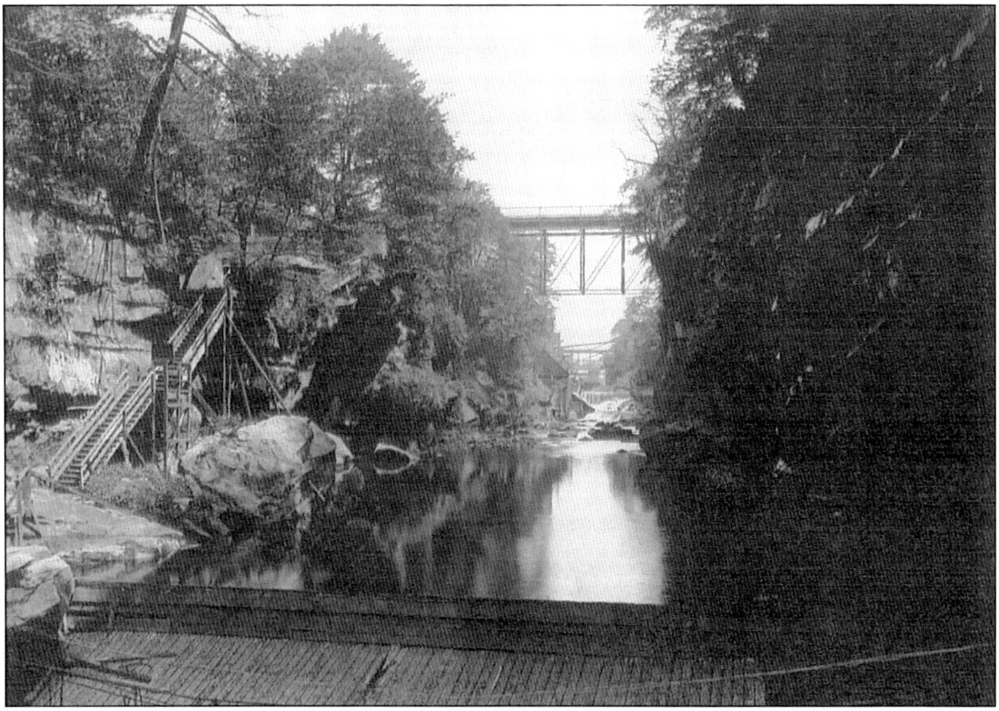

Many of the park's visitors strolled over the swinging suspension bridge to view the river scenery. In this photo, the Prospect Street bridge can be seen in the distance.

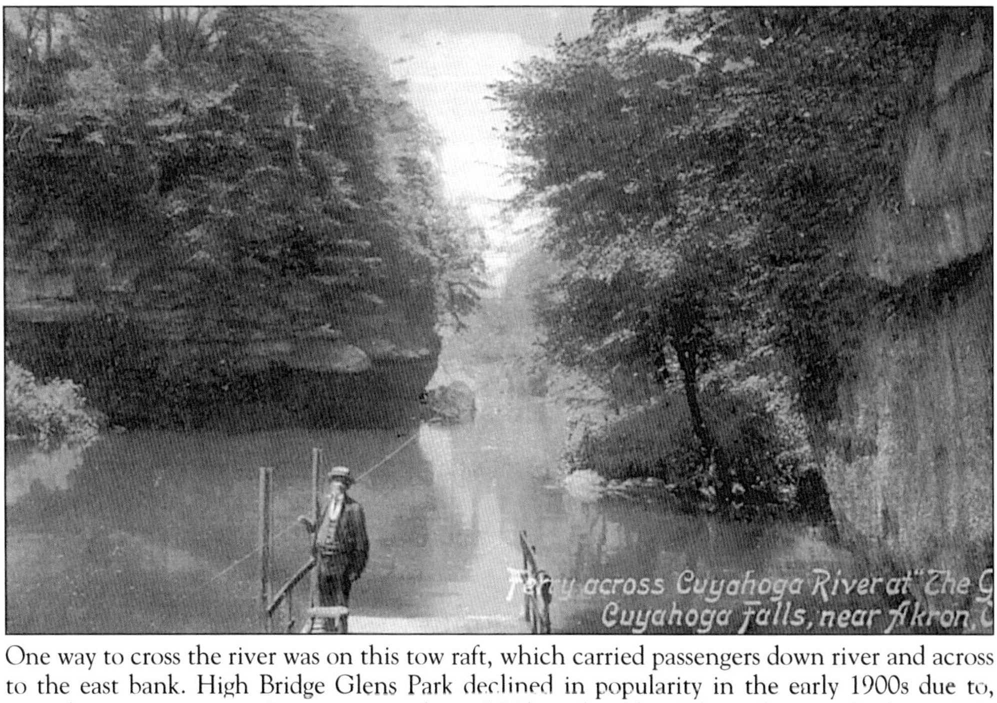

One way to cross the river was on this tow raft, which carried passengers down river and across to the east bank. High Bridge Glens Park declined in popularity in the early 1900s due to, according to one source, "excessive rowdyism." When the Ohio Edison dam was built in 1912, most of the site was flooded, and that marked the end of the amusement park.

Tourists enjoyed the High Bridge Glens even in the winter. The woman is shown on a footpath on the east side of the Glens, and the man is standing on the suspension bridge, 75 feet south of the High Bridge. The suspension bridge was held by heavy wire cable with a 6-foot-wide floor. Only heavy ropes on each side kept this man from falling over into the icy, rock-studded river.

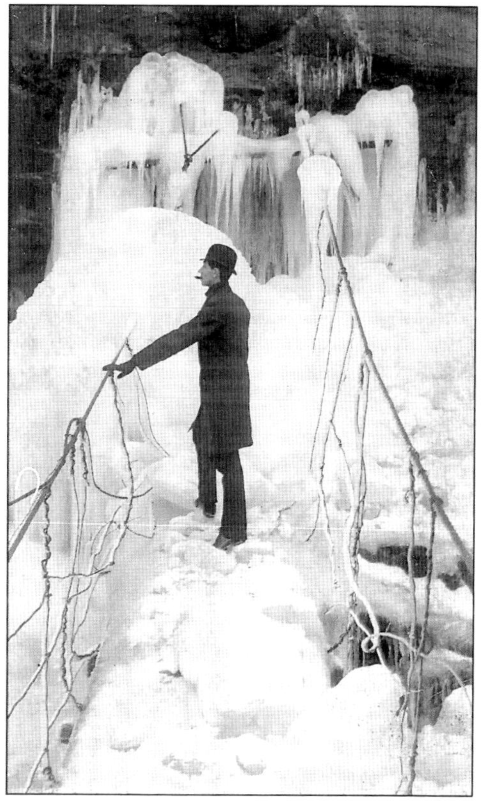

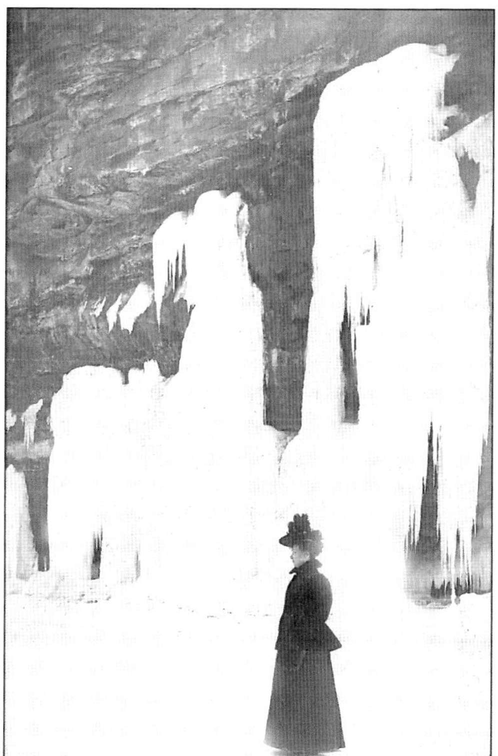

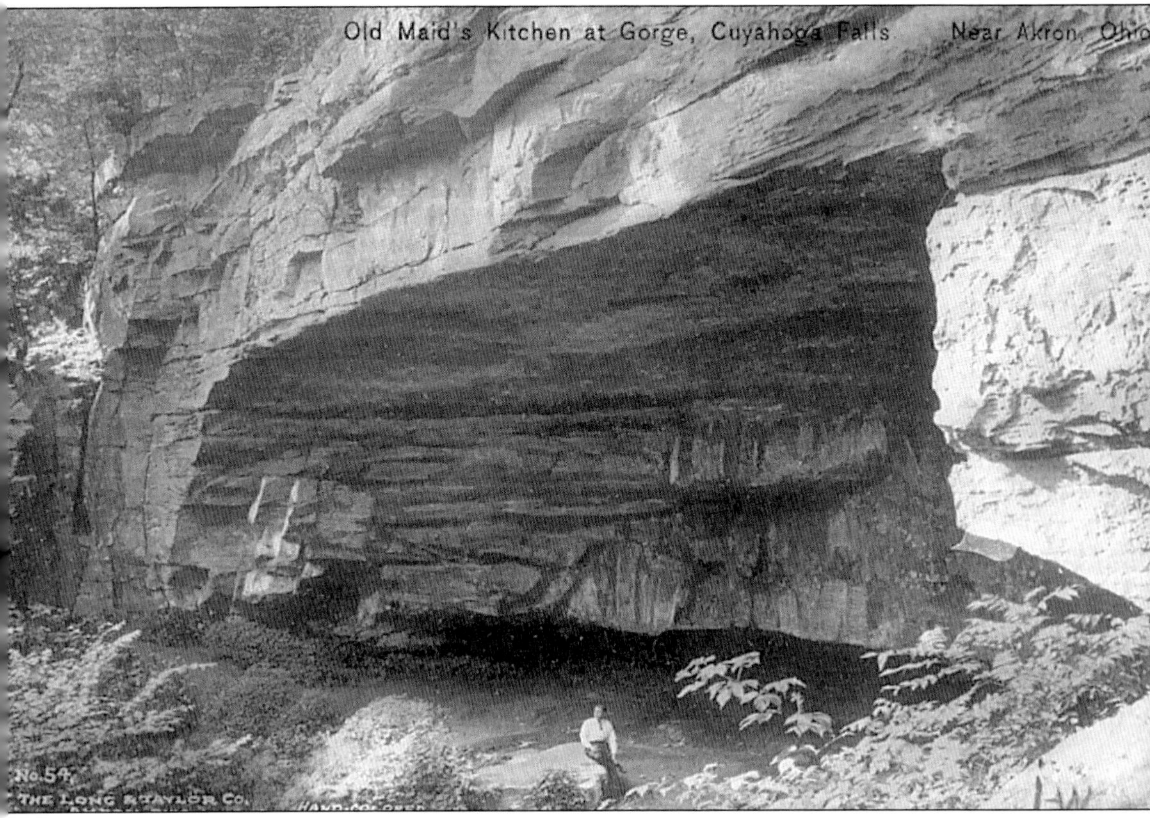

Old Maid's Kitchen in Gorge Metropolitan Park is also known as Mary Campbell Cave. A plaque at the entrance to the cave states that in 1759, a young girl was captured by a raiding party of Delaware Indians. According to the legend, the warriors and their captives, including Mary, took temporary shelter in this cave. Netawatwees, the chief of the tribe, adopted young Mary Campbell. When the British and Indian tribes of the region made a treaty in 1764, Mary was returned to her family in Pennsylvania. Her descendants occasionally have family reunions at the site.

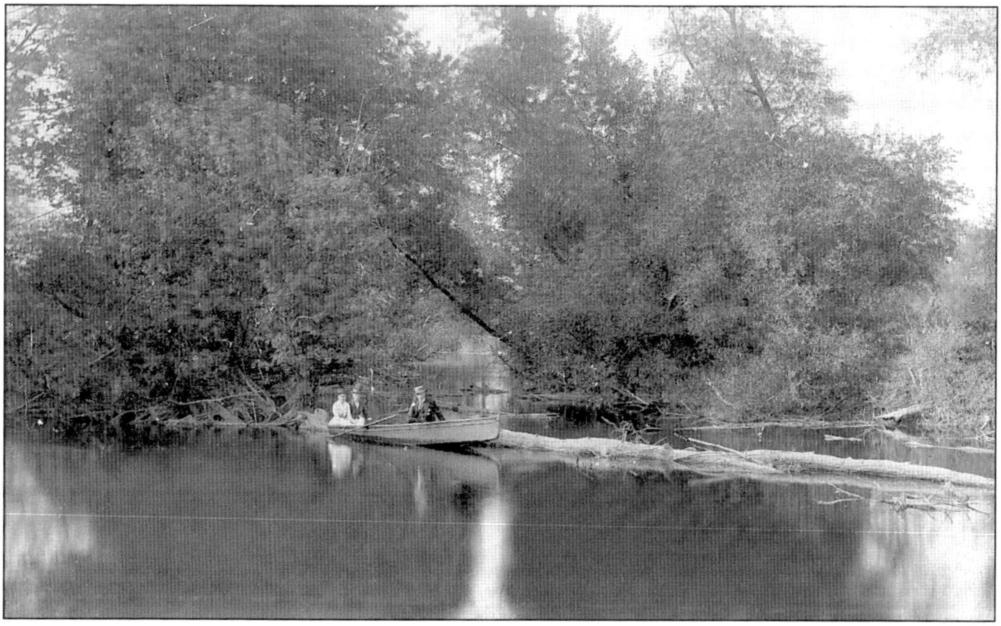

Sightseers could rent rowboats and explore the Cuyahoga River upstream of the High Bridge Glens. This photograph was probably taken near Goose Egg Island, close to the present day Waterworks Park.

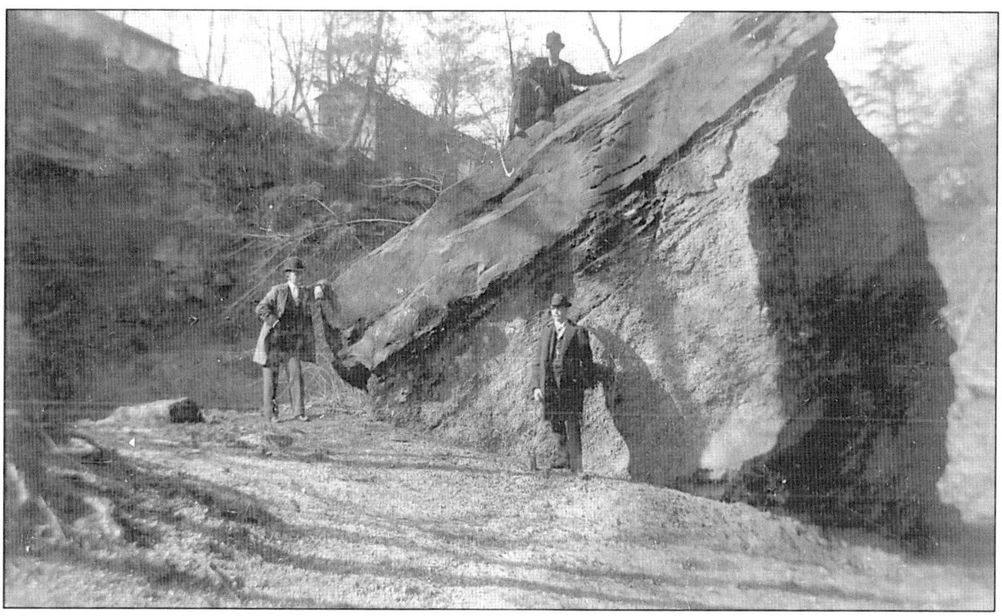

Many scenic rock formations drew visitors to hike the river trails. This rock is believed to be Anchor Rock, which was used as the east abutment of the dam built by Portage Canal & Manufacturing Company (a.k.a. The Chuckery). Marathon Rubber Company later used the rock for the same purpose, and today the rock is standing just above water on the east side of the river, below the Prospect Street observation bridge.

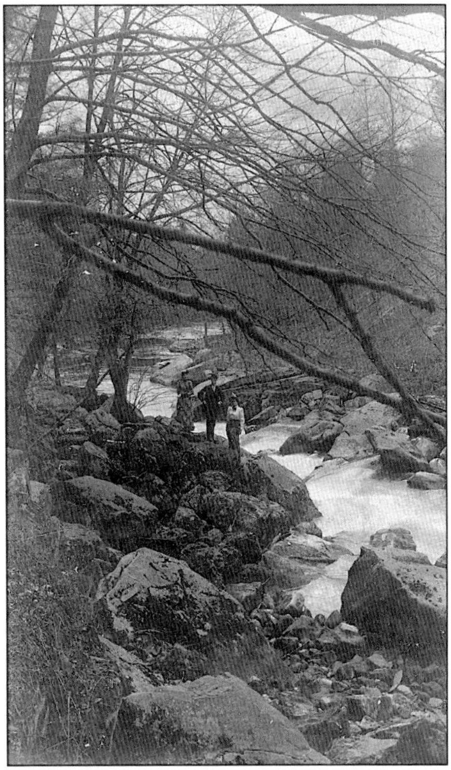

In this photograph, visitors to the High Bridge Glens Park climb the rocks along the river. This area is now submerged.

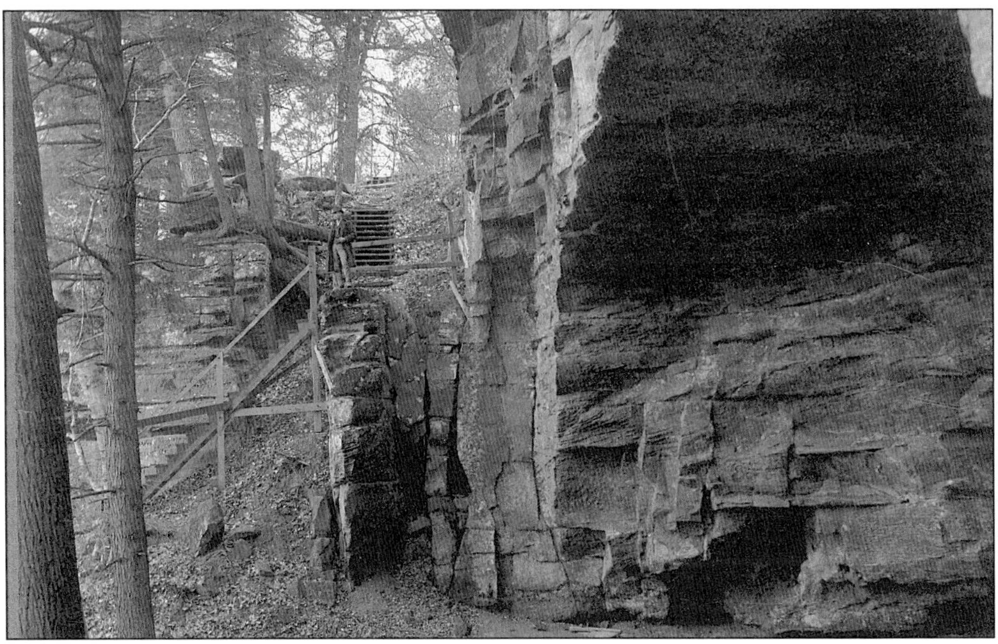

Steps from Mary Campbell Cave once led up out of the valley to the Falls Hotel, built on the plateau above. Mrs. Fosdick made the hotel restaurant famous with her chicken dinners. The hotel and restaurant probably closed in the 1920s or 1930s. The steps are now gone, but hikers still enjoy the trail that passes in front of the cave.

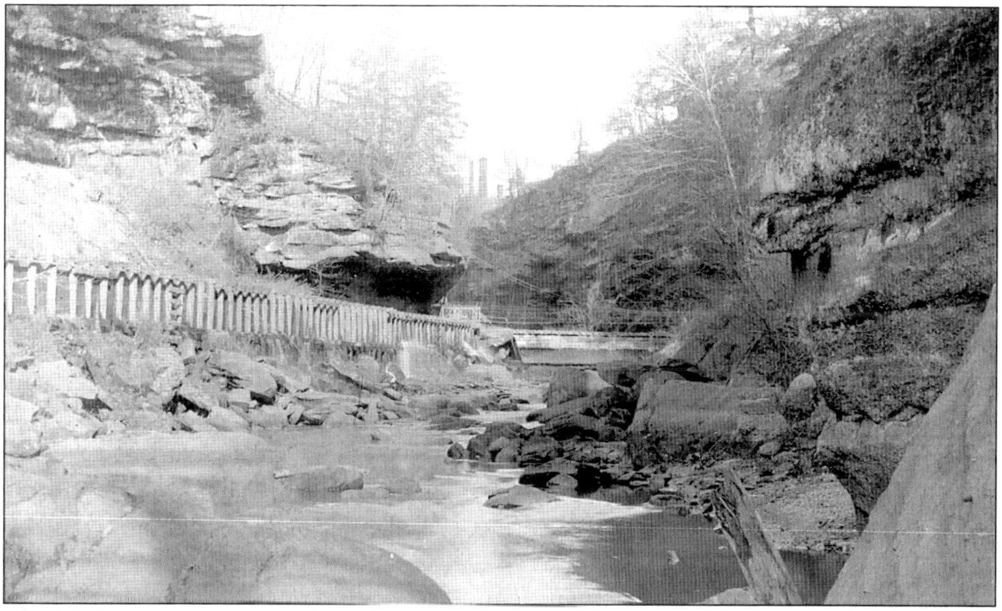

This photograph, looking north, shows a spillway along the river in the back of Marathon Rubber and Lange Welding. The wooden structure on the left is probably a flume to send water to the mill. A suspension bridge spans the river in the center of the photograph.

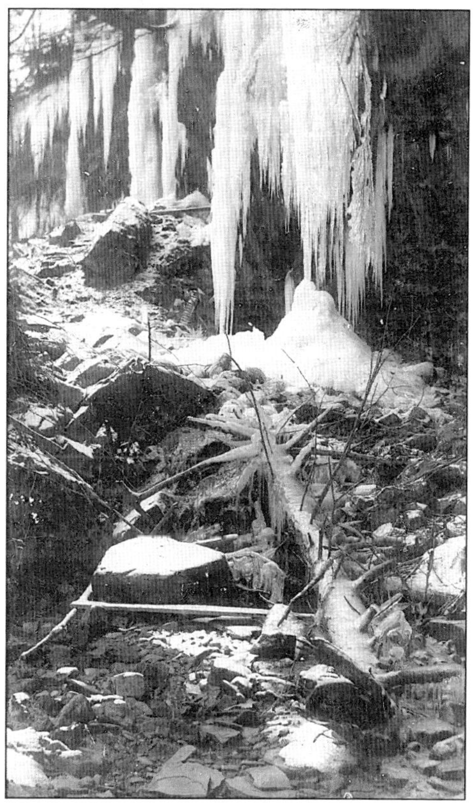

Icicles hang from the cliffs along the path of the east bank of the Cuyahoga River below the suspension bridge.

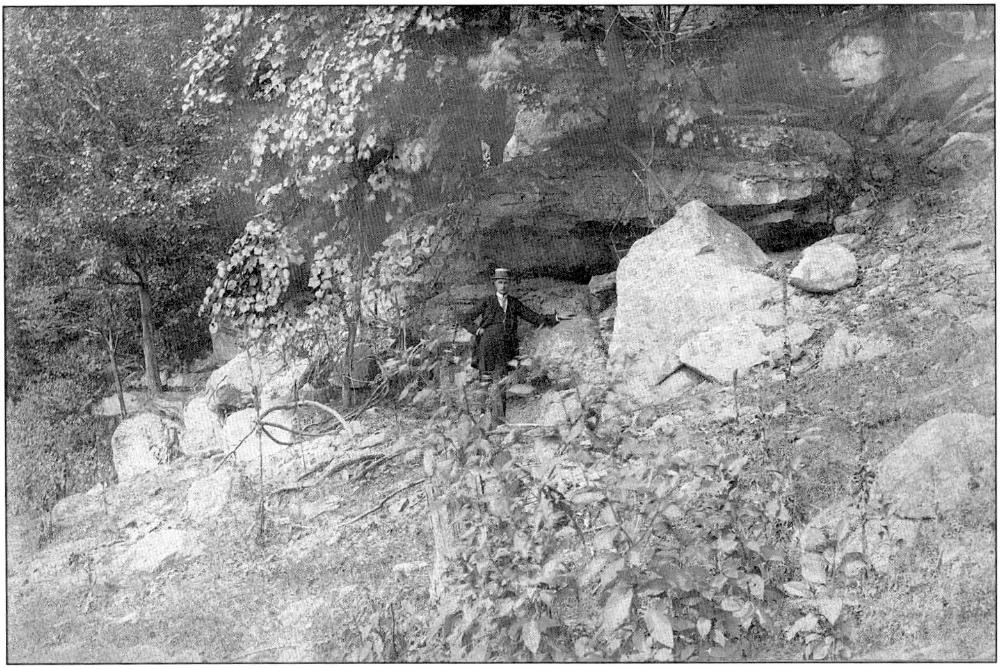

In this photograph, a tourist poses for a summation photograph taken on the "West Promenade" at the High Bridge Glens Park.

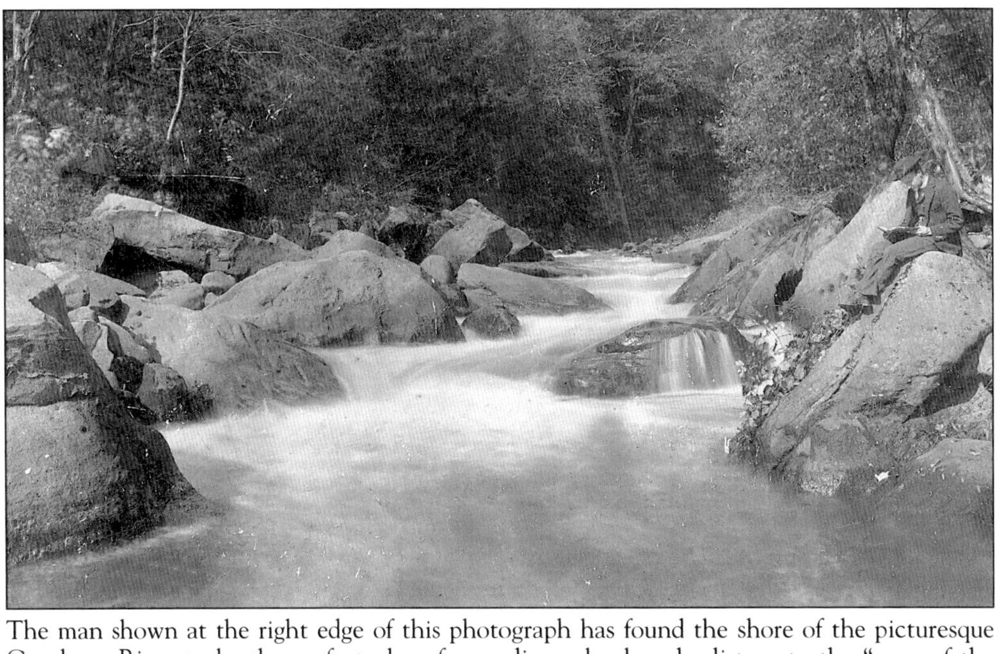

The man shown at the right edge of this photograph has found the shore of the picturesque Cuyahoga River to be the perfect place for reading a book as he listens to the "song of the waters." The natural beauty of the area still attracts hikers and explorers today, even though the landscape has changed since this picture was taken.

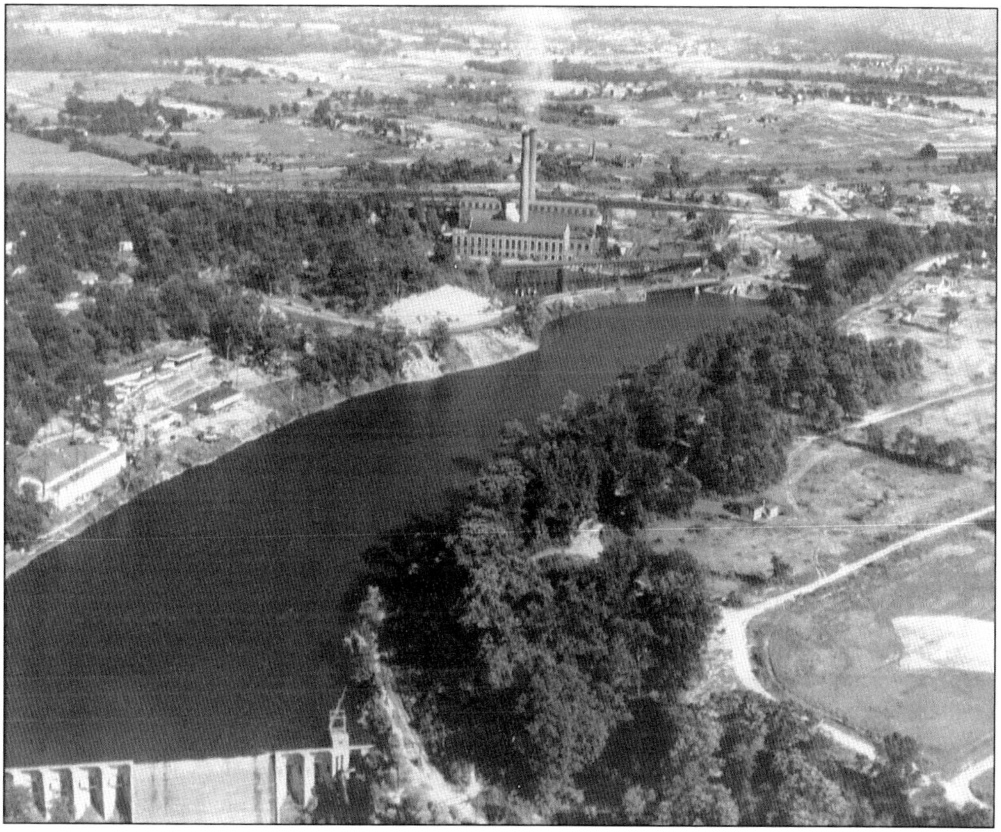

Another popular park along the river was Riverview Park, as seen on the left edge of this aerial view. The Ohio Edison power plant is at the top center of the photograph.

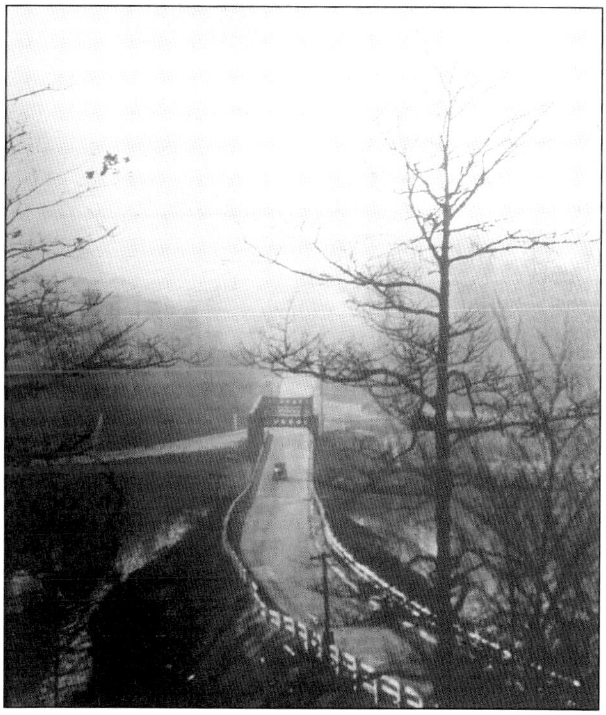

Front Street was one route that brought people into Riverview Park. This view is looking towards Akron, and the power plant is on the left.

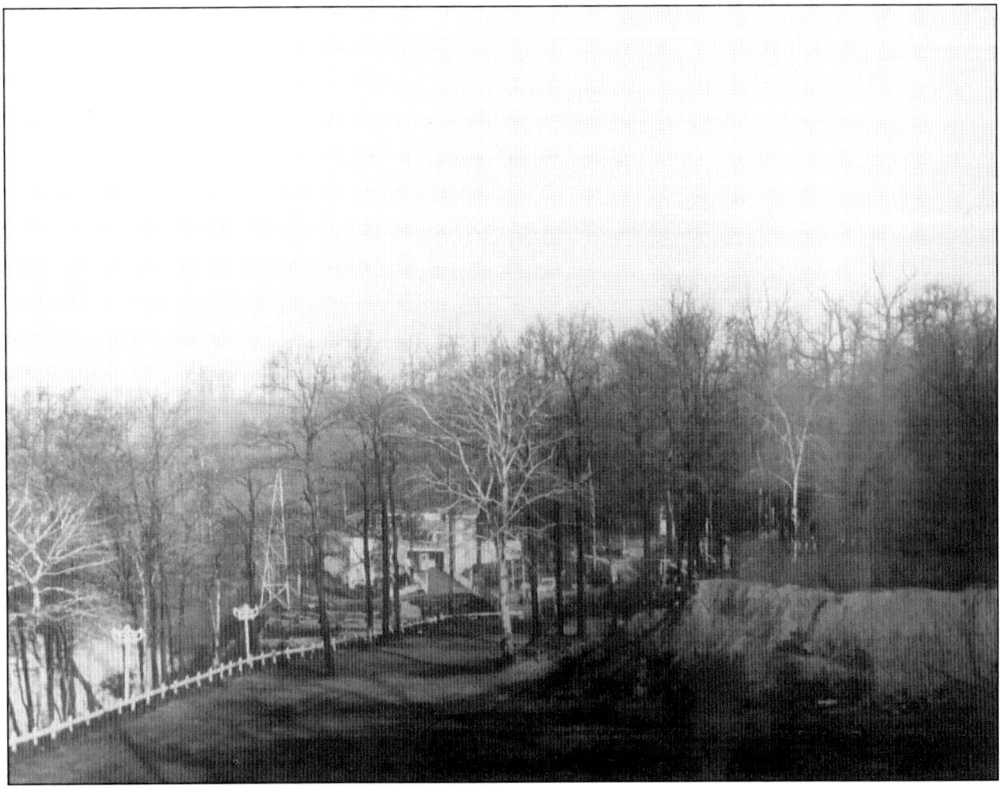

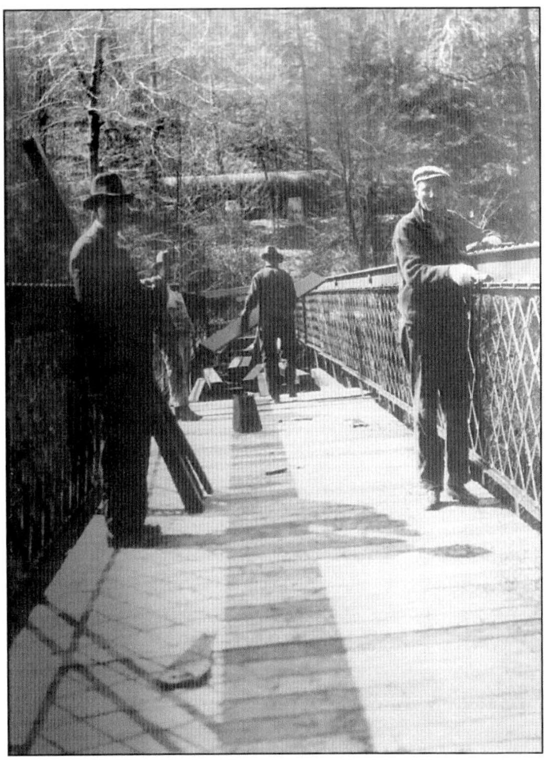

This driveway leads to the entrance of Riverview Park. The dance pavilion and the tower for a swinging chair ride can be seen in the distance. The Cuyahoga River is at the left edge of this photograph.

Visitors to Riverview Park could cross the river to the Akron side by way of a footbridge below the dam. Here workers are repairing the wooden deck of the bridge. The pipe in the background is a penstock that ran to a turbine generator located near the present high-level bridge.

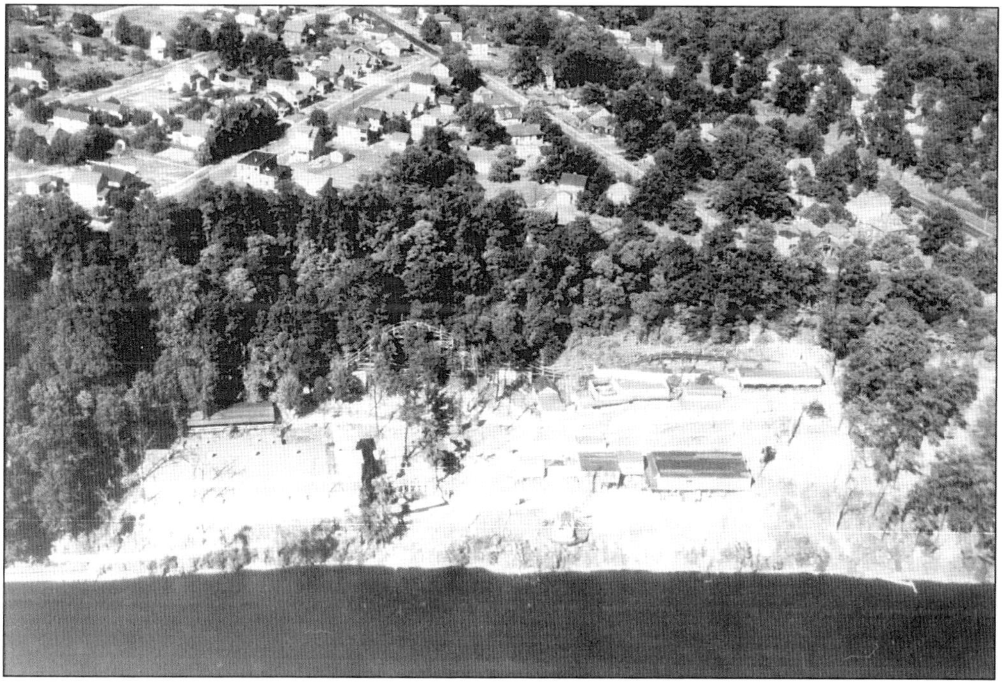

Riverview Park was located at the present site of the Gorge Metropolitan Park and was popular during the early twentieth century. A major attraction of the park was the "Sky Rocket" roller coaster seen in the center of this aerial view.

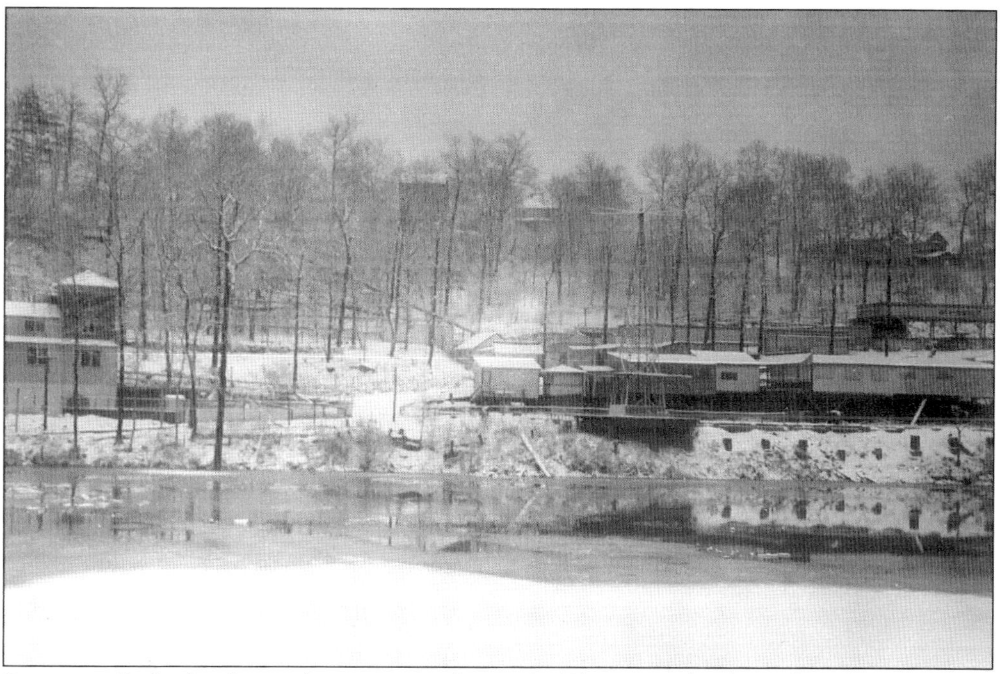

Riverview Park also featured a swinging chair ride. The tower for this ride is located in the center of this view. One resident remembers that the park also contained a crocodile and several monkeys.

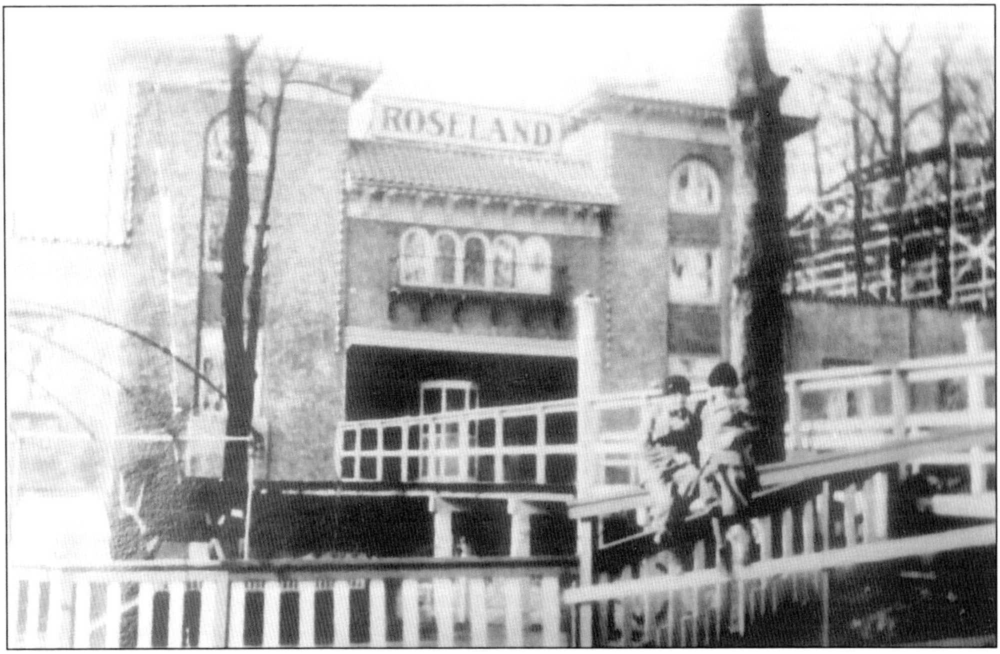

Roseland Dance Pavilion was another attraction of Riverview Park. It was located near the present entrance to Gorge Metropolitan Park. One long-time resident remembers that separate skating and dance pavilions were originally located at this site; however, when one of the buildings burned, the remaining one accommodated both skaters and dancers. The building was eventually moved to Elizabeth Park in Akron, where it burned to the ground. This photograph was taken in 1928.

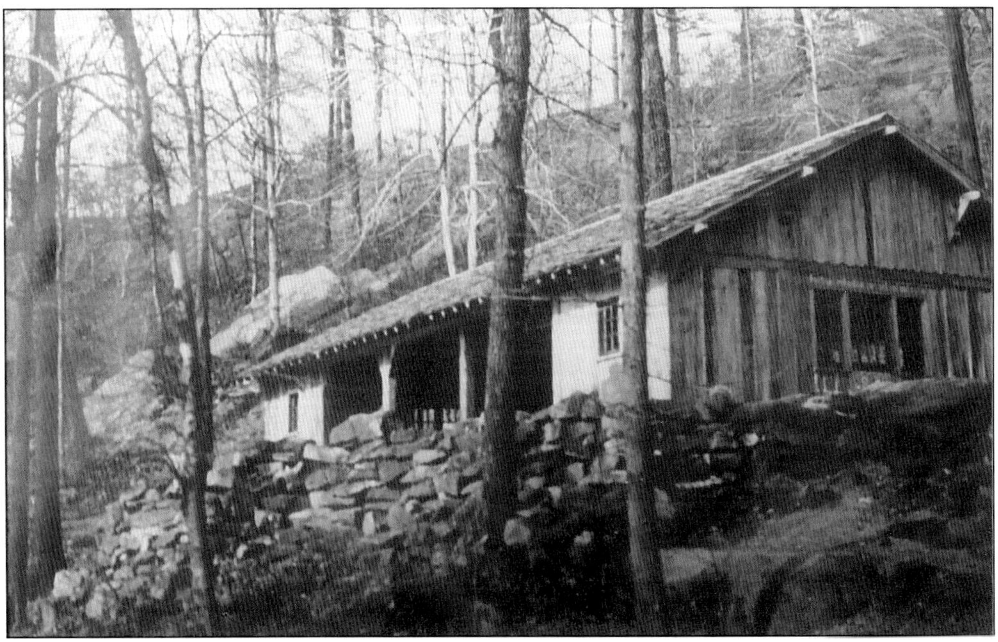

The old Riverview Park shelter house seen here has been replaced with an open-air picnic shelter on the same site, just east of Mary Campbell Cave in the Gorge Metropolitan Park.

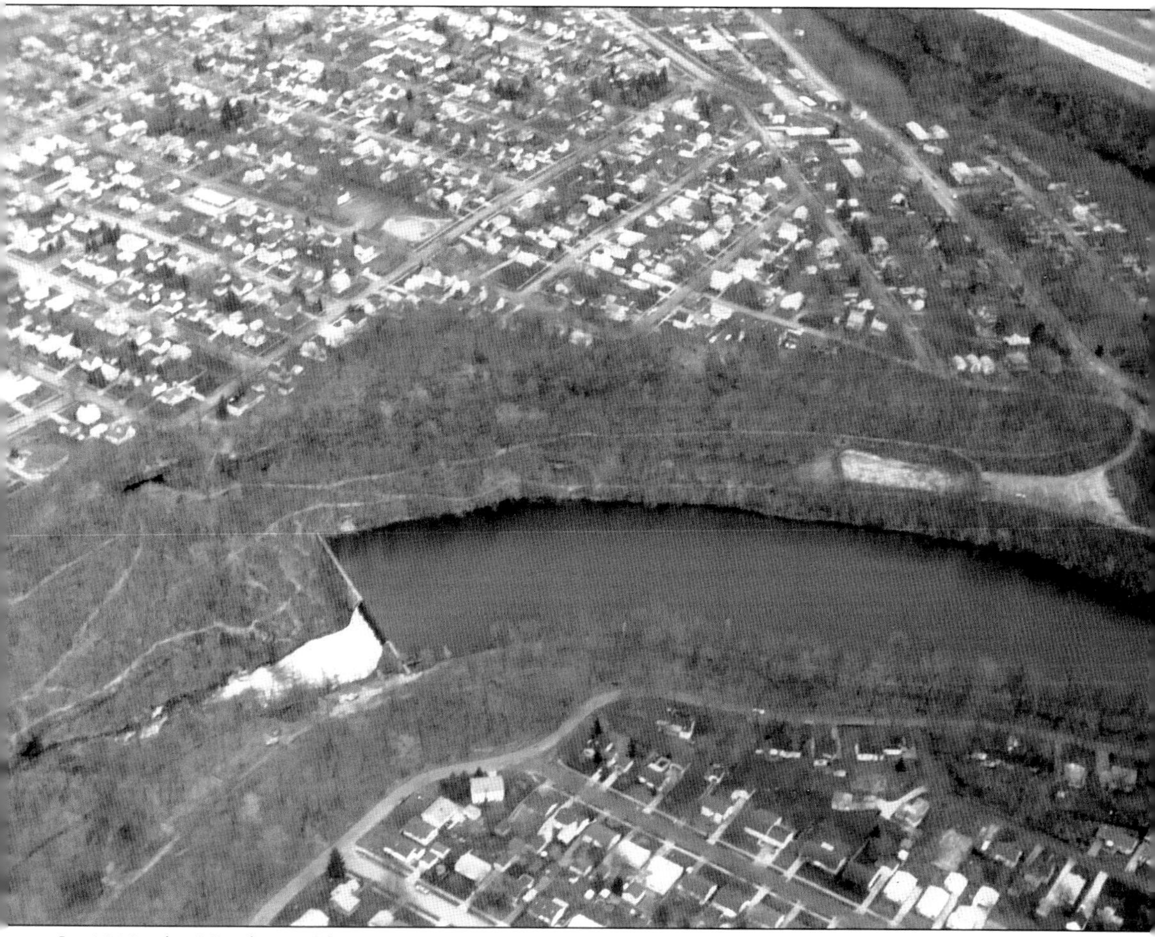

In 1912, the Northern Ohio Traction and Light Company constructed the 70-foot dam seen in this aerial photograph. The dam supplied electricity to homes and industries, as well as to rail lines north of the Summit-Stark county line. The powerhouse was one of the largest coal-hydroelectric plants in Ohio. Coal was delivered to the powerhouse yard and was dumped down the side of the gorge to the plant. The operation later evolved into the Ohio Edison Company. This aerial view is looking east at the Gorge Metropolitan Park, and Mary Campbell Cave is at the left edge of the photo. The Ohio Edison right-of-way (Chuckery) and flume pipe from the dam can be seen in the lower left corner. This photo was taken in 1976 by Bob Cunningham.

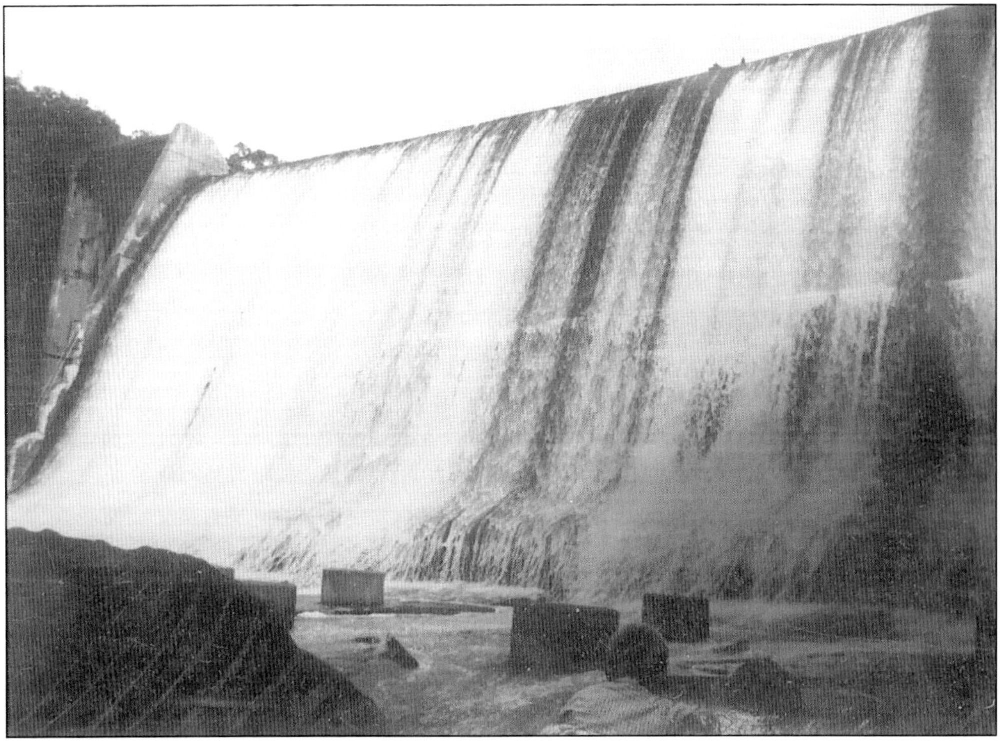

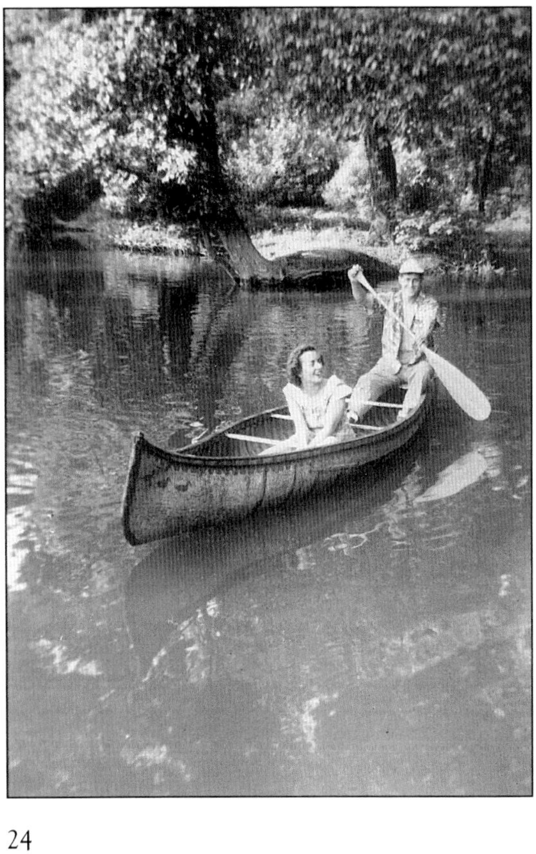

Although the company no longer harvests the energy created by the Ohio Edison dam, the falls remain a centerpiece of the Gorge Metropolitan Park, and the lake behind it is popular for fishing.

Even after the Ohio Edison dam flooded much of the Glens area once used for recreation, the river upstream continued to be popular with boaters. This undated photo by Harold E. Ekers won third place in an exhibit sponsored by the Goodyear-Akron Photographic Society.

Two

The Hum of Busy Wheels

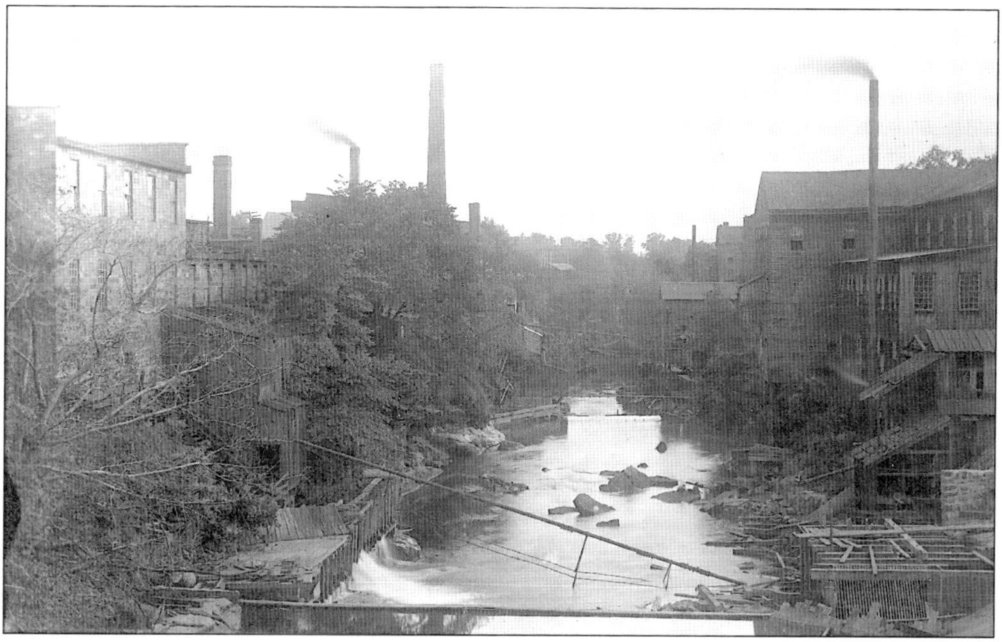

Cuyahoga Falls was once considered the most promising commercial location in the area, and might have developed as a major urban center if it had not been for three events. First, in 1825, the planners of the Ohio & Erie Canal routed the waterway through Akron instead of Cuyahoga Falls. Then in 1842, Akron—not Cuyahoga Falls—was chosen as the Summit County Seat, and just two years later "The Chuckery" project failed. The Chuckery was a canal flume that was supposed to divert water from the Cuyahoga River and channel it to a new industrial center to be named Summit City. The plans were ambitious from the beginning, but the originator of the idea, Dr. Crosby, finally secured funding for the construction of the flume in 1841. The gates were opened on May 27, 1844, and water flooded the canal bed, but within an hour the gates had to be closed due to water seepage. The company went bankrupt, and Cuyahoga Falls lost its last chance to become a premier industrial center. Nevertheless, business and industry thrived in Cuyahoga Falls, as demonstrated in this early photograph.

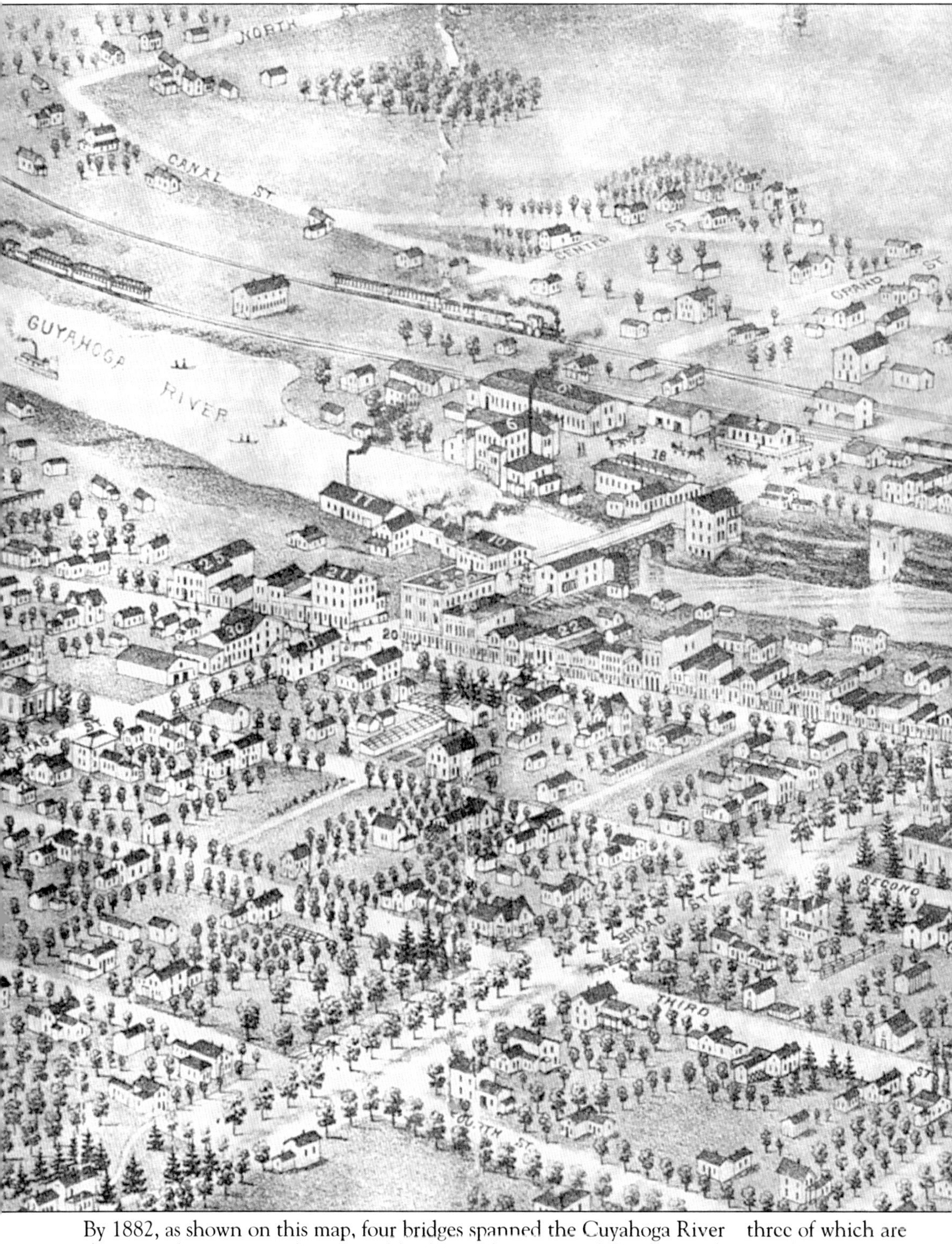

By 1882, as shown on this map, four bridges spanned the Cuyahoga River three of which are shown in this picture. The covered bridge in the center of the map is the Broad Street (now Broad Boulevard) bridge. At this time, five dams generated power for industries on both sides

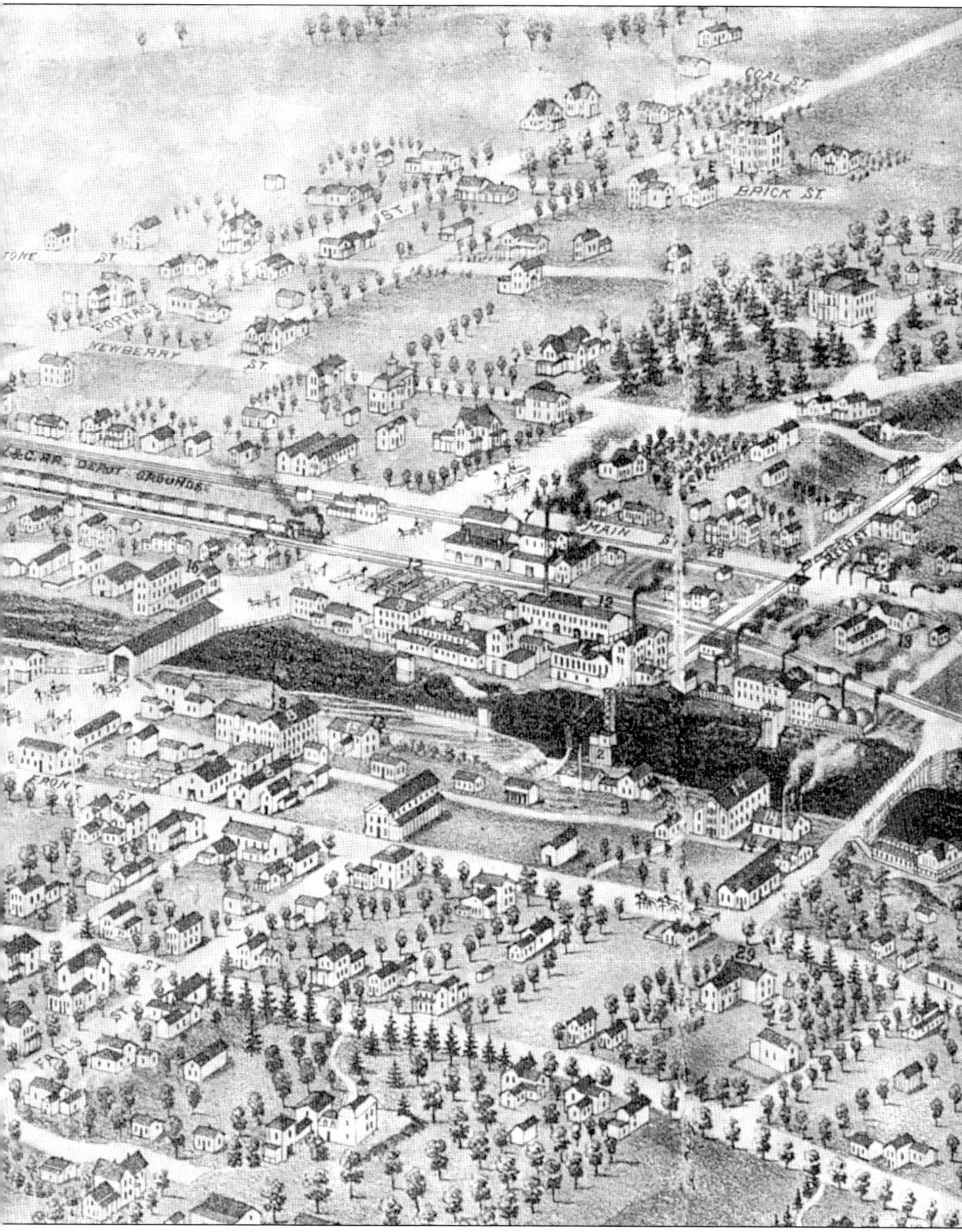

of the river within the distance of a quarter mile. The power generated by the falling Cuyahoga was estimated by one source at nearly 3,500 horsepower.

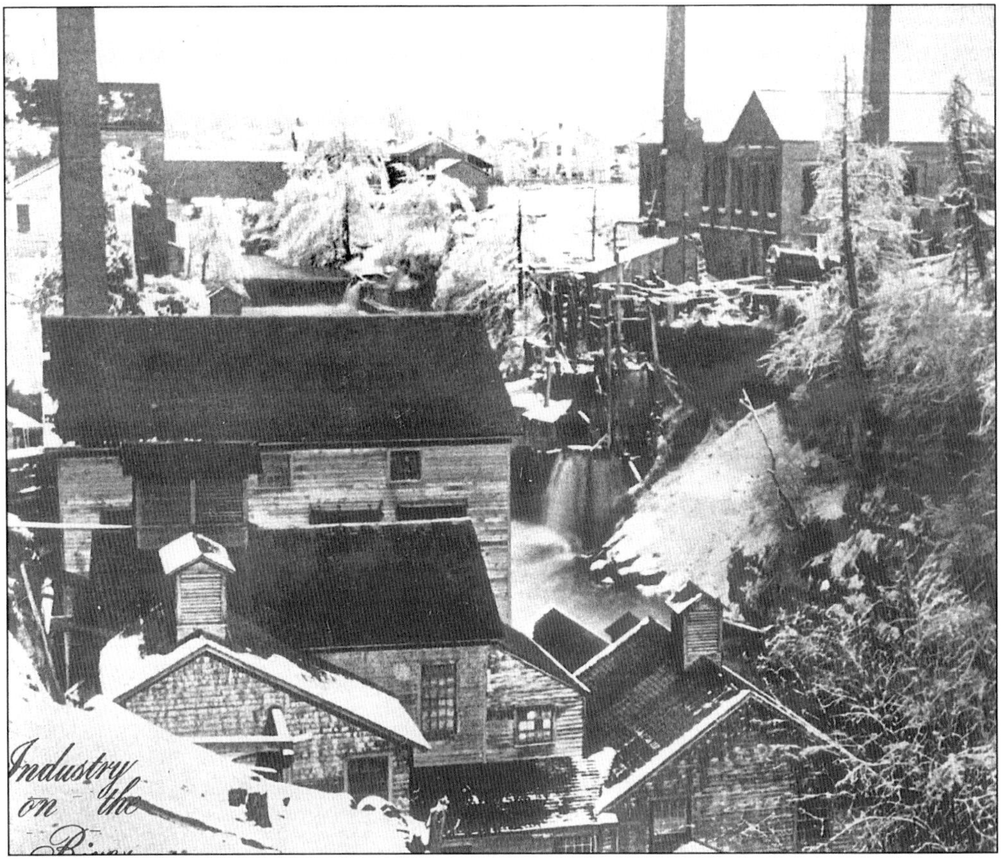

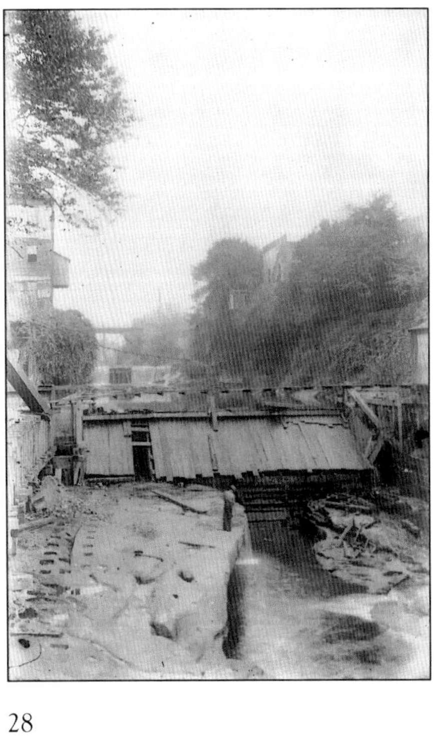

Business boomed along the Cuyahoga River, as shown in this early photograph that captures a section of industry south of Broad Street. As the town grew, industry moved down river from Portage Street (now Portage Trail) to Prospect Street. The covered bridge spans the river at the top of this photograph.

Industries on both sides of the 5 miles of the river that runs through Cuyahoga Falls have included manufacturing of paper, flour, rivets, doors and blinds, linseed oil, pipe, brick and tile, machinery, candles, wire, clocks, pottery, and wool, to name a few. This photograph shows one of the dams and spillways that generated some of the power.

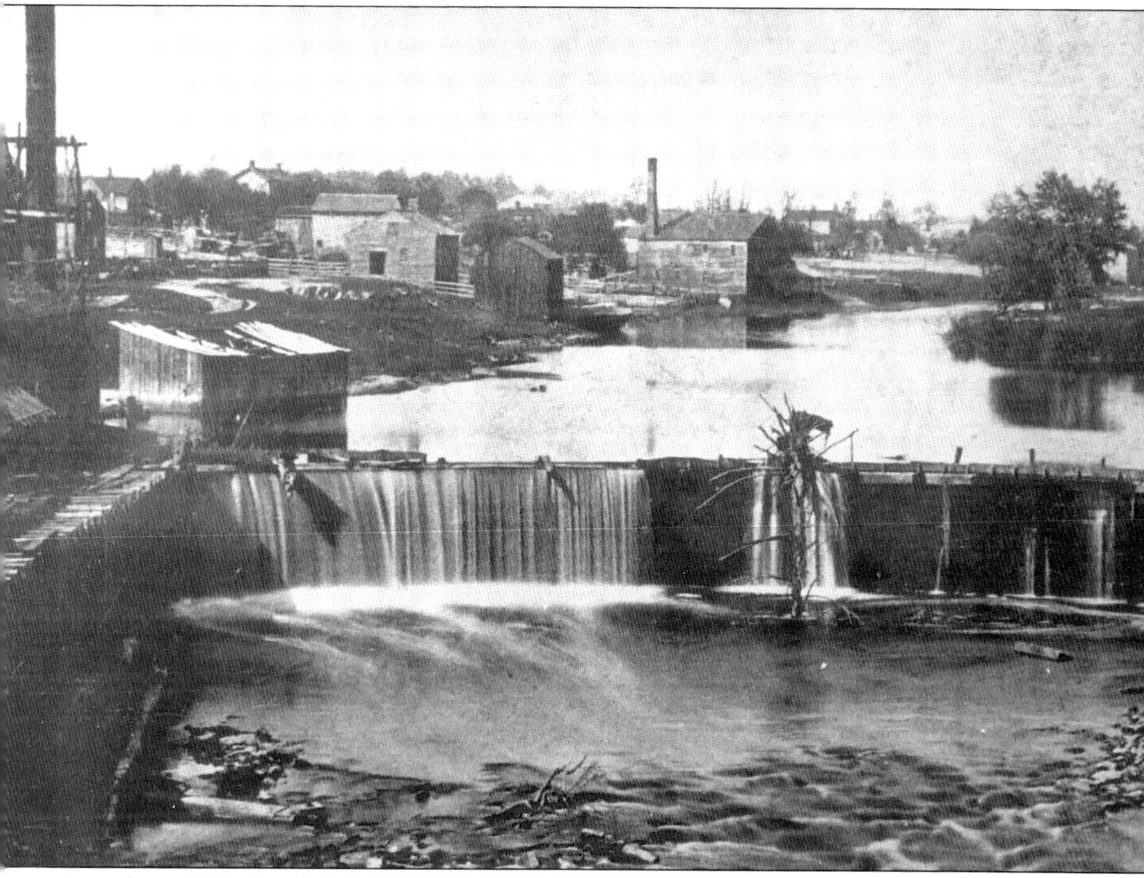

As early as 1837, Cuyahoga Falls was an important manufacturing center. The population was 1,200, and the town was one of the fastest growing communities in northern Ohio. The town contained three churches, an academy, a bank, a printing office, four blacksmiths, two paper mills, two saw mills, a chair factory, a machine shop, and dozens of retail establishments—including a bookstore. This photograph is probably the north side of the old Portage Street dam in the late nineteenth century. The Cuyahoga River dams generated much power for industries during this time, inspiring one poet to write: "I'm the mighty Cuyahoga/ At Cuyahoga Falls and Kent/ And at Munroe, in running mills/ My mighty power is spent./ I used to run canal boats/ It wasn't much to brag on/ For thus they stole my water/ To run the mills at Akron./ Tho' the 'Falls' has dammed me badly/ It didn't cause such feelings,/ As the many d—ns they uttered/ About the water stealing." (O.R. in *Reporter*, Feb. 14, 1874)

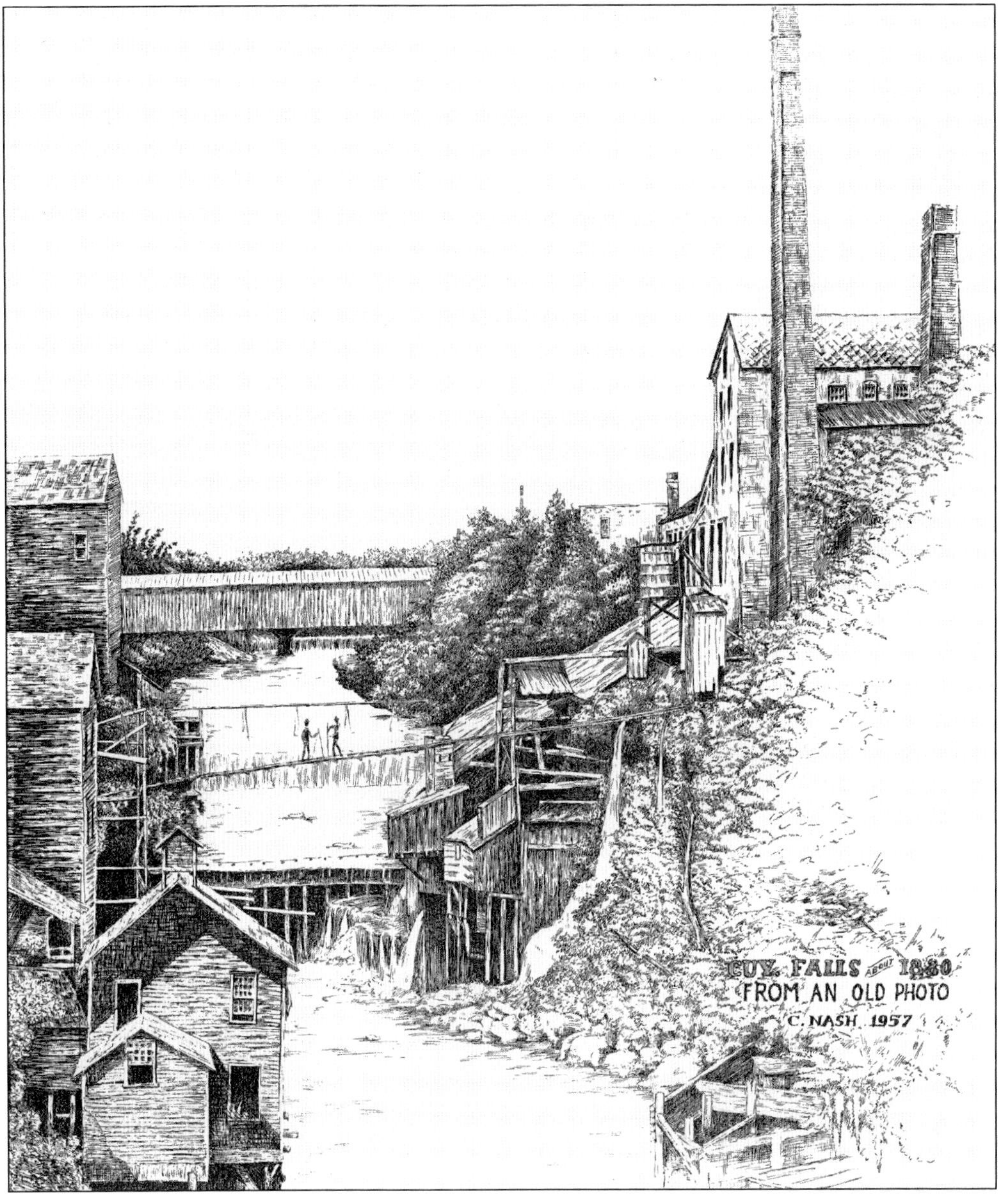

This drawing of Cuyahoga Falls industry was made from a photograph taken about 1880. The Broad Street covered bridge is in the distance. Businesses changed hands frequently during this era, and fires in the wooden structures were common. We do know that in 1891, a dam built by Mr. Newberry in 1826 was still being used to supply power to the Turner, Vaughn, Taylor Machine Shop at the left of this drawing. Walsh Lumber Company may be one of the businesses on the other side of the river. The square chimneys predate knowledge of rounded construction.

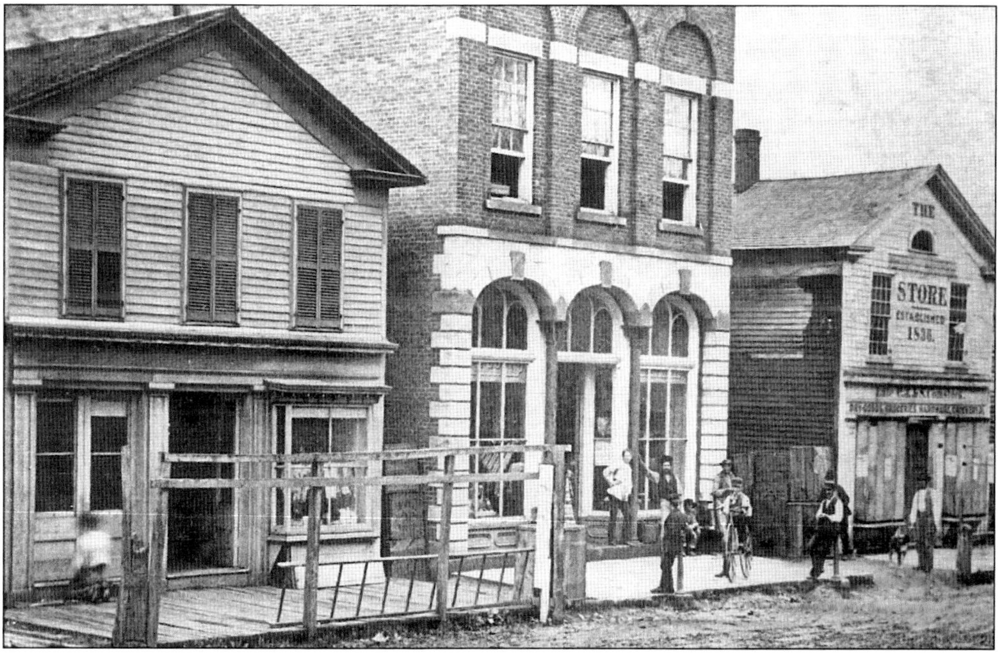

Cuyahoga Falls businessman Ezra S. Comstock visited Chicago in 1836. Upon returning to Cuyahoga Falls, he dismounted from his horse and said, "I saw Chicago. There is nothing there but a few log cabins, a trading post and a lot of drunken Indians. Cuyahoga Falls has Chicago skinned in a dozen ways. Chicago will never amount to much but Cuyahoga Falls will." For years, Comstock and his brother were leading merchants in the city. They operated a general store in the Comstock Building shown in the center of this photograph.

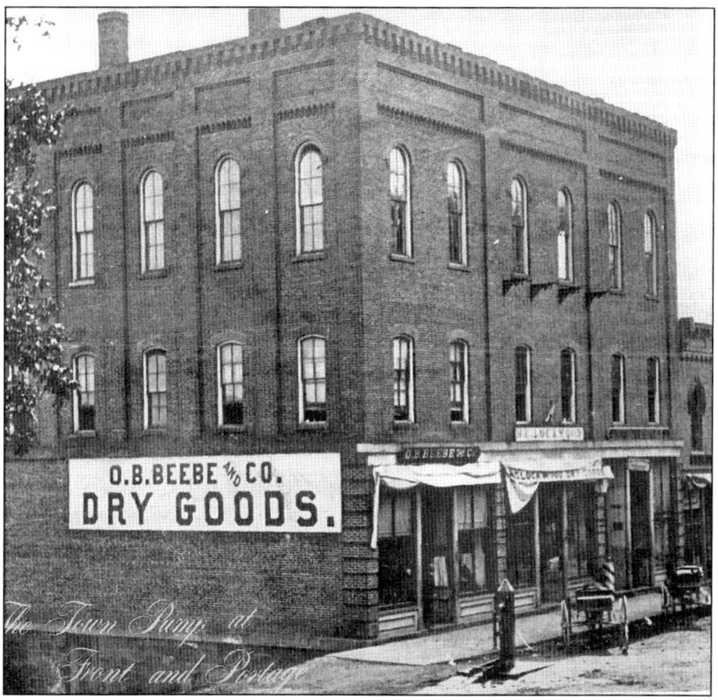

This building was located on the southeast corner of Portage and Front Streets. The Apollo Opera and Entertainment Center, with a seating capacity of 500, was housed on the third floor. The town pump is located in the front center of the photograph. The rail along the street was used for securing the horses while their owners shopped. The building is named for Oliver Beebe, a bookbinder and stationer, who later maintained a successful dry goods trade.

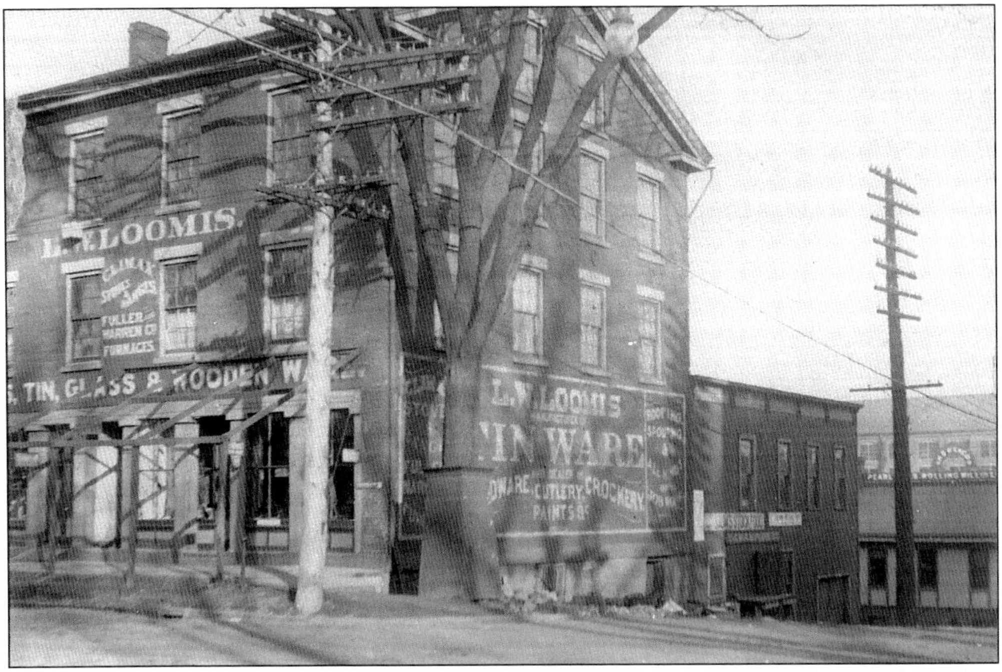

Loomis Hardware was located at Front and Portage Streets. This photograph, probably taken sometime at the turn of the century, shows shoppers gathered in front of the store. Merchandise included stoves, tin, sheet-iron and copperware, crockery, glassware, and notions.

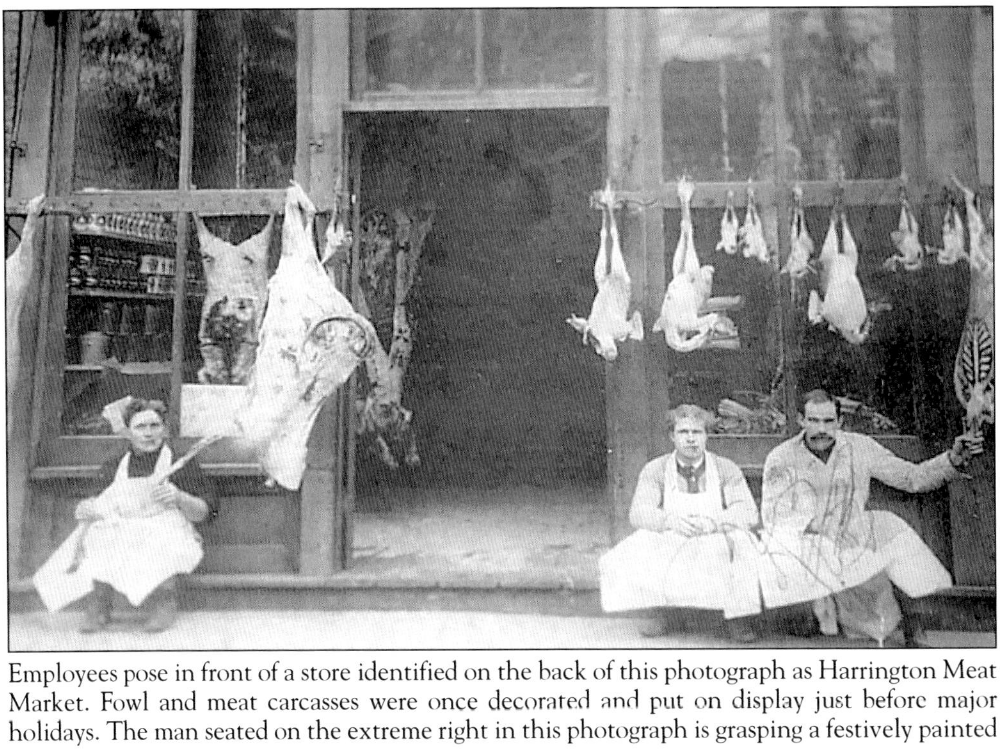

Employees pose in front of a store identified on the back of this photograph as Harrington Meat Market. Fowl and meat carcasses were once decorated and put on display just before major holidays. The man seated on the extreme right in this photograph is grasping a festively painted meat carcass.

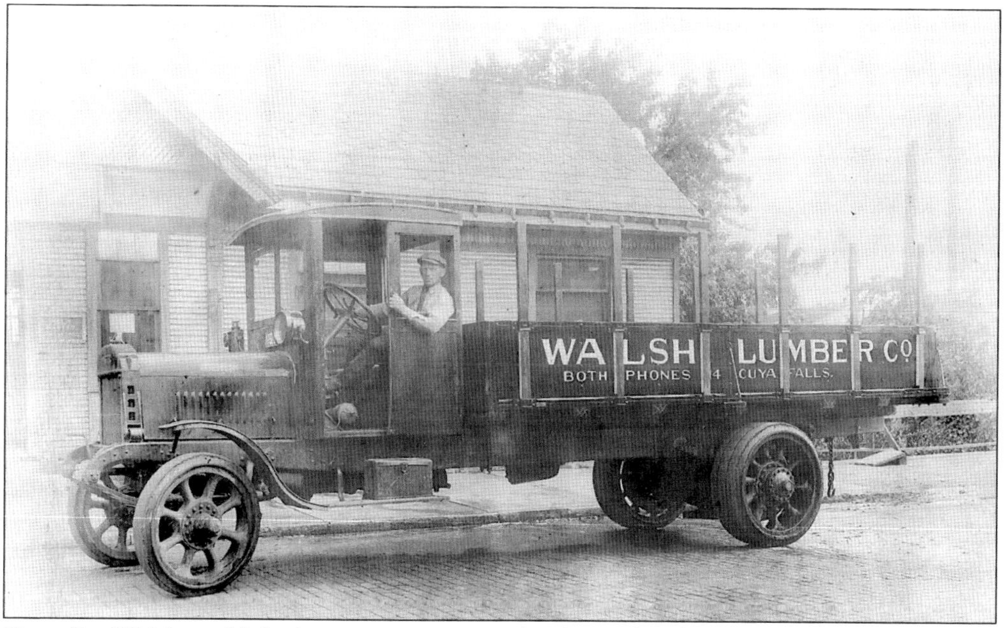

Cornelius Walsh established a paper company, a lumberyard, a flourmill, and the Falls Hollow Staybolt Company at the turn of the century. The Walsh Lumber Company office shown in this photograph was located on Portage Street, and the driver of the truck is identified on the back of this photo as Bill Hiser.

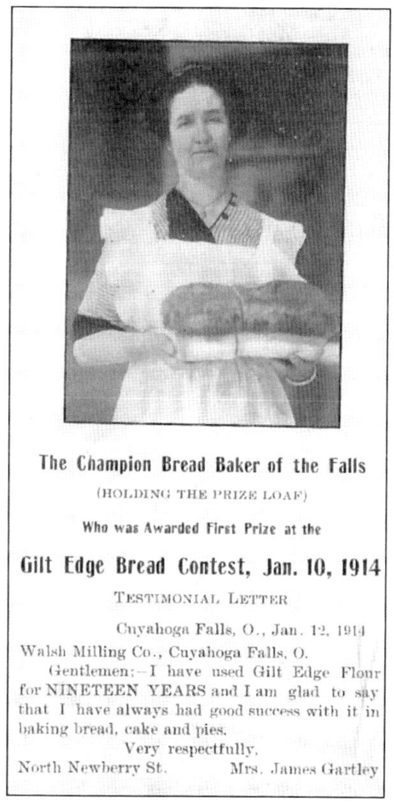

In 1914, Mrs. James Gartley won first prize for her bread recipe. Her testimonial is printed on the bottom of this advertisement for Gilt Edge flour produced by the Walsh Milling Company.

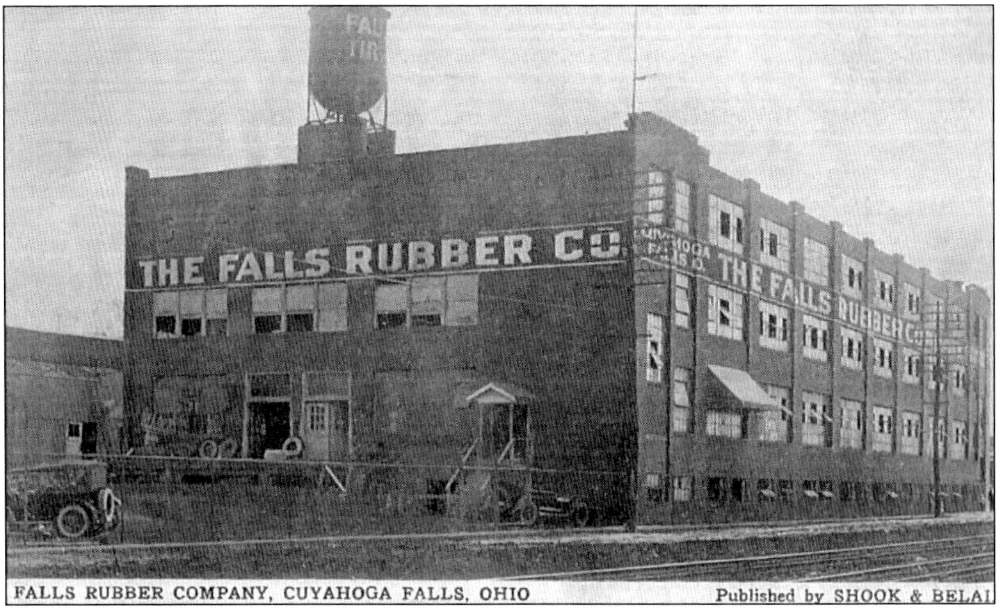

The Falls Rubber Company was founded in 1909 and merged with the Cooper Corporation in 1930. In 1919, the company was located at this site, now the Schwebel Baking Company, formerly Lawson's. The rubber company became famous for "Road Master" tires.

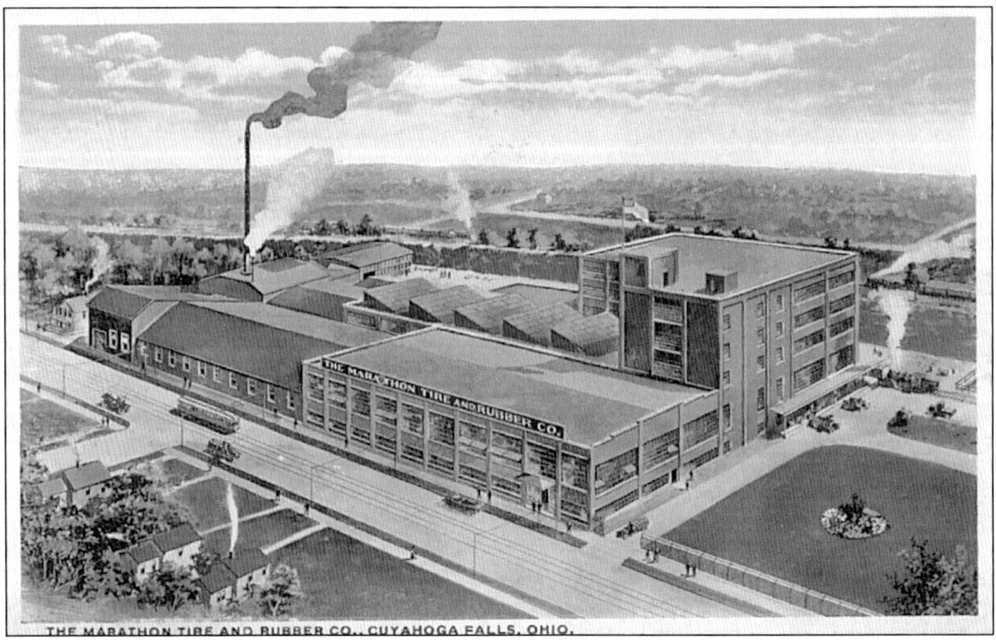

The Marathon Tire and Rubber Company opened in 1912. The company, located on South Front Street, built tires, inner tubes, and accessories; in fact, Marathon held the patent on red inner tubes. The street intersecting Front Street at the left edge of this postcard is Sackett Avenue.

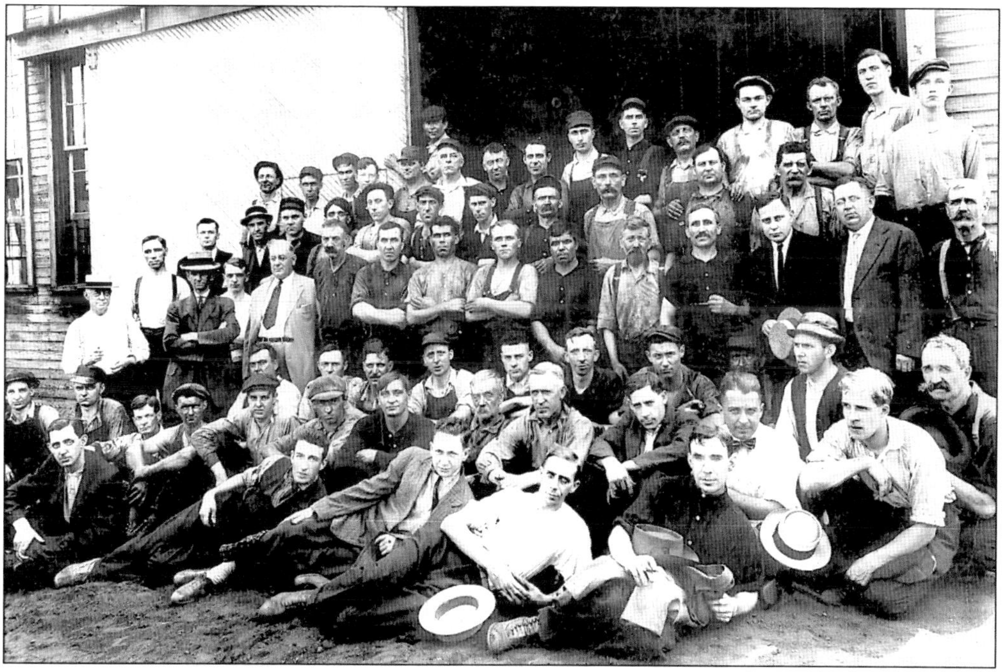

The Vaughn Machine Company, formed in 1856 as Turner, Park and Company, was once located at the site of the present-day Sheraton Suites. When employees posed for this photograph in 1915, the company was a leader in the manufacture of cold drawing equipment for the steel, copper, and aluminum industries.

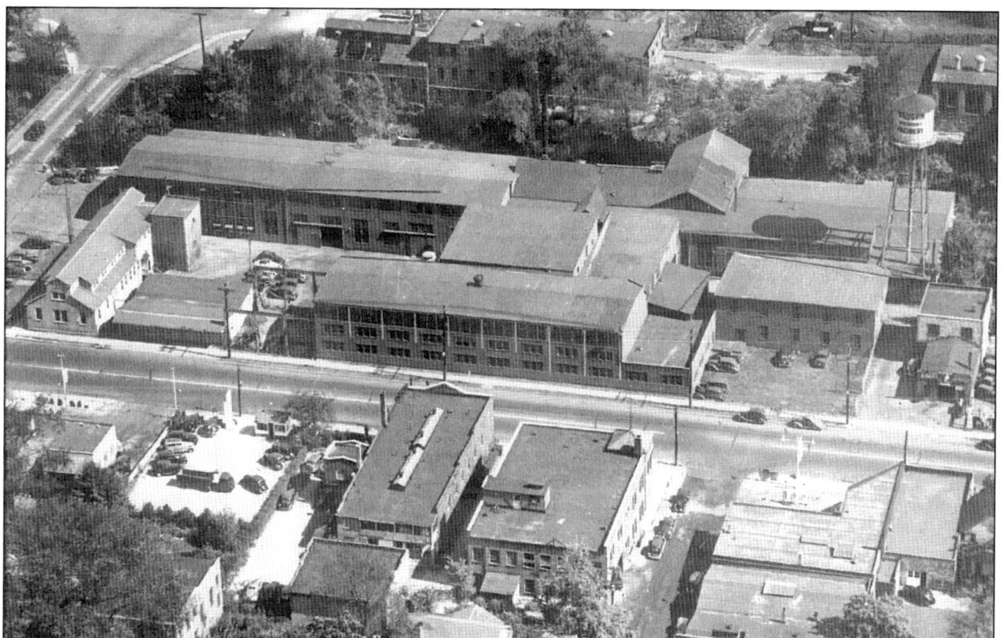

Most of the sprawling Vaughn Machine Company shown here was demolished, but you can still view the old Vaughn generator building which has been incorporated into the Sheraton Suites building. (Courtesy of Taylor Memorial Public Library.)

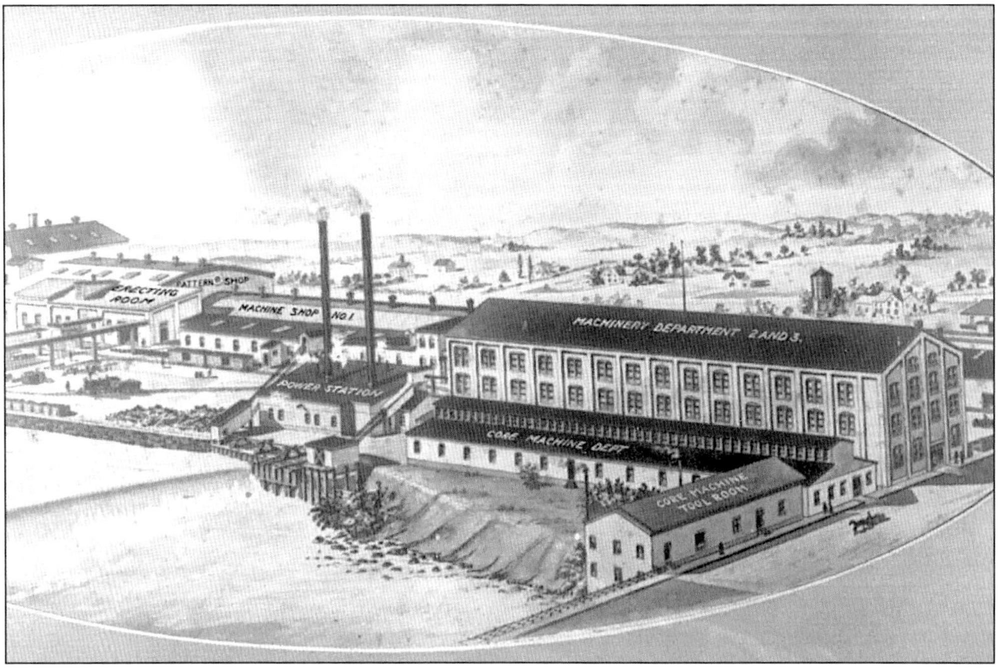

Falls Rivet and Machine Company was established in 1873 and manufactured rivets and steel-rim pulleys. The Upper Works, shown at the top of this page, was located on the river near Portage Street and later became Kent Machine Company. Portage Street (now Portage Trail) is on the right side of this image.

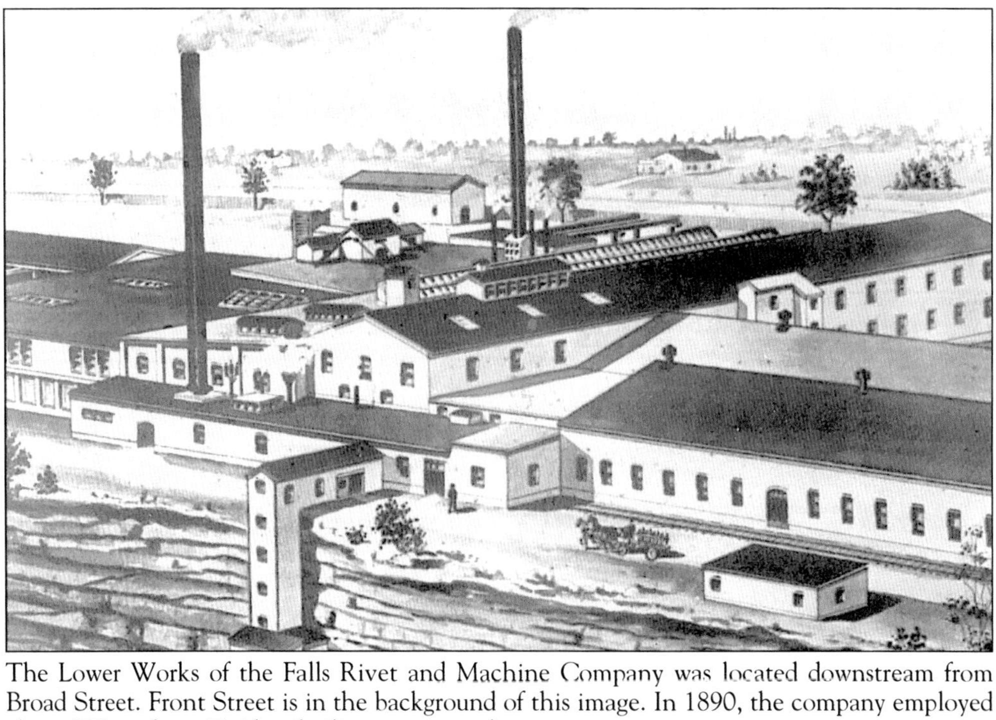

The Lower Works of the Falls Rivet and Machine Company was located downstream from Broad Street. Front Street is in the background of this image. In 1890, the company employed about 250 workers. Neither facility remains today.

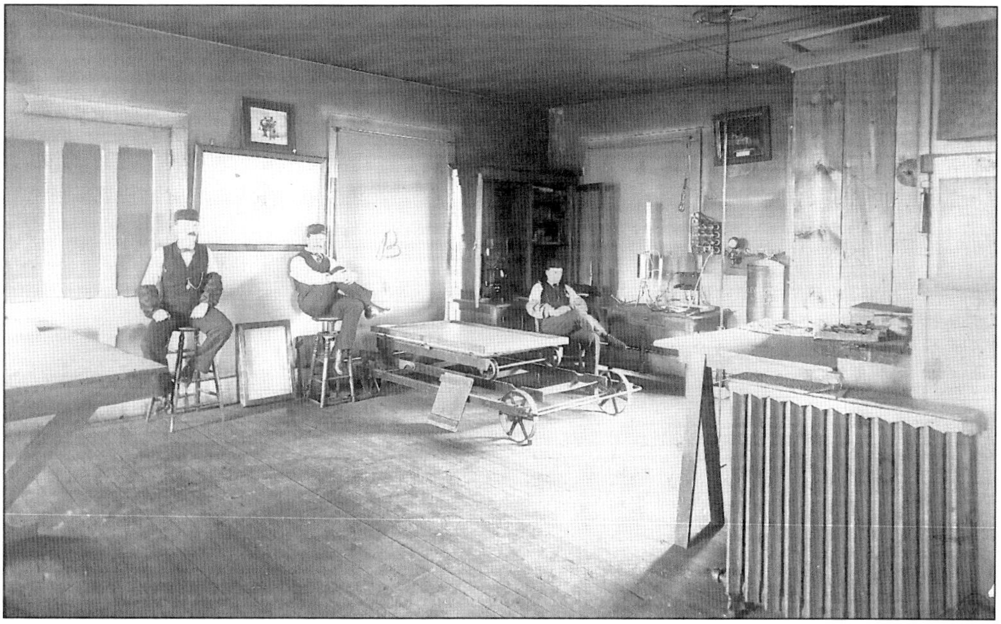

Pictured here, from left to right, are: George Irvin, Charles Falor, and George Hinchman in the drafting room of the Falls Rivet Company.

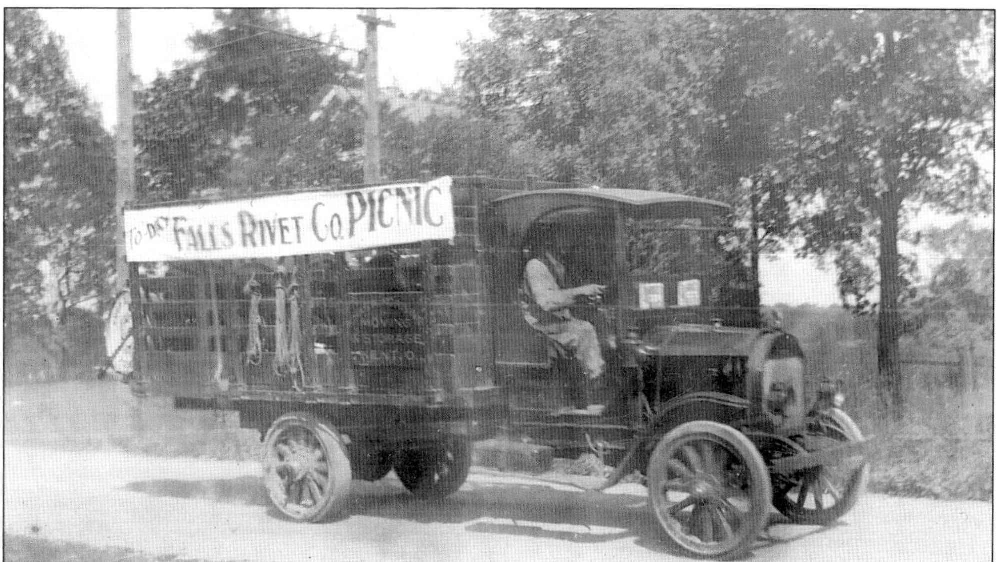

The banner on this truck advertises the Falls Rivet Company picnic. The small sign on the truck advertises Charles Horning Moving and Storage of Kent, Ohio.

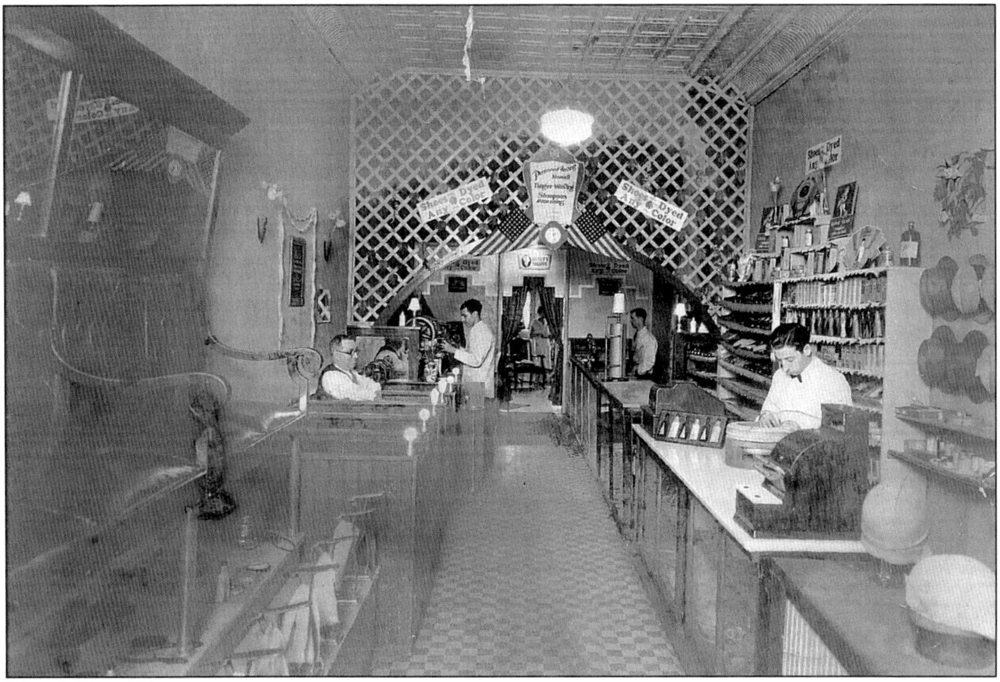

This photograph was taken around 1929 at Modern Hat Cleaning Company. At this business, located at 2046 Front Street, you could have your hat cleaned and re-blocked in 24 hours. A beauty salon operated in the rear. Pictured here, from left to right, are: unidentified seated man, shoemaker Ralph Camito, Mary Camito (seated), Kathy Romanski, shoe shiner William Caruso, and owner Paul Sullivan. At age 19, Sullivan was believed to be the youngest businessperson on Front Street.

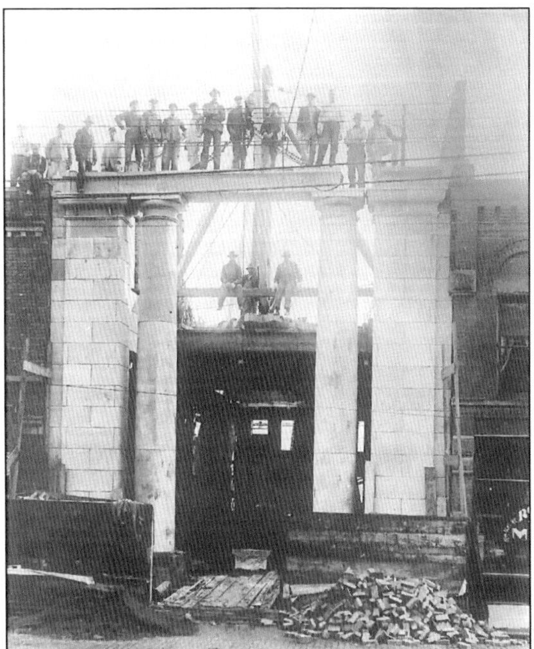

In this photograph, workers pose atop a beam hoisted onto the stone pillars during the reconstruction of the Falls Savings Bank, later First National Bank, on November 3, 1915. The building, located at 25 South Front Street (streets were renumbered in 1929), has been home to several banks and is now used as the Cuyahoga Valley Art Center. The beautiful stone pillars seen here have been covered with a new façade.

During the Depression, Cuyahoga Falls dairy merchant J.J. Lawson lost customers because milk cost too much. Lawson decided to sell milk by the gallon on a cash and carry basis through his own stores in order to lower prices. The first such store opened in 1939 at the corner of the Lawson's dairy plant located on the east side of the river at Broad Street. Here customers could save 16¢ a gallon over regular delivery prices. The plan was so successful, that by 1951 every neighborhood in Summit County had a Lawson's store. The "gallon-jug plan" for selling milk made J.J. Lawson famous locally, but his idea soon spread across the nation.

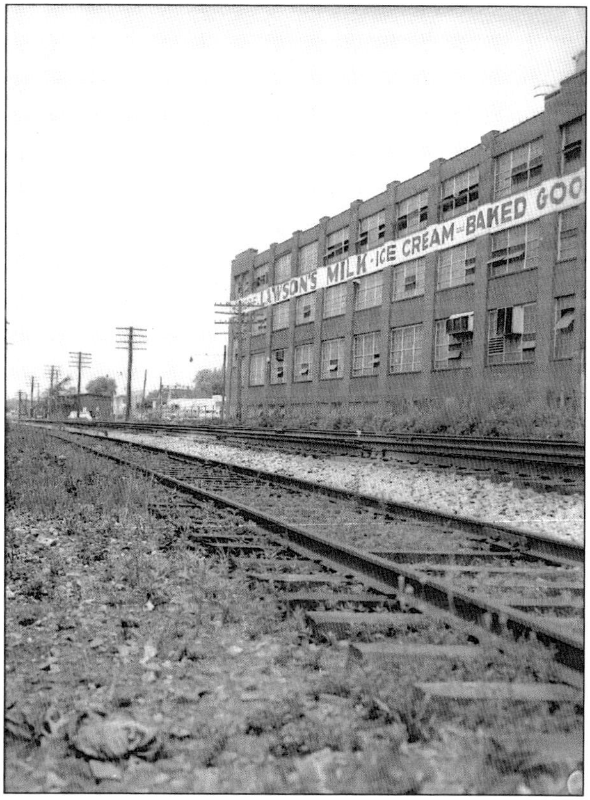

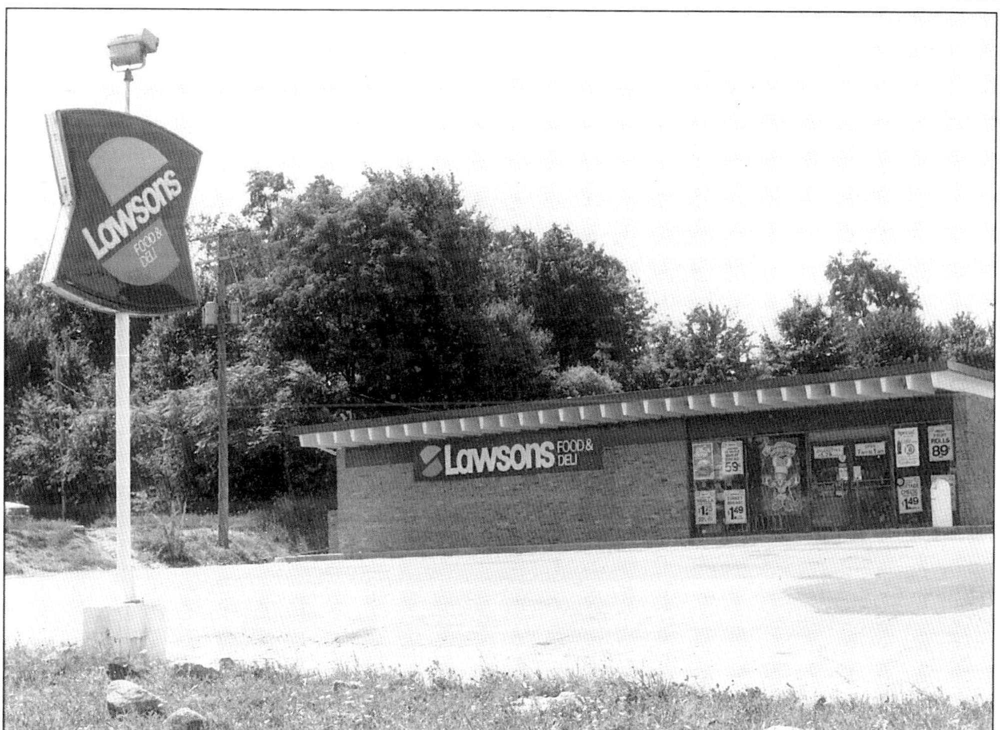

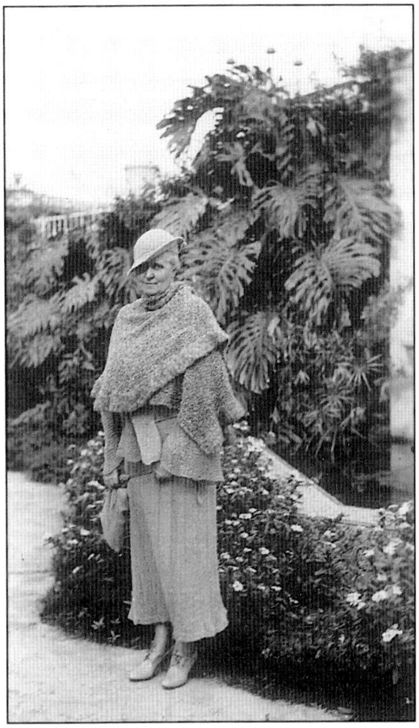

Byrdana Whipple operated her business, Byrdana's Hand Knitted Apparel, out of a shop at her home on Broad Boulevard. Her husband, C. Horton Whipple, operated the Whipple Furniture Company on Front Street. In this photograph, Madame Byrdana—as she was known professionally—poses in one of her creations.

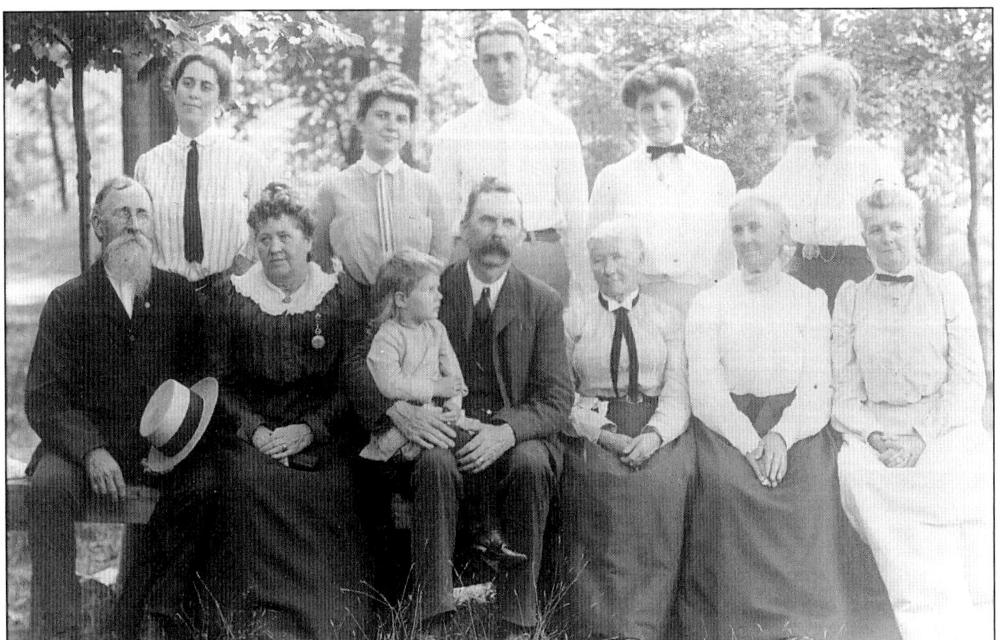

Byrdana's father, Josiah Brown, a cabinetmaker, was believed to also be the first undertaker in Cuyahoga Falls. Byrdana and her father are pictured here in a 1903 family reunion photograph. Front row: Josiah Brown, Emily Brown, Irwin Warner on the lap of his grandfather, W.W. Warner, Mary Baldwin, Ann Warner, and Harriet Frances. Back row: Byrdana, Mabel Warner, Frank Manchester, Nina Manchester, and Josie Warner.

Carol Whipple, daughter of Byrdana and C. Horton Whipple, poses in one of her mother's hand-knitted outfits. Carol was a certified teacher of the Unity Church denomination, and in her later years she fought to save her ancestral home from the wrecker's ball—hoping the house would become a museum. Carol died in 1998.

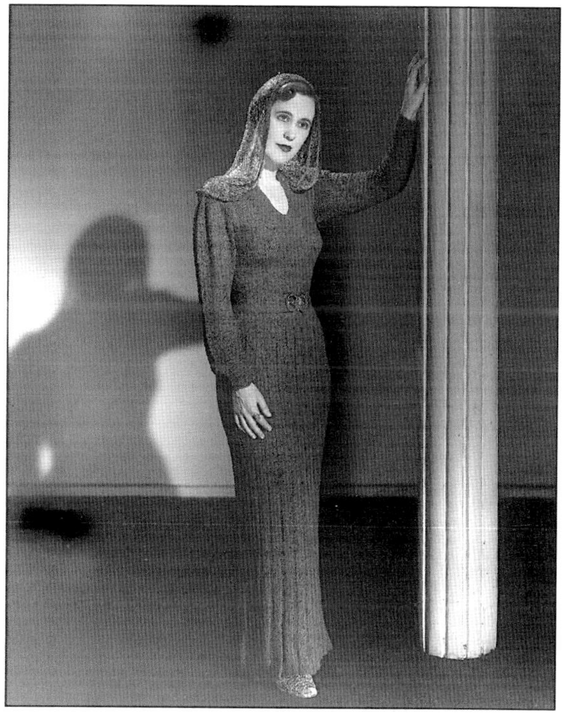

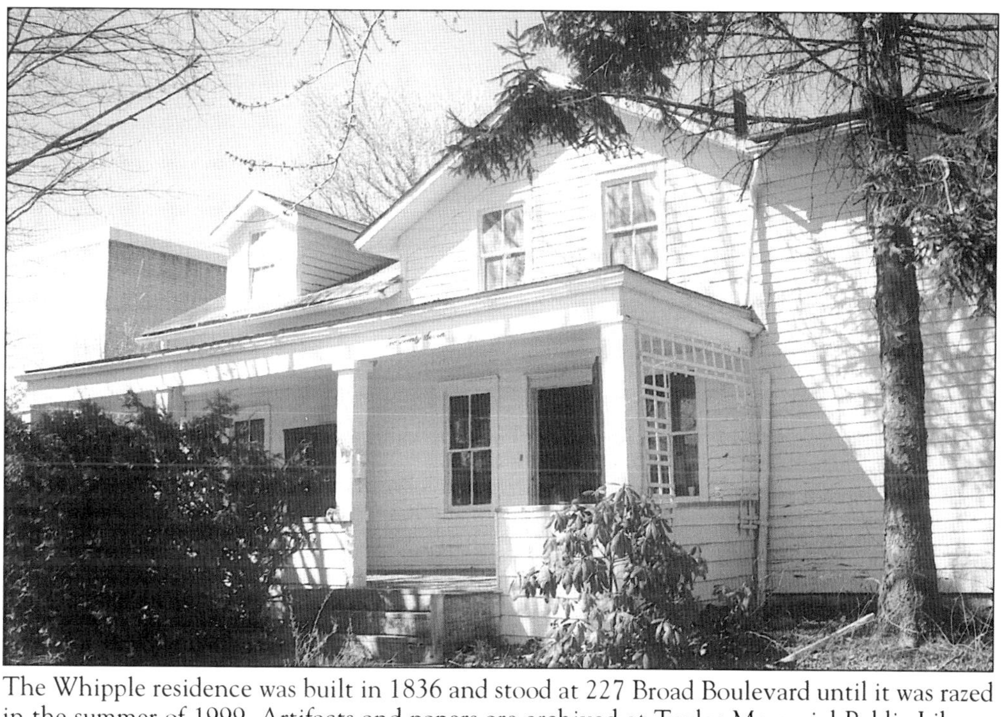

The Whipple residence was built in 1836 and stood at 227 Broad Boulevard until it was razed in the summer of 1999. Artifacts and papers are archived at Taylor Memorial Public Library (next to the Whipple house site) and at the Cuyahoga Falls Historical Society Museum. Although the house could not be saved as Carol Whipple had hoped, her family's legacy has been preserved.

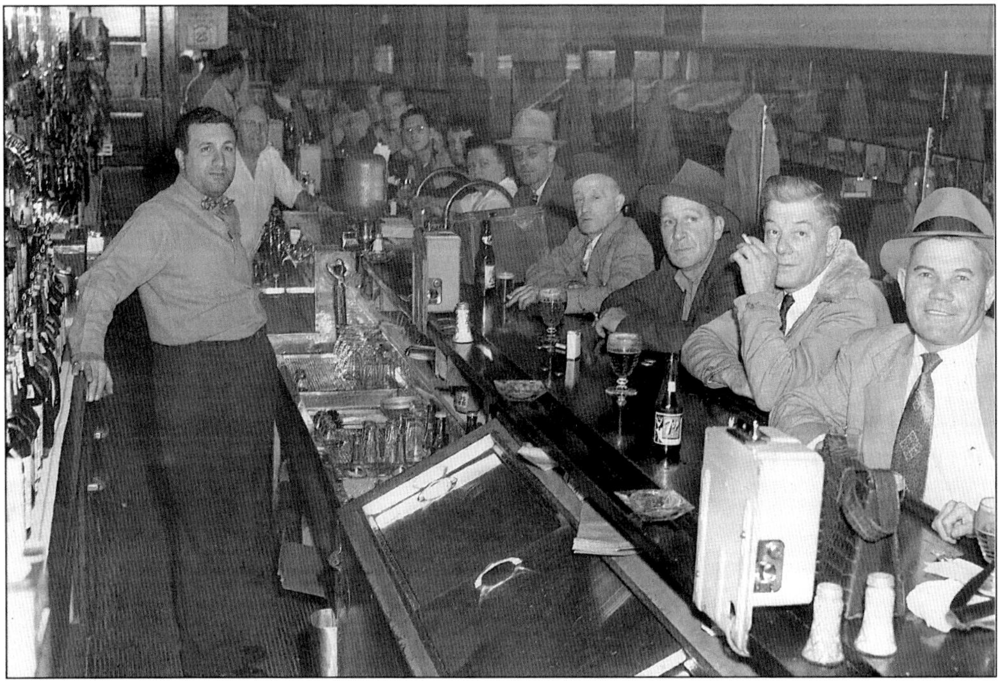

Tommy's Café at 2225 Front Street was a popular eating and drinking establishment in the mid-1900s. In this photograph, proprietor Tommy Bruno stands behind the counter.

TOMMY'S CAFE

2225 FRONT STREET
CUYAHOGA FALLS, OHIO

Dinners Ala Carte

LARGE T-BONE STEAK	1.50
BREADED VEAL CUTLET	.95
GRILLED PORK CHOPS (2)	1.00
ROAST PRIME RIBS OF BEEF	1.25
GRILLED HAM STEAK	.95
GRILLED HAMBURGER STEAK with Onions	.95
ROAST FRESH HAM	.95
GRILLED CUBE STEAK	.90

Cooked To Order

SPAGHETTI AND MEAT BALLS	.95
SPAGHETTI WITH PLAIN SAUCE	.75
HOME-MADE RAVIOLI WITH SAUCE	1.10
SPAGHETTI WITH MUSHROOM SAUCE	1.25

Sea Food

BREADED SHRIMP, Fan Tail	.90
BREADED SCALLOPS	.90
BLUE PIKE	.95

ABOVE ORDERS INCLUDE
Potatoes, Bread, Butter and One Side Dish, Coffee or Tea, Milk Extra

21 SHRIMP IN THE BASKET	1.25

WE FEATURE CHICKEN IN THE BASKET
Half Spring Chicken, French Fried Potatoes, Celery, Carrot Sticks, Olives, Hot Buttered Bun and Coffee
1.25

Hot Sandwiches

Hot Beef or Pork with Potatoes and Gravy	.60

Cheese & Cracker Plates

Large Plate	.50
Small Plate	.30
Olives, per order	.25

Sandwiches

Hamburg	.30
Cheeseburg	.35
Swiss or American	.25
Grilled Cheese	.35
Cube Steak	.45
Meat Ball	.30
Fried Fish	.30
Baked Ham, Pork or Beef	.40
Fried Ham	.45
Fried Egg	.25
Bacon, Lettuce and Tomato	.45
Ham and Egg Combination	.55

Tomato .05 extra

Cocktails

BACARDI	.65	MARTINI	.55

Long Drinks

TOM COLLINS	.55	JOHN COLLINS	.55

You could get a good meal for under a dollar at Tommy's Café. The front of this menu displays a drawing of Tommy (smoking his trademark cigar) and a drawing of a bear. The caption reads "The bear fact is, for food in the Falls, it's Tommy's Café."

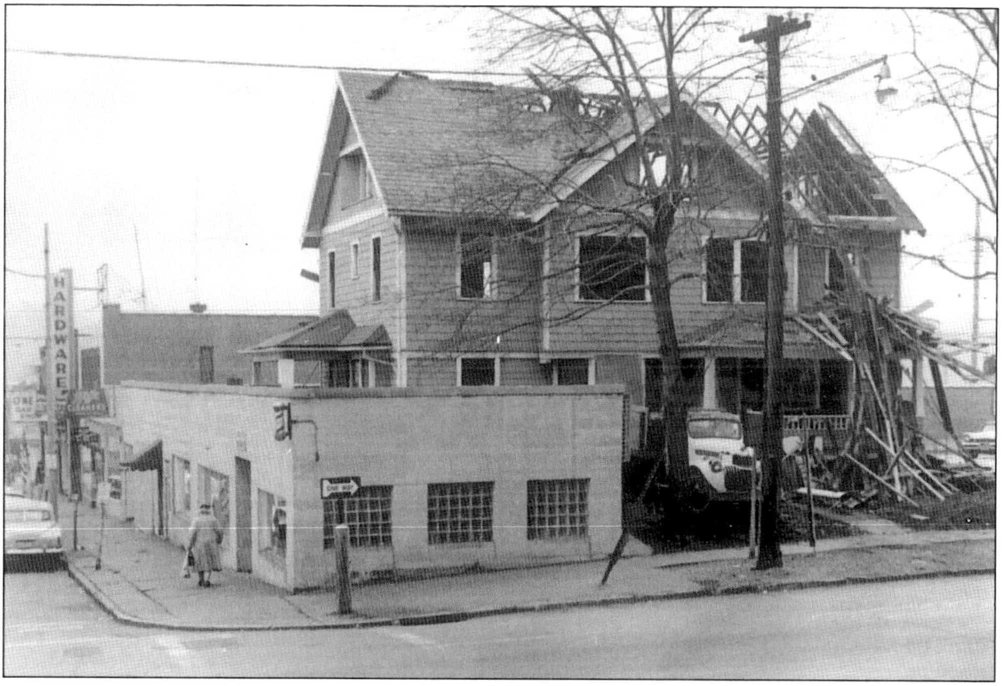

Valley Savings and Loan first opened its doors in 1923 at a location on the southeast corner of Portage Trail and Second Street. In 1962, the buildings on the corner of Portage and Second Streets, shown above, were razed and remodeled to construct the present facility shown below. A special section of the *Falls News*, which announced the grand opening, proclaimed: "Valley Savings writes happy ending for the corner's Cinderella story." Notice that in 1962, Second Street was a one-way route.

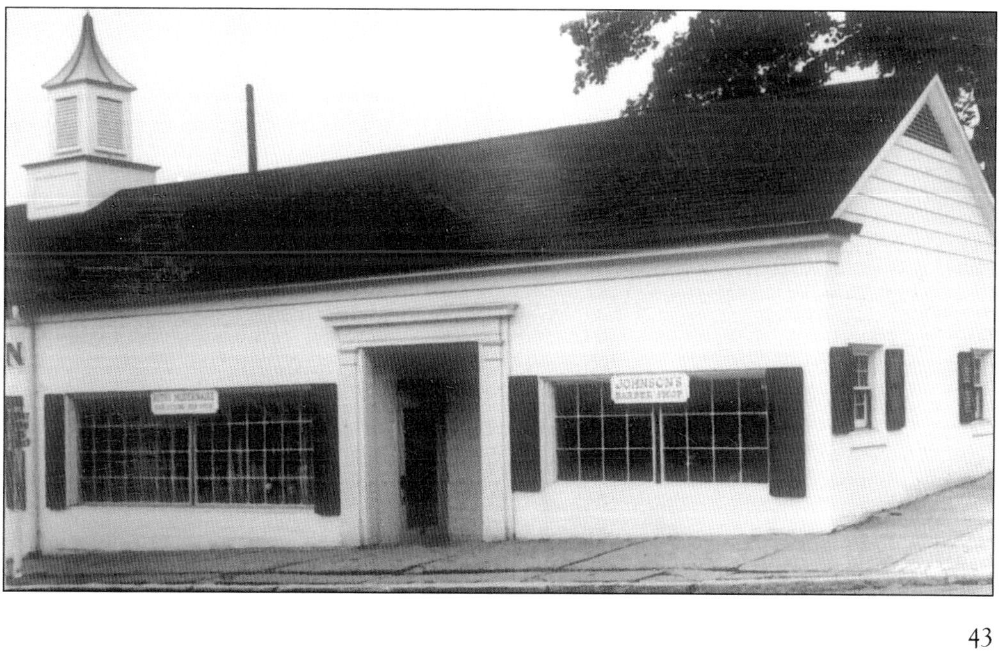

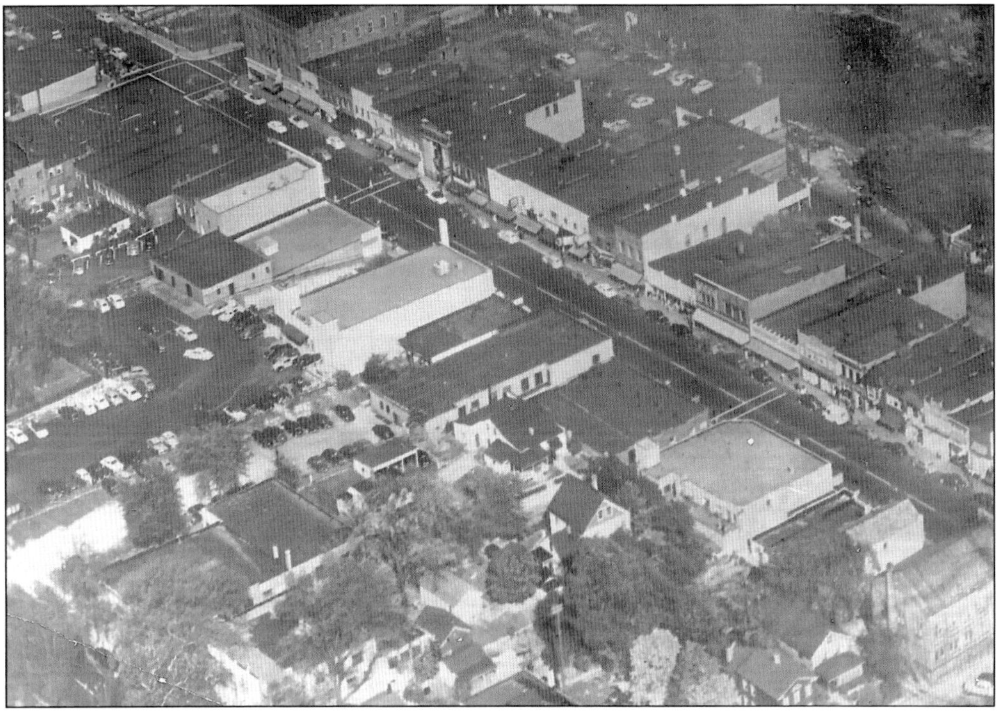

This aerial view photographed by Richard B. Miles shows Front Street in 1948. The corner lot at Front and Portage is empty in this view, because fire destroyed the Falls Hardware Company and Falls Chocolate Shop building that once occupied this space. Businesses along Front Street during this time included Pioneer Café, F.W. Woolworth's 5&10, Leiter Hardware, Knight Cleaners, Falls Department Store, Isaly's, Kippy's, Kroger's, Levinson's, O'Neil's, and Falls Theatre.

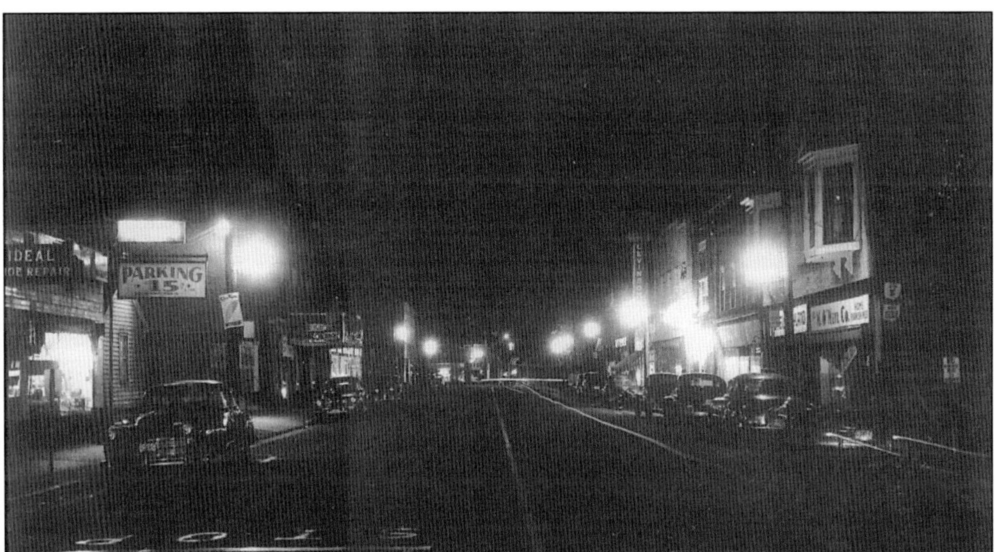

This night view of Front Street looking north from Portage Trail was taken in 1949. Early streets of Cuyahoga Falls were once lit by gasoline vapor lamps, but electric lighting was in use as early as 1891.

Three

BUILDING A COMMUNITY
PEOPLE, PLACES, AND PROTECTORS

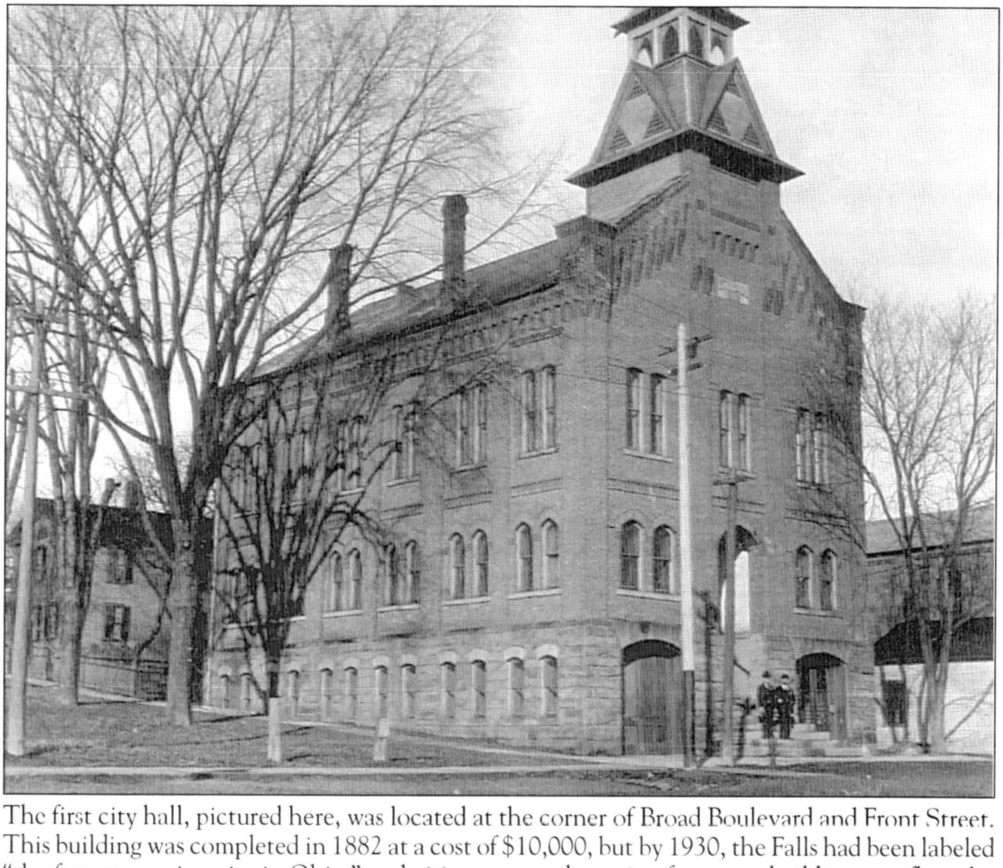

The first city hall, pictured here, was located at the corner of Broad Boulevard and Front Street. This building was completed in 1882 at a cost of $10,000, but by 1930, the Falls had been labeled "the fastest growing city in Ohio," and citizens were clamoring for a new building to reflect the city's image. An editorial appearing in the *Falls News Reporter* in January of 1930, declared: "The present one (city hall) is antiquated.... The size of the city grows, but yet we have the same old city hall which muchly [sic] resembles an old schoolhouse.... In the face of this, we should have a new building, something which will be a monument to the present generation who made the Falls the wonderful American city it is today." In 1952, a new city hall was built at 2310 Second Street. This chapter illustrates some of the people, places, and safety forces that helped to make Cuyahoga Falls the thriving city it became in its early years.

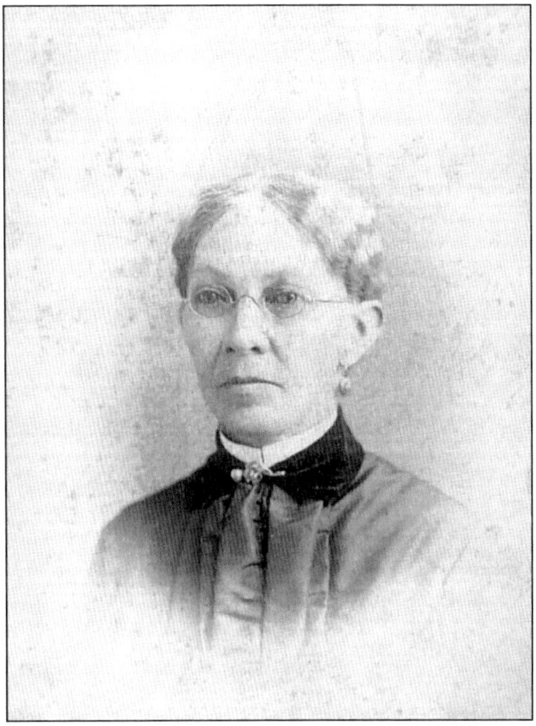

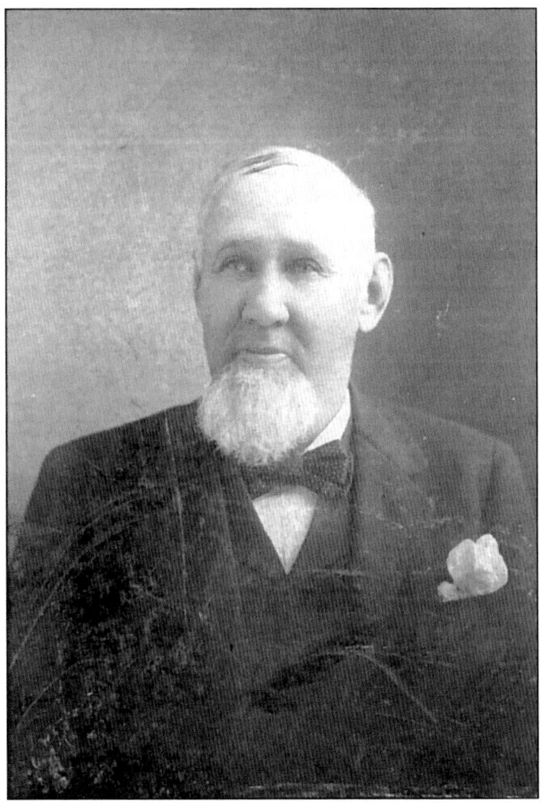

William A. Taylor was born in Vermont in 1830. He was a prominent industrialist and executive of the Turner, Vaughn & Taylor Company (later the Vaughn Machinery Company). William A.'s nephew, William H. Taylor, served as postmaster and mayor of Cuyahoga Falls. W.A. died in 1907, and when Margaretta Taylor died two years later, she left $15,000 for "a library and a place to display relics, works of art, and specimens" in Cuyahoga Falls. She also donated $3000 for books. In August of 1912, a red brick library was built for this purpose and was named for the Taylors.

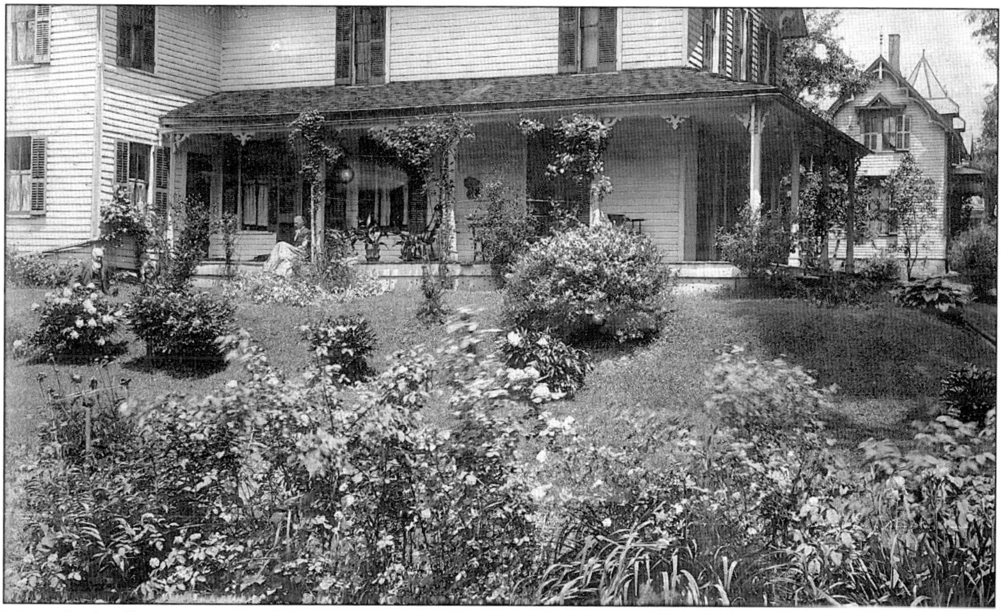

The Taylor home pictured here was a stately 12-bedroom house located at 2028 Second Street. The location is now the new Taylor Memorial Public Library parking lot.

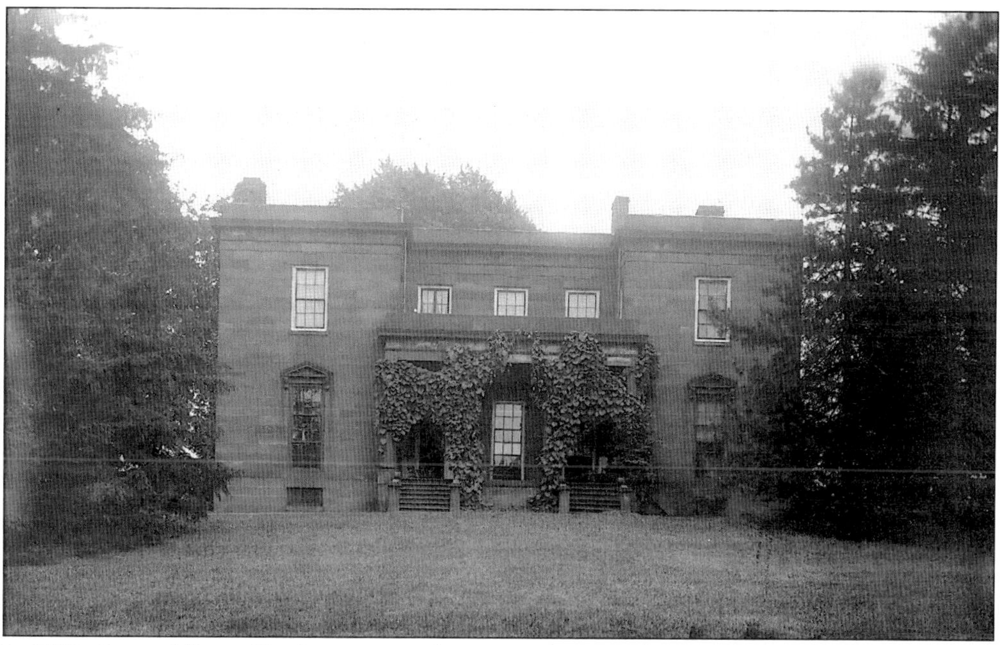

In 1798, General Roger Newberry won a drawing and received a 1000-acre grant in the Western Reserve of Connecticut in Ohio country. A large portion of present-day Cuyahoga Falls was part of this grant. General Newberry died in 1814 and left the land to his son, Henry, who built this mansion. The house overlooking the Cuyahoga River was completed in 1840, and the Newberry family lived there until 1892. The structure was later used as a sanitarium known as Fair Oaks Villa. In 1956, the building was torn down in favor of a modern hospital (Fallsview).

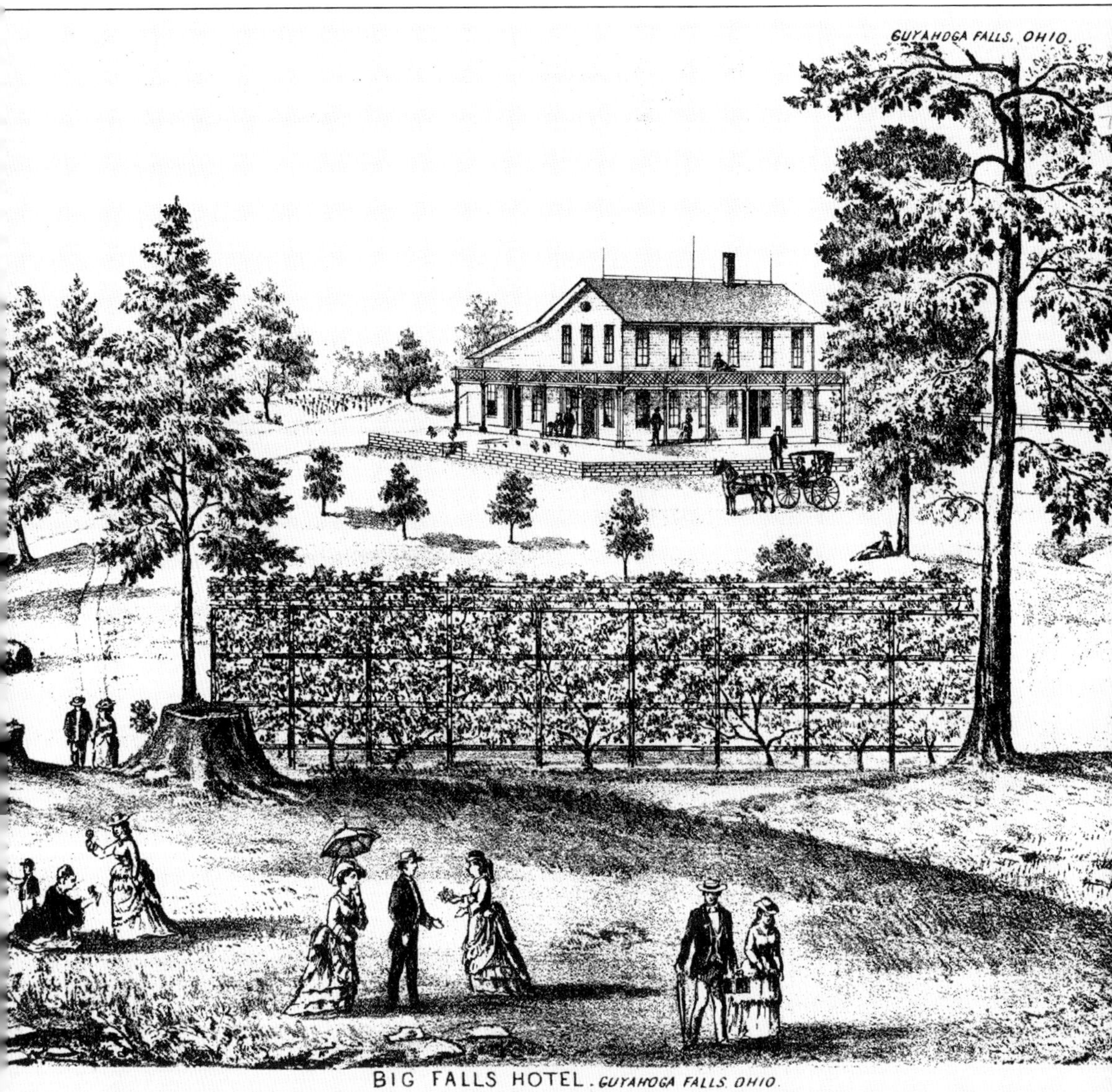

The Big Falls Hotel was located directly above Mary Campbell Cave, overlooking the Cuyahoga River. The establishment was the location for many dances and parties. Rapid transit cars transported people and their bags to the hotel to enjoy the many recreational activities available. Outside the hotel, steps led down to the gorge where a wooden dance floor was laid in Mary Campbell Cave. Guests could also enjoy the High Bridge Glens amusement area. The building pictured here burned down in 1913 and was never rebuilt as a hotel.

The Wetmore House was built in 1835 for Cuyahoga Falls pioneer Henry Wetmore, who built a paper mill on the east side of the river in 1830. The paper made at his mill was the first machine-made paper in Ohio. This home originally faced Front Street, but was later changed to have its address on Second Street.

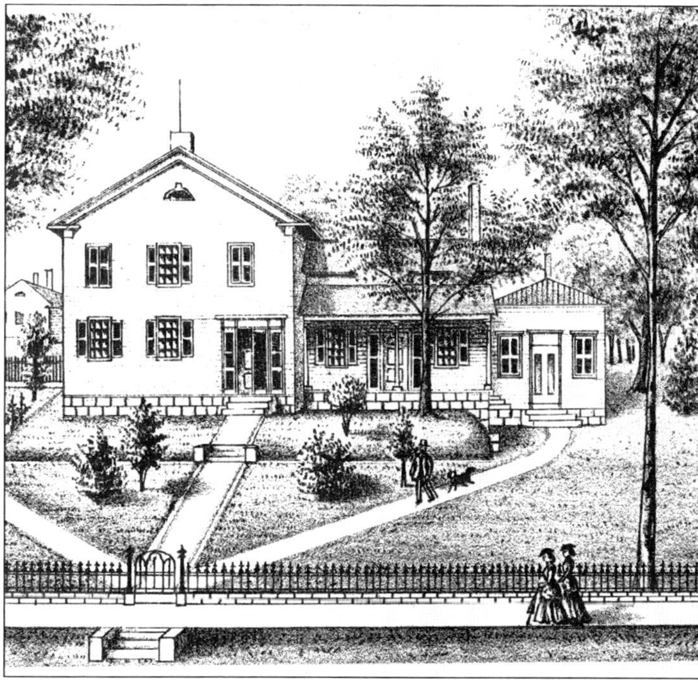

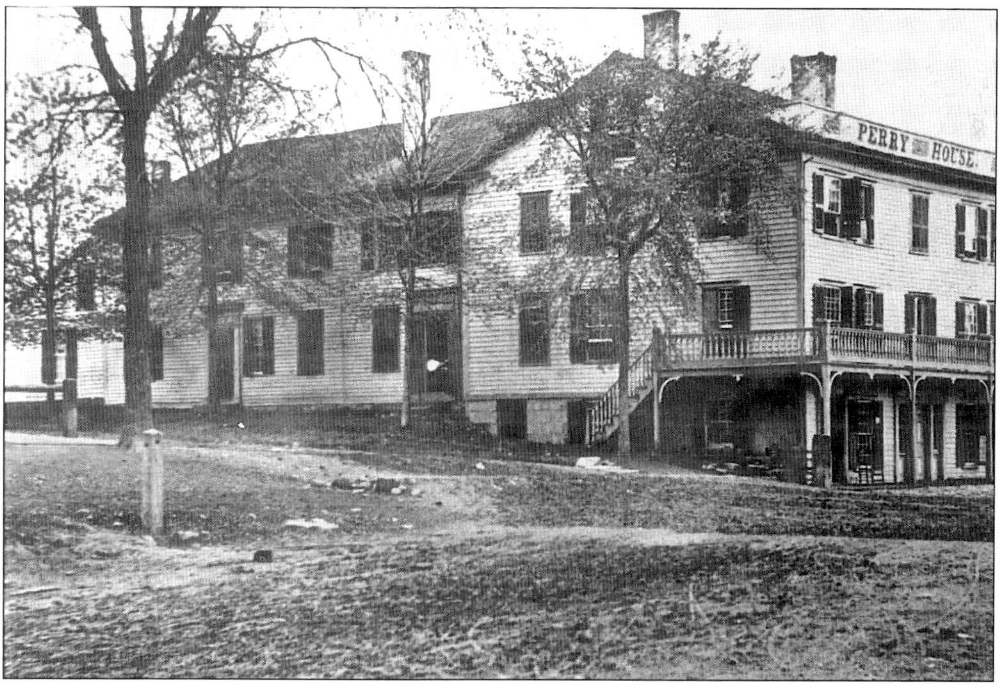

The Perry House was located at the corner of Portage Trail and Front Street. Built in 1827 by William Wetmore, brother of Henry Wetmore, it was used as a home and later as an inn. It was one of the first places at which early settlers could stay while they waited for their new homes to be built. In later years, the Perry house had a barbershop on the first floor. As a social activity on Saturday nights, people of the community came to the Perry House to sit on the benches and discuss the week's news.

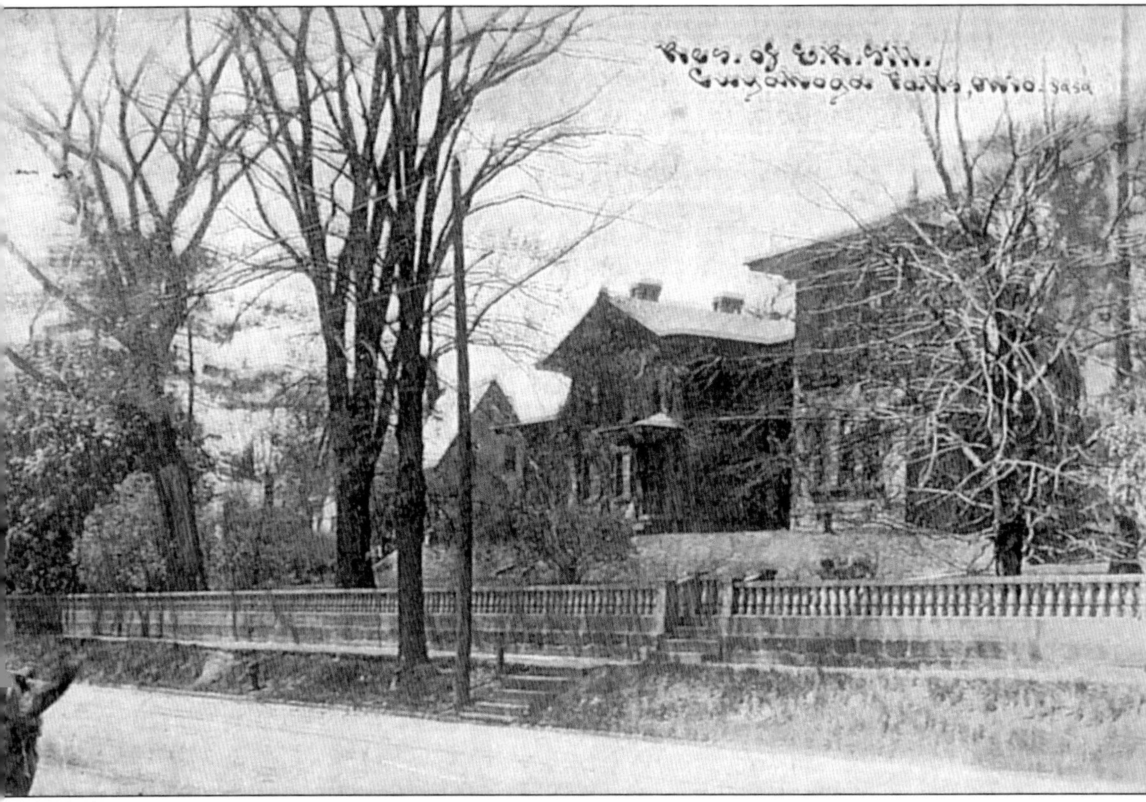

The Sill House was once home to one of Cuyahoga Falls' most famous early residents. Edward Rowland Sill moved to Cuyahoga Falls from Connecticut in 1853, at the age of 12. He was educated at Yale University and became an accomplished poet. He traveled extensively, taking many trips to California. Sill married his cousin, Elizabeth Strong. He helped organize Cuyahoga Falls High School and served as the head of Falls schools from 1869-1871. Later, the Sills moved to California, and Edward became a professor of English at Berkley, but eventually he came back because he missed his home in the Falls. Sill, who was in poor health for most of his life, died in 1887 after going to the hospital for a minor operation. On his deathbed he wrote these lines:

"The end's so near,
It is all one
What track I steer,
What works begun.
It is all one
If nothing done
The end's so near."

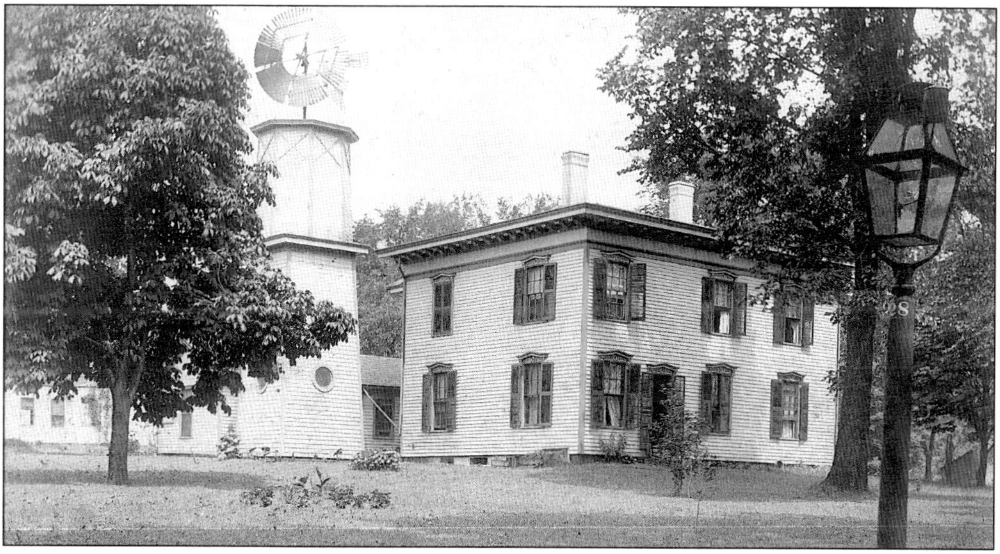

The Old Hanford Homestead pictured here was located at the corner of Broad Boulevard and Second Street. This was once the largest and most modern house in Cuyahoga Falls. E.L. Babcock, owner of the Falls Rivet and Machine Company, bought the home in 1885. He installed the first telephone in Cuyahoga Falls and built a private sewer system long before sewers became common. The panic of 1893 caused the Babcock business to fail, and the family was forced to sell the building to Dr. W.B. Middleton, who converted it into a hospital. The building was razed in 1938.

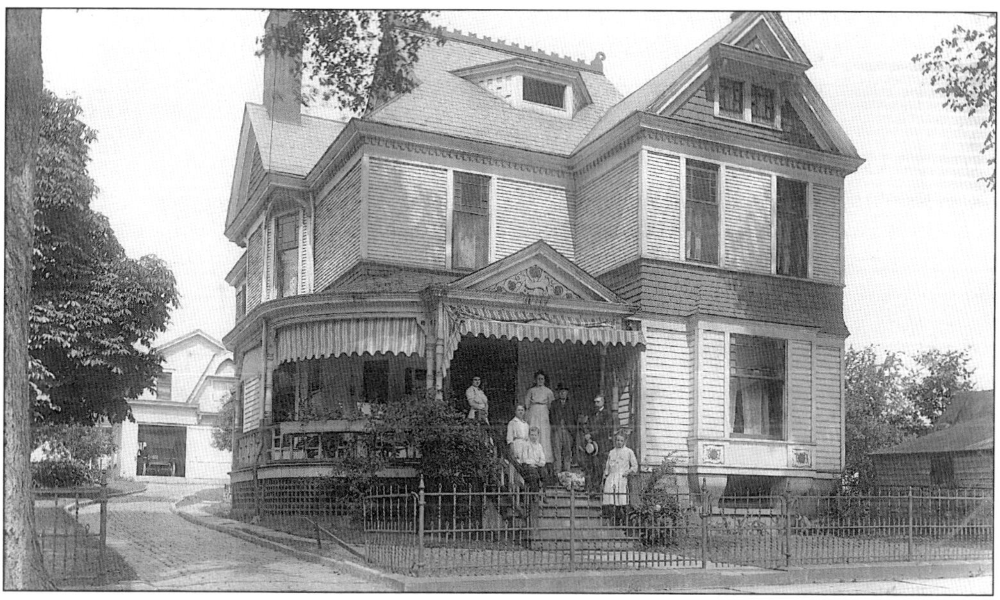

Dr. Floyd Smith (man holding hat) and his family pose in 1920 on the steps of their home at 14 North Front Street. Floyd was the son of Harvey Smith, a pioneer in homeopathic medicine. Floyd graduated from the Cleveland Medical College in 1896 at age 20. Dr. Smith was called to a case of hiccoughs only a few days after beginning his practice, and since hiccoughs was a rare affliction, he wasn't sure how to treat the man. While pondering what to do, a mysterious voice said, "Give him chloroform." Dr. Smith believed it was his dead father who spoke to him.

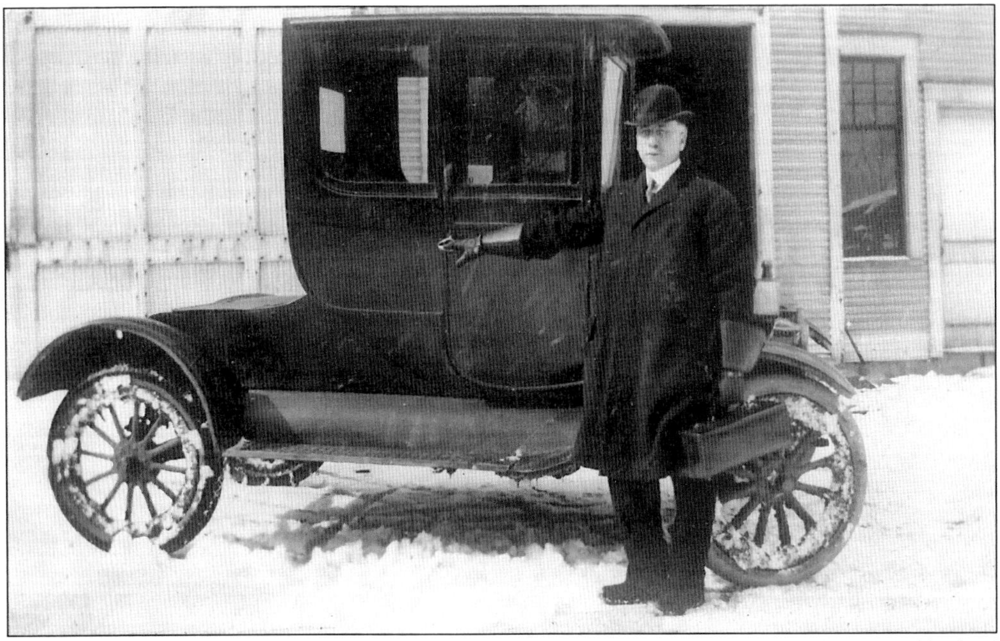

Dr. Floyd Smith stands in front of his car in the driveway of his home. Dr. Smith claimed he had one of the first automobiles in Cuyahoga Falls. For most of the winter, he stored the car in the garage and used horses until the weather improved.

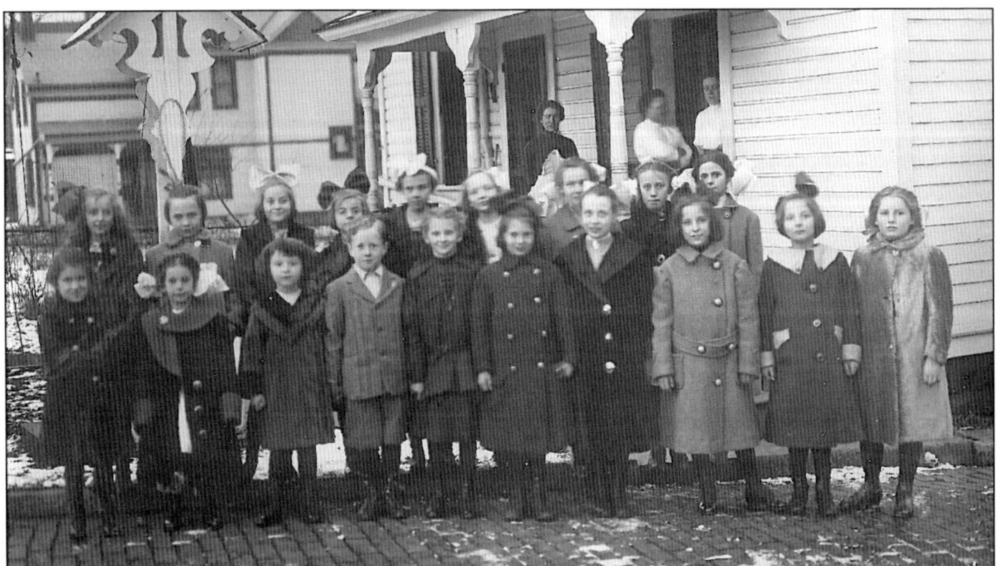

On November 12, 1927, Ethel Mae Smith, daughter of Dr. Floyd Smith, celebrated her eleventh birthday with her friends pictured here. At this particular party, no gifts were given, but instead, the children sat in a circle around Ethel and wished her the gifts that they wanted to give. Pictured from left to right, are: (front row) Harriet Long, Sarah Bolich, Wilbur Smith, Jean Duffy(?), Edith Humm, Ethel Smith, Dorothy Messner, Ethel Doan, Dorothy Armstrong; (back row) Nettie Murry, Norma Dunn, Dorothea Bayles, Harriet Miller, Julia Wills, Ruth Alspaugh, Dorothy Hibbard, Lois Tilock, and Helena Swain.

Harvey Snyder (top) was fire chief of Cuyahoga Falls in 1882 when the fire department was composed strictly of volunteers. In 1888, the department was reorganized, and all volunteers were given a certificate from the State of Ohio that exempted firemen from paying any road tax, performing jury duty, and serving in the military. William I. Clarkson (below), who was chief in 1891, was one of the first to serve as chief under this new system.

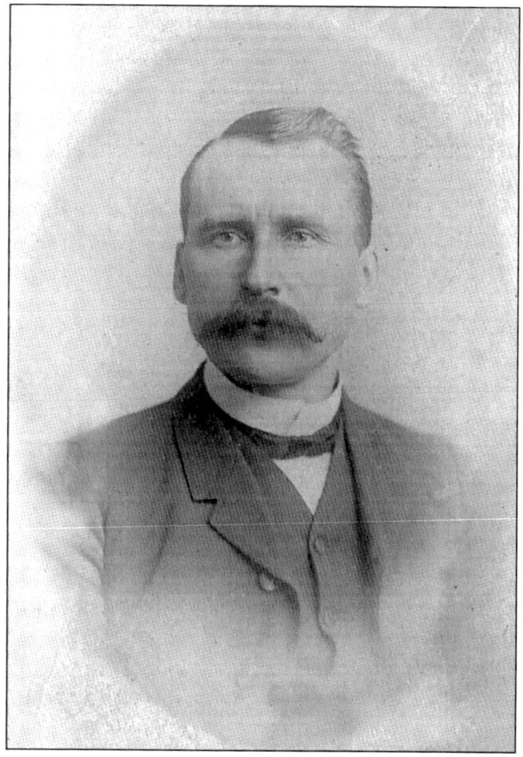

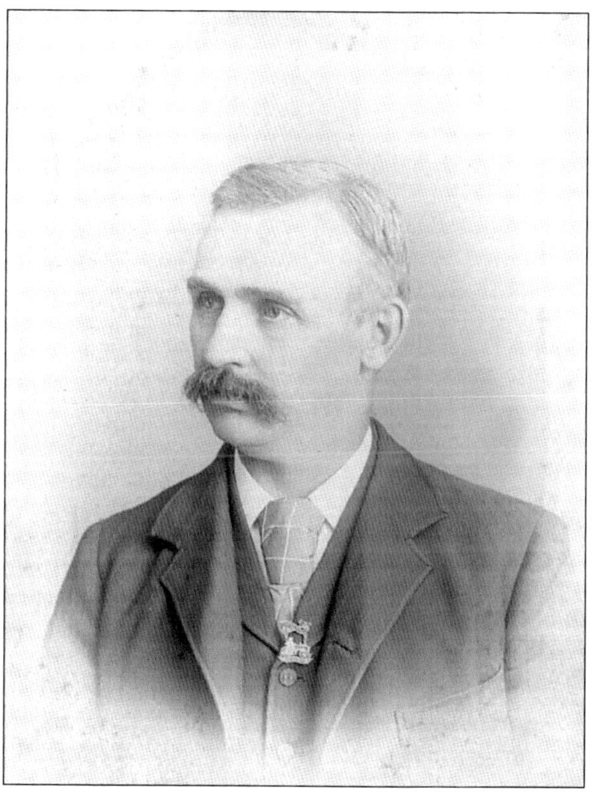

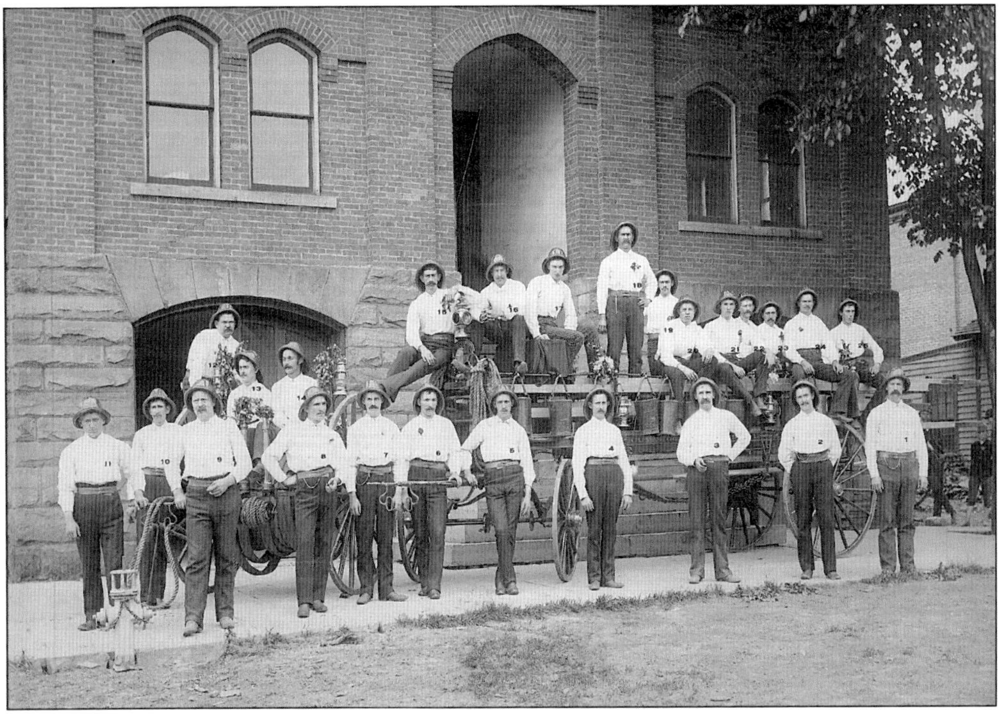

This photo shows the 1917 Cuyahoga Falls Volunteer Fire Department. The men are standing in front of the old city hall. Ten years later, the city created a full-time department, and headquarters was moved to Front Street. The department has since added two additional stations—a High Street station at the east end of Portage Trail, and an east-side station on Portage Trail near Bolich Middle School.

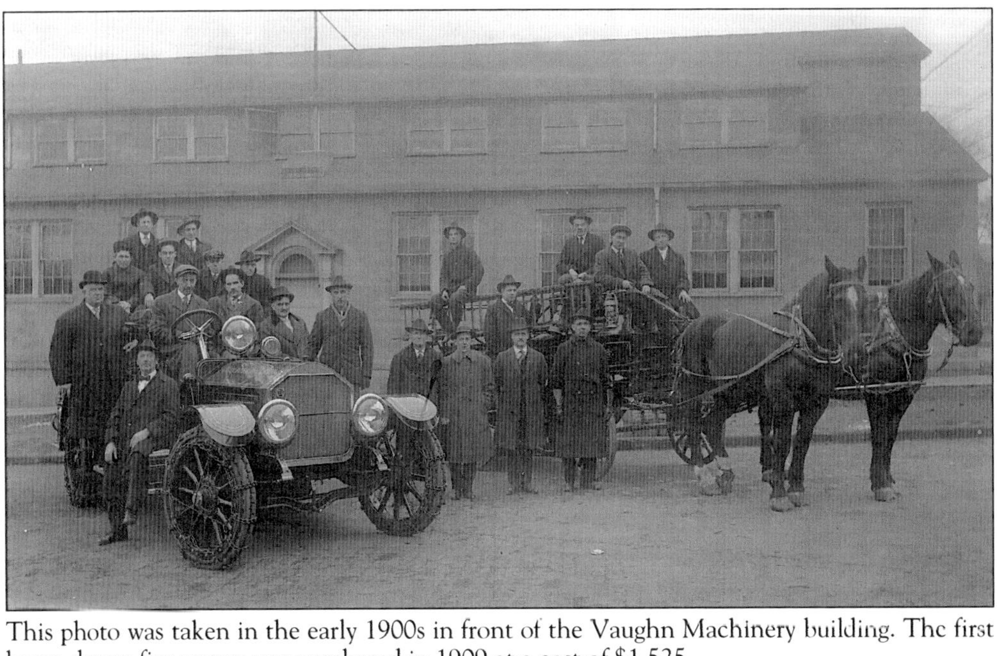

This photo was taken in the early 1900s in front of the Vaughn Machinery building. The first horse-drawn fire wagon was purchased in 1909 at a cost of $1,525.

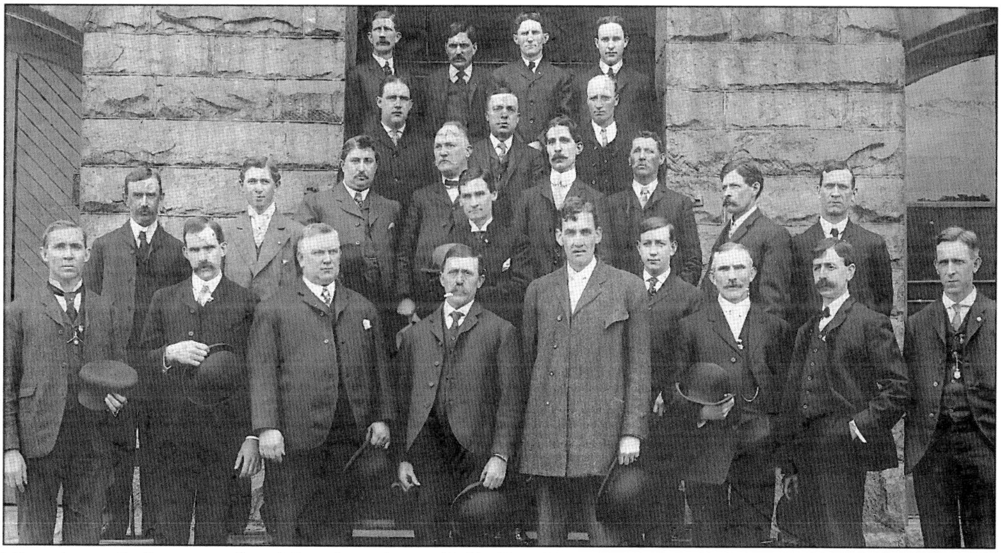

This formal photograph of the Cuyahoga Falls Fire Department was taken in the mid-1920s in front of the old city hall. The fire wagon was housed behind the arched door on the left.

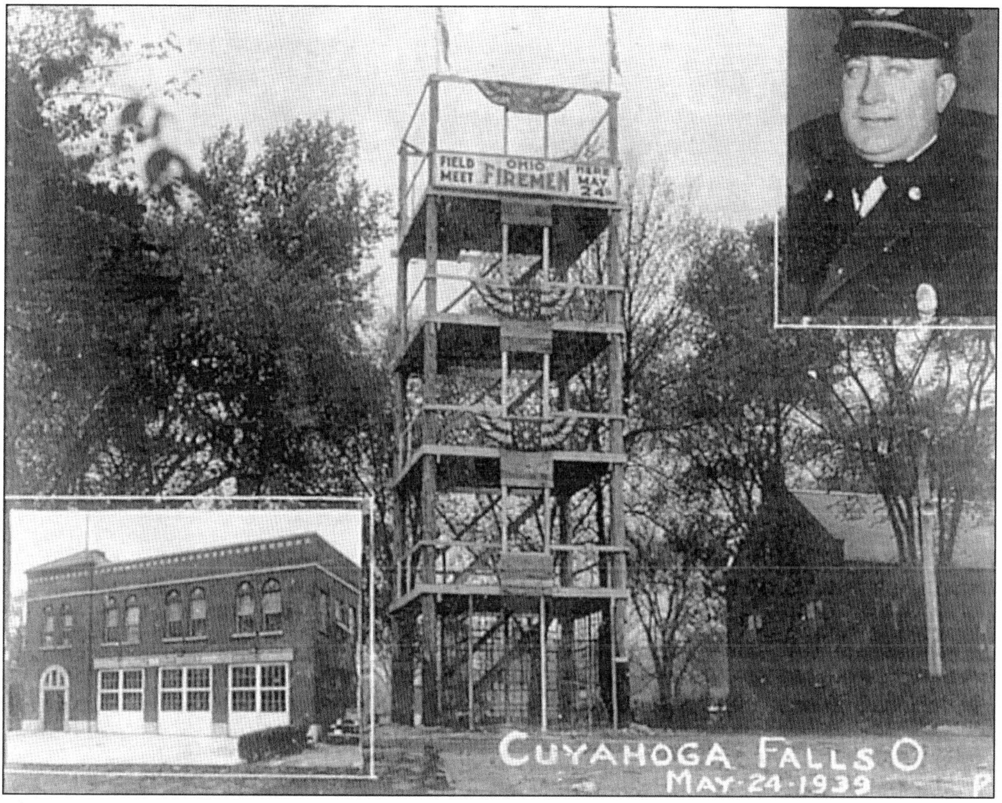

This early postcard view shows the tower used at the Ohio Firemen field meet on May 24, 1939. The tower was used in meet competitions held at a location near the old Taylor Library on the right. In the bottom left inset is a picture of the Fire Department headquarters located on Front Street. The top right inset is fire department Chief Louis Seiler.

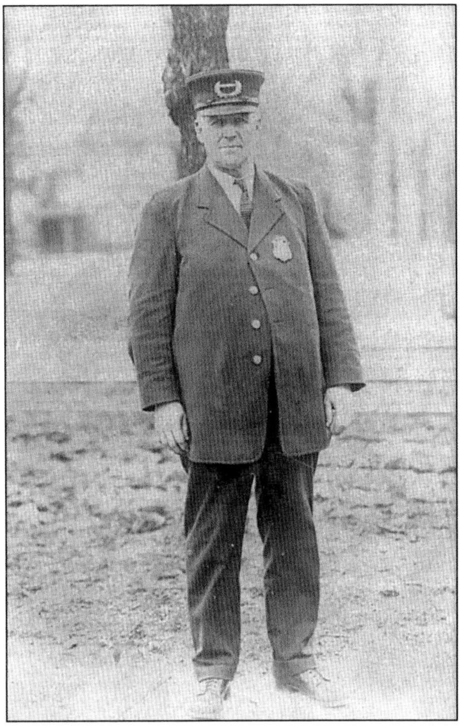

William Sanderson served as the last town marshal in Cuyahoga Falls from 1916 to 1922, when the new police department was established. Until then, Cuyahoga Falls had been protected by a lone marshal and a few volunteers. The qualifications for the job were "to know right from wrong and be strong enough to stand up to tough situations."

Five Cuyahoga Falls policemen pose here in front of the old city hall in 1946 or '47. Pictured here, from left to right, are: Dan Skidmore, Clarence Chance, Henry Greenwood, Robert DeHart, and Louis Felmly. Chance died in the line of duty.

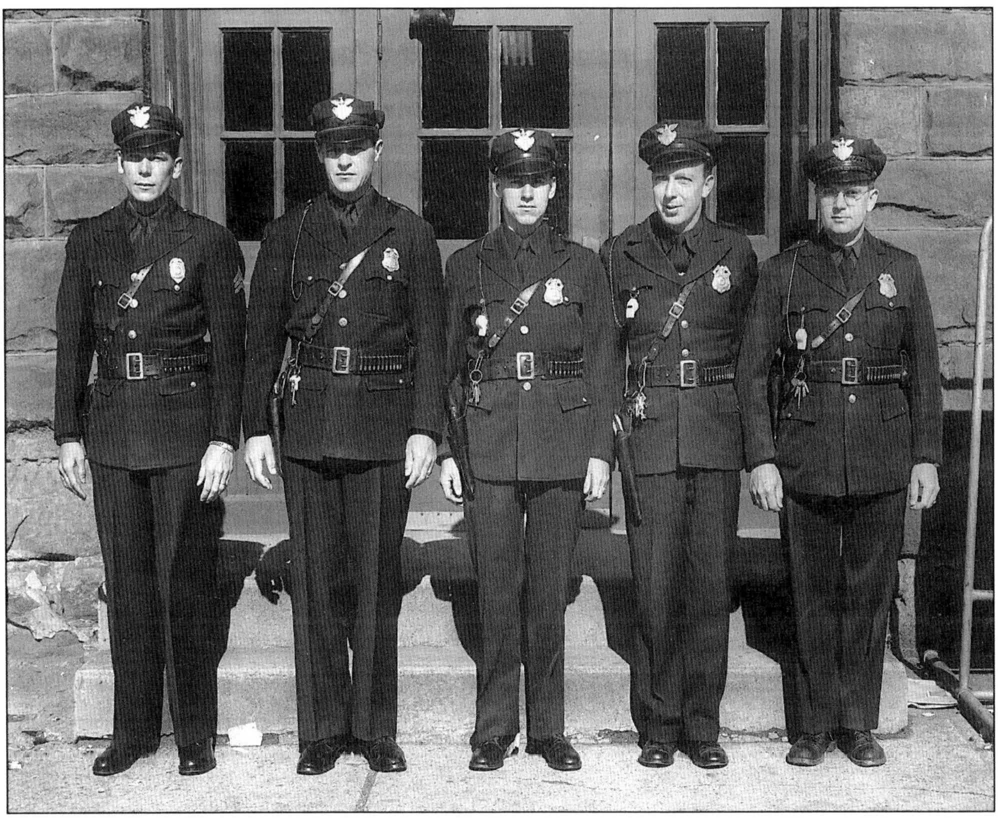

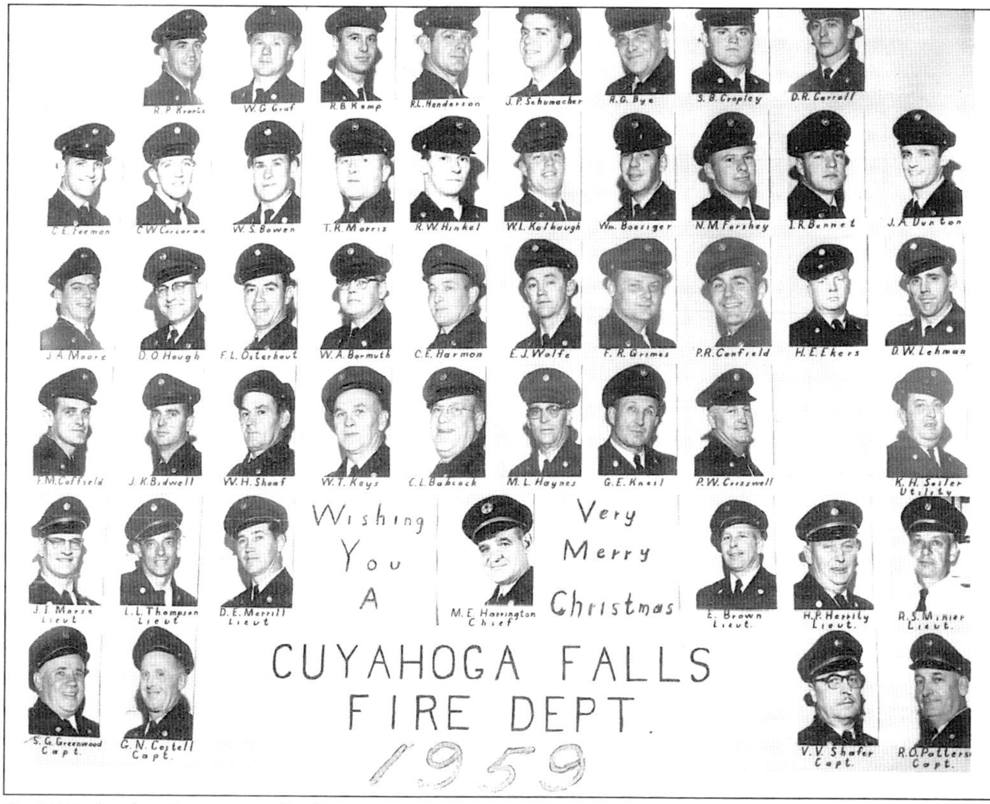

By 1959 the fire department had grown to over 40 members. They are pictured here, from left to right: (bottom row) S.G. Greenwood, G.N. Castell, V.V. Shafer, R.O. Patterson; (second row) J.J. Morse, L.L. Thompson, D.E. Merrill, M.E. Harrington, E. Brown, H.P. Herrity, R.S. Minier; (third row) F.M. Coffield, J.K. Bidwell, W.H. Shoof, W.T. Keys, C.L. Babcock, M.L. Haynes, G.E. Kneil, P.W. Grisswell, K.H. Seiler; (fourth row) J.A. Moore, D.O. Hough, F.L. Osterhout, W.A. Bormuth, C.E. Harmon, E.J. Wolfe, F.R. Grimes, P.R. Canfield, H.E. Ekers, D.W. Lehman; (fifth row) C.E. Freemen, C.W. Corcoran, W.S. Bowen, T.R. Morris, W.W. Hinkel, W.L. Kalbaugh, Wm. Boesiger, N.M. Forshey, J.R. Bennet, J.A. Dunton; (top row) R.P Krantz, W.G Graf, R.B. Kemp, R.L. Henderson, J.P. Schumacher, R.G Bye, S.B. Cropley, and D.R. Carroll.

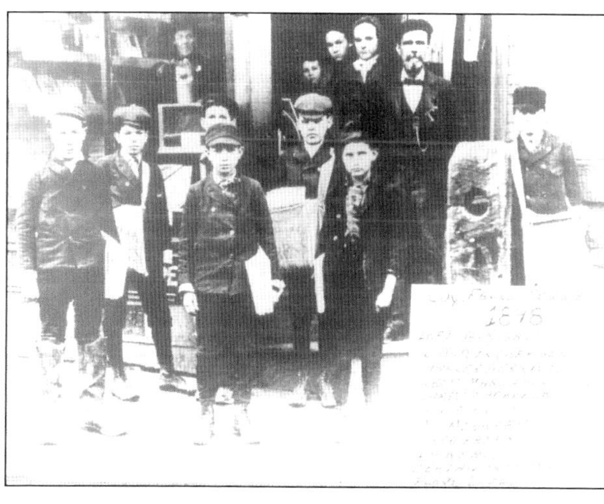

In the early years of Cuyahoga Falls, "newsies" were used to distribute the newspaper to the public. This 1898 photograph of the Cuyahoga Falls Newsies and friends shows, from left to right: (front row) Dutch Fryberger, Harley Herrick, Leon Marshall, Carlton Herrick, Dave Price, V.J. Medkeff, Fred Freer; (back row) Bertha Freeman, and Floyd Steel (?).

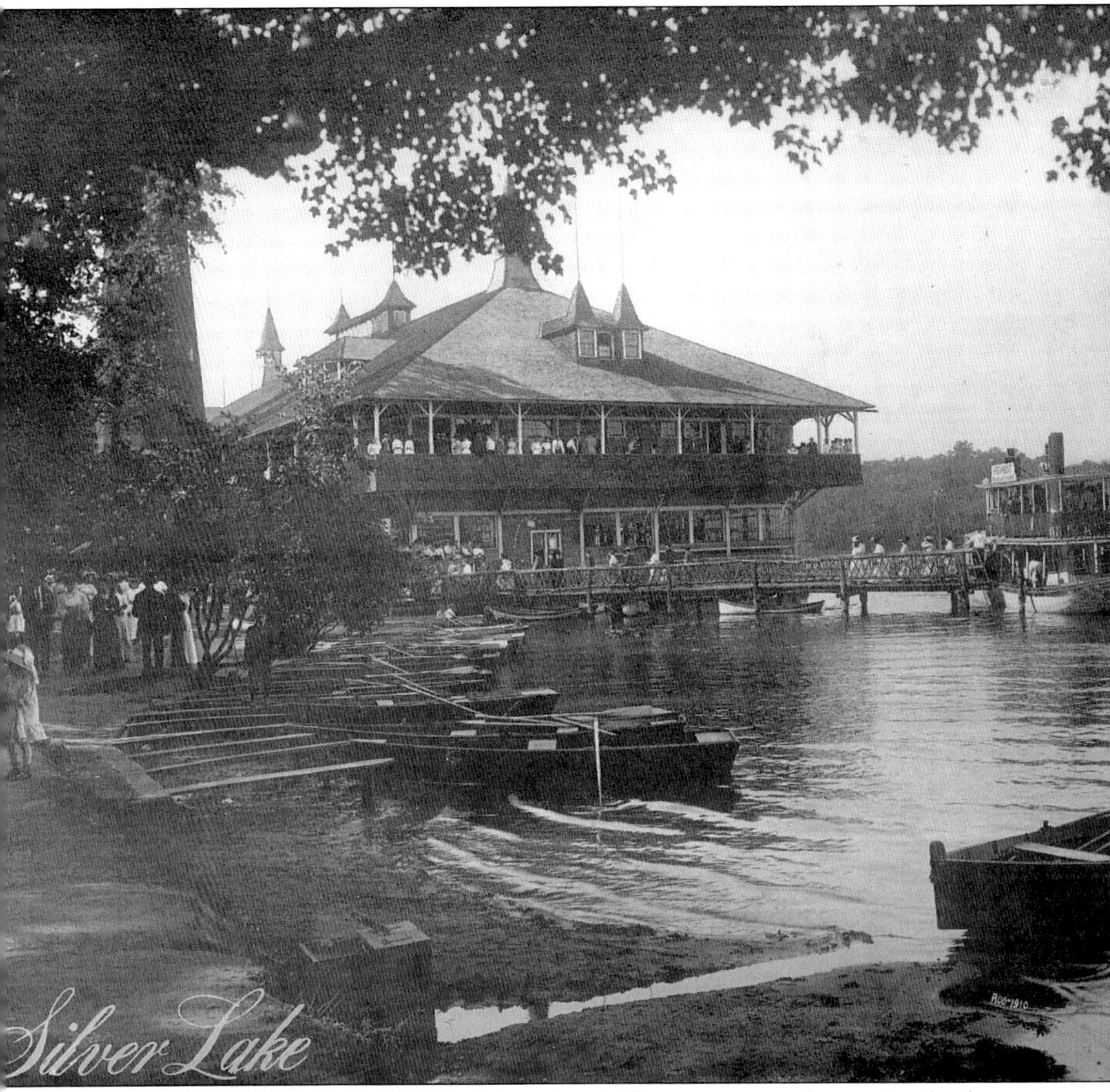

By the close of the nineteenth century, Cuyahoga Falls was a center of recreation for the entire state. At this time, Silver Lake Park was the main attraction in Ohio. At the height of its popularity, Silver Lake Park had a steamboat that made trips around the lake, a bathhouse, bear pits, an aquarium, a skating rink, a zoo, a merry-go-round, a roller coaster, rowboats, picnic facilities, a miniature railway, an airport, and the largest dance hall in Ohio, and would accommodate up to 20,000 people in a single day.

The first black bears were brought to Silver Lake from the north shore of Lake Superior. A total of 78 bear cubs were raised here—the first black bear cubs to be raised in captivity in America.

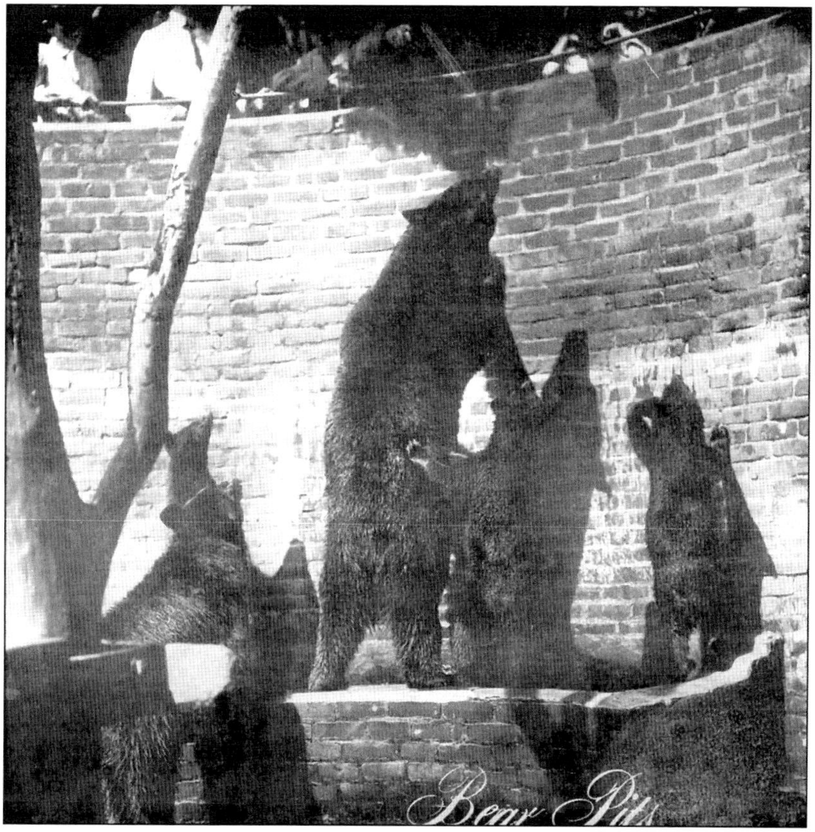

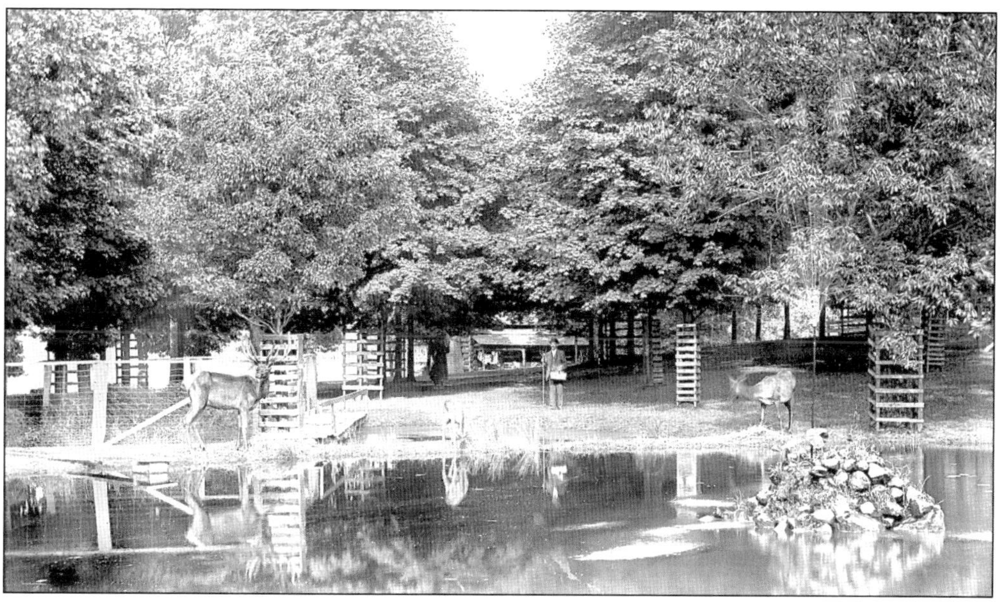

The bears weren't the only beasts to inhabit the shores of Silver Lake. The zoo contained raccoons, foxes, a bald eagle, monkeys, badgers, woodchucks, beavers, skunks, hawks, swans, an owl, a prairie wolf, a mountain lion, and a herd of elk. Three elk are pictured here.

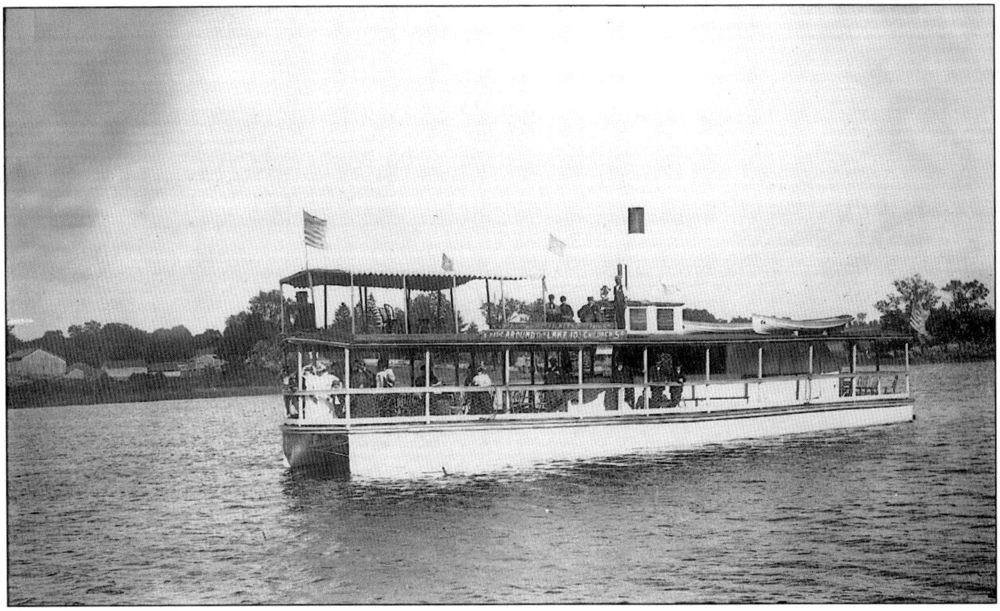

Three steamboats were in operation and offered rides around the lake for 10¢ per person—5¢ per child. The most popular of these three was the *Silver Queen*, which is pictured here.

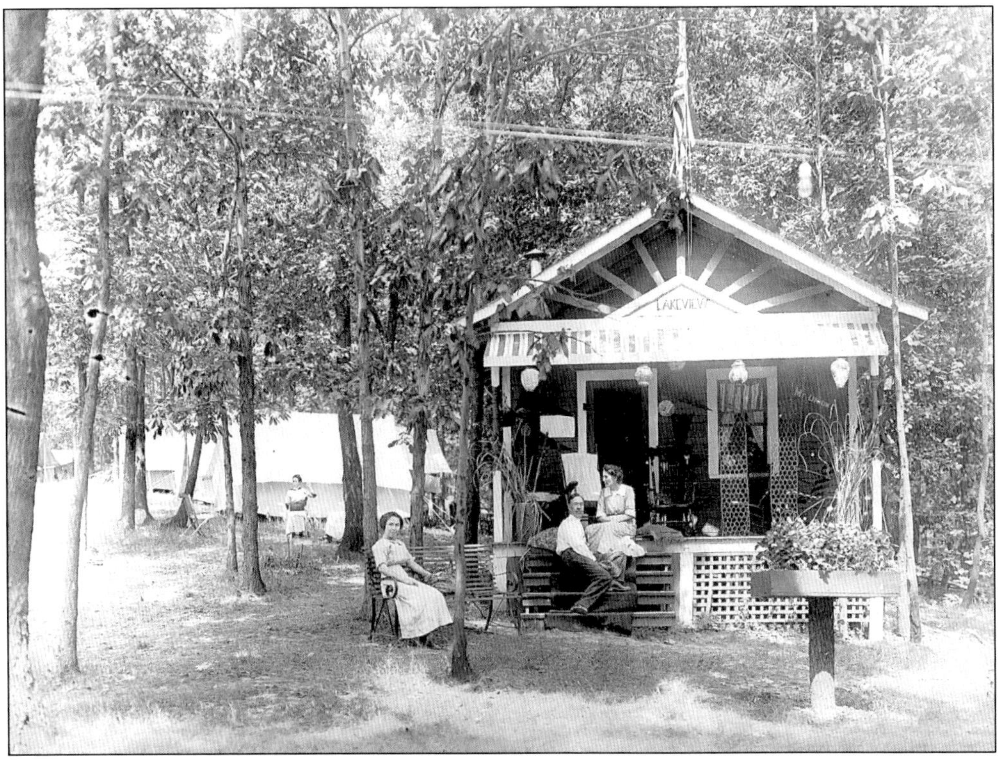

Several campsites and many cottages were located around the edge of Silver Lake in the late nineteenth century. This cabin was owned by the Domer Family. They are pictured here, from left to right: Lucille Domer, Rev. F.A. Domer, and Mrs. Domer.

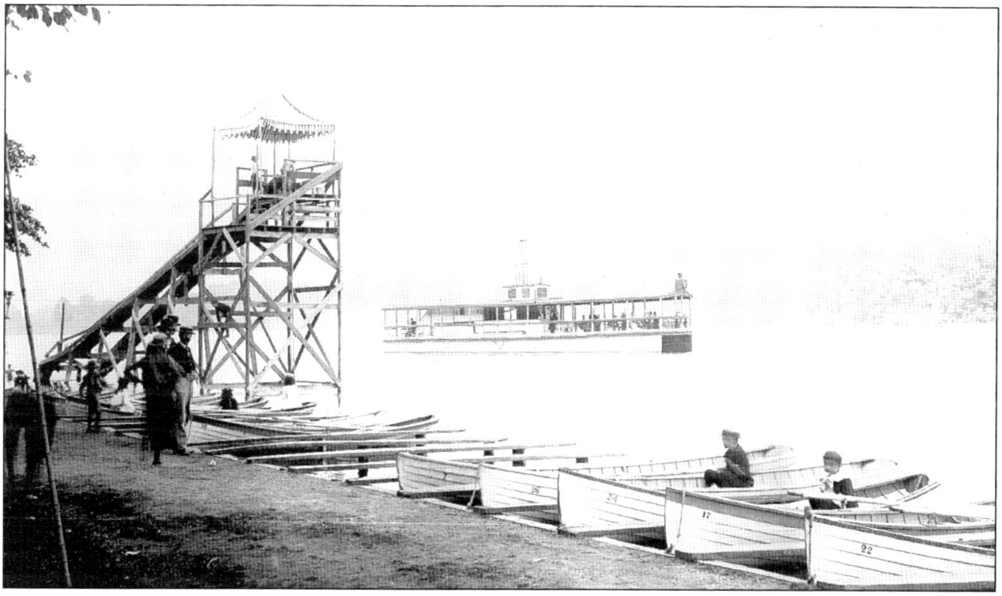

At Silver Lake Park rowboats could be rented for 25¢ an hour. To please the anglers, Silver Lake was stocked with several different kinds of fish in addition to its native species.

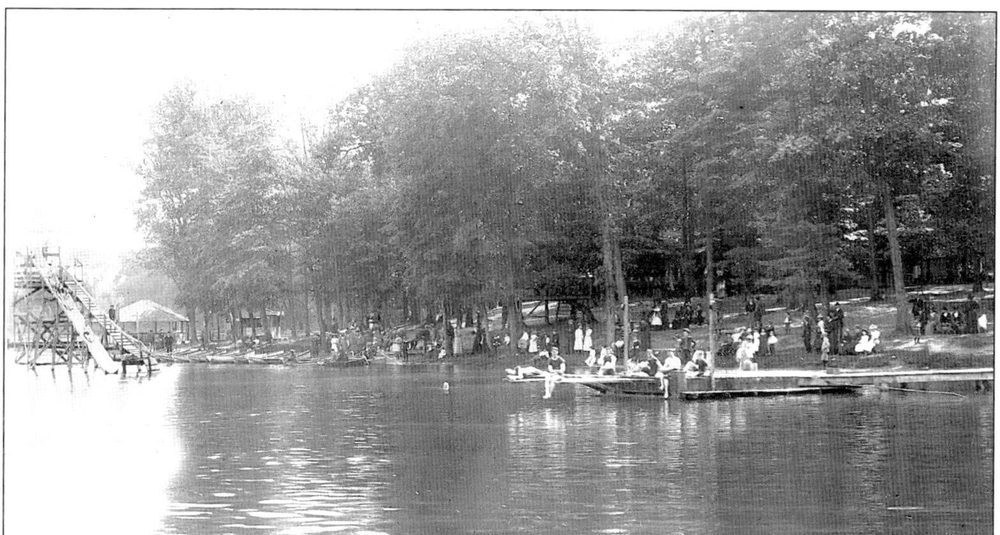

The toboggan chute at the left of this photo was a 25-foot tower with a chute that extended into the water at a 45-degree angle. Snow toboggans were carried up to the top of the tower, and several people could ride down at once. William Lodge, son of park developer Ralph Hugh Lodge, once described the toboggan chute: "They would ride lying down with two to six on at once, depending on the length of the sled. Fat men and fat ladies would go down the chute and go right out of sight, nothing to be seen but a big splash; while others would skim along the top 60 to 75 feet with spray splashing all over them."

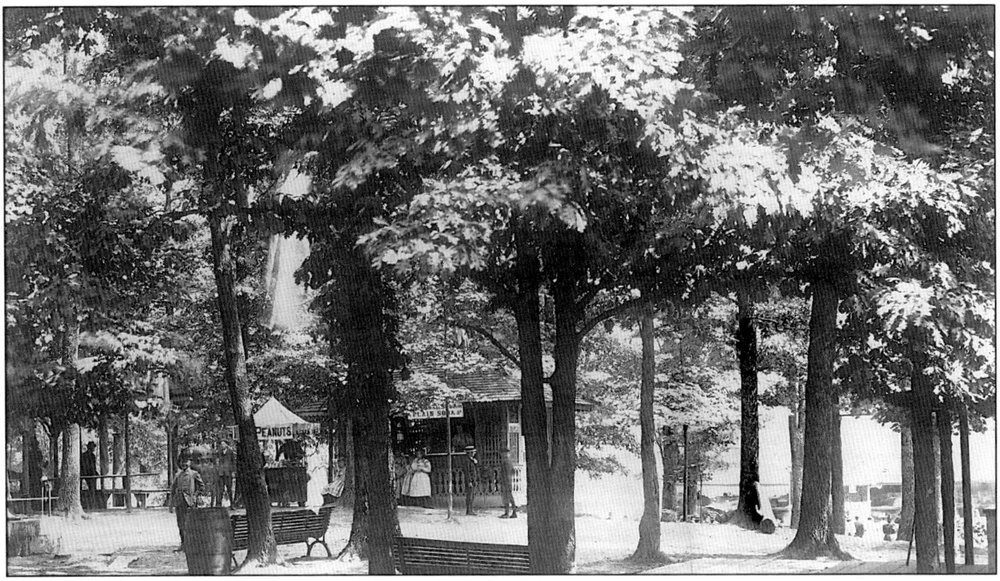

A picnic area with concessions was built to accommodate the many guests that visited Silver Lake Park.

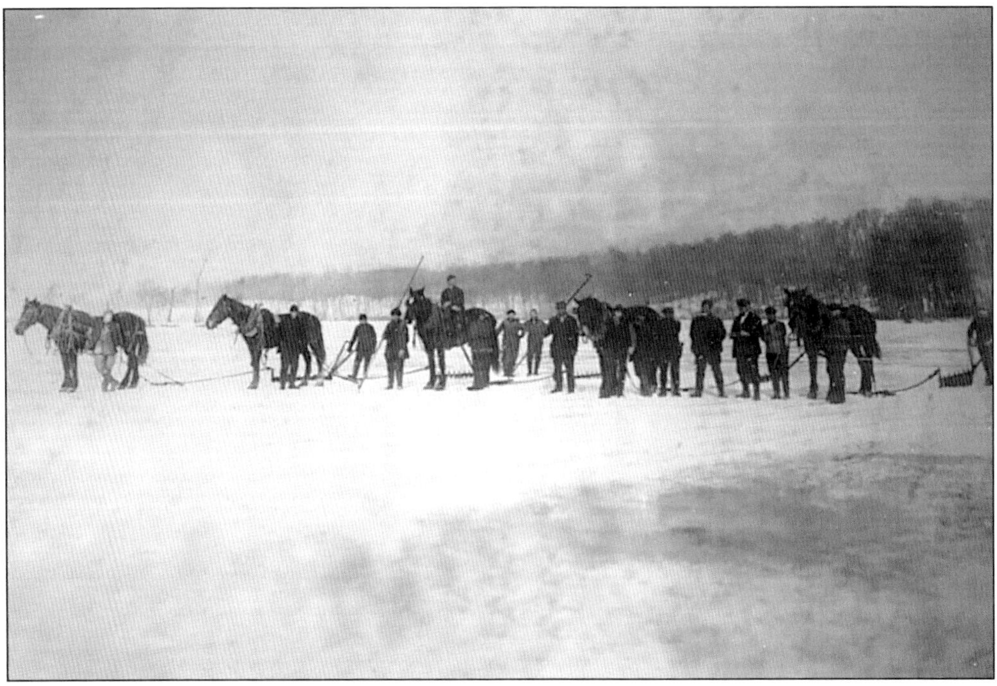

Located north of Silver Lake is Crystal Lake, where this photo was taken. Here visitors could enjoy another center of entertainment—Randolph Park, which included an auditorium and pavilion. In this photo, the M.E. Harrington Company is cutting ice out of the frozen Crystal Lake. Ice was harvested and then sold in the days before modern refrigeration.

Four

TRANSPORTATION
A CITY AT THE CROSSROADS

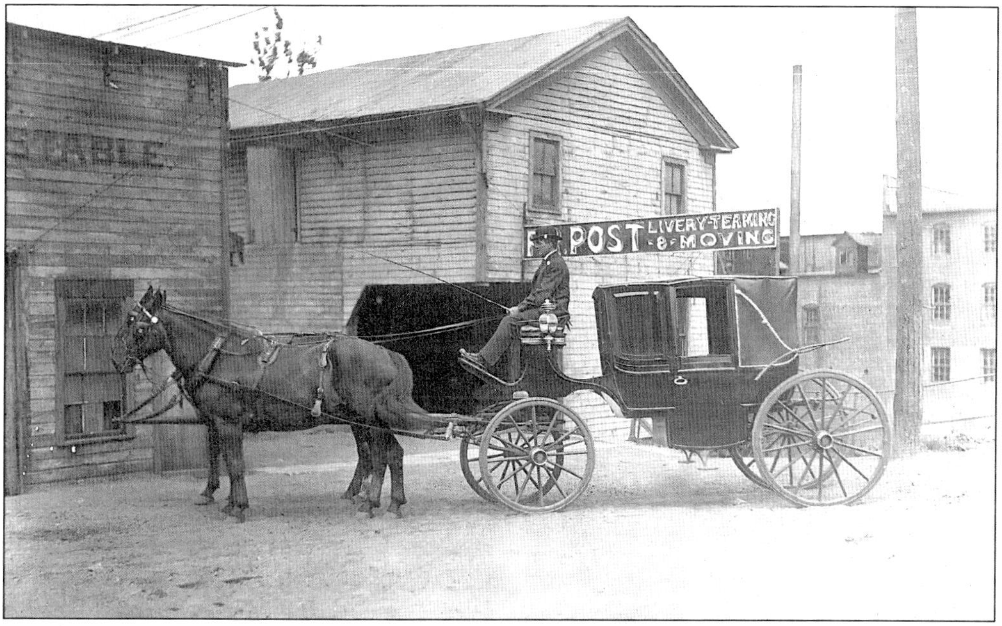

Cuyahoga Falls has always been a crossroads of sorts, even before the Europeans settled in the area. An important route for Native Americans was the Mahoning Trail, which passed through the area and intersected the portage between the Cuyahoga and Muskingham Rivers. In 1807 a hunter asked an early Ohio settler what the prospects of the frontier area were. The settler replied that a new road had been built along the Cuyahoga River past the rapids and then, following a ravine southeast, proceeded on to Canton. "I wouldn't be surprised to see a big town built there at the water falls. There is a lot of water power there," said the settler.

The settler's words were actualized in ways that he could never imagine. The river that had long been a major transportation route for Native Americans now became a principal power source for the early industries of the community of Cuyahoga Falls. After the construction of the Ohio & Erie Canal in 1827, planners thought it necessary to construct another waterway between Lake Erie and Pittsburgh. This canal passed through Cuyahoga Falls, but its usefulness was eclipsed when railroads were laid through the area. By 1852, a track ran near the bank of the river through the whole town. Streetcars and automobiles would soon follow, making Cuyahoga Falls accessible to all. This photograph shows a Cuyahoga Falls street when a horse-drawn vehicle was the primary mode of transportation.

Front Street

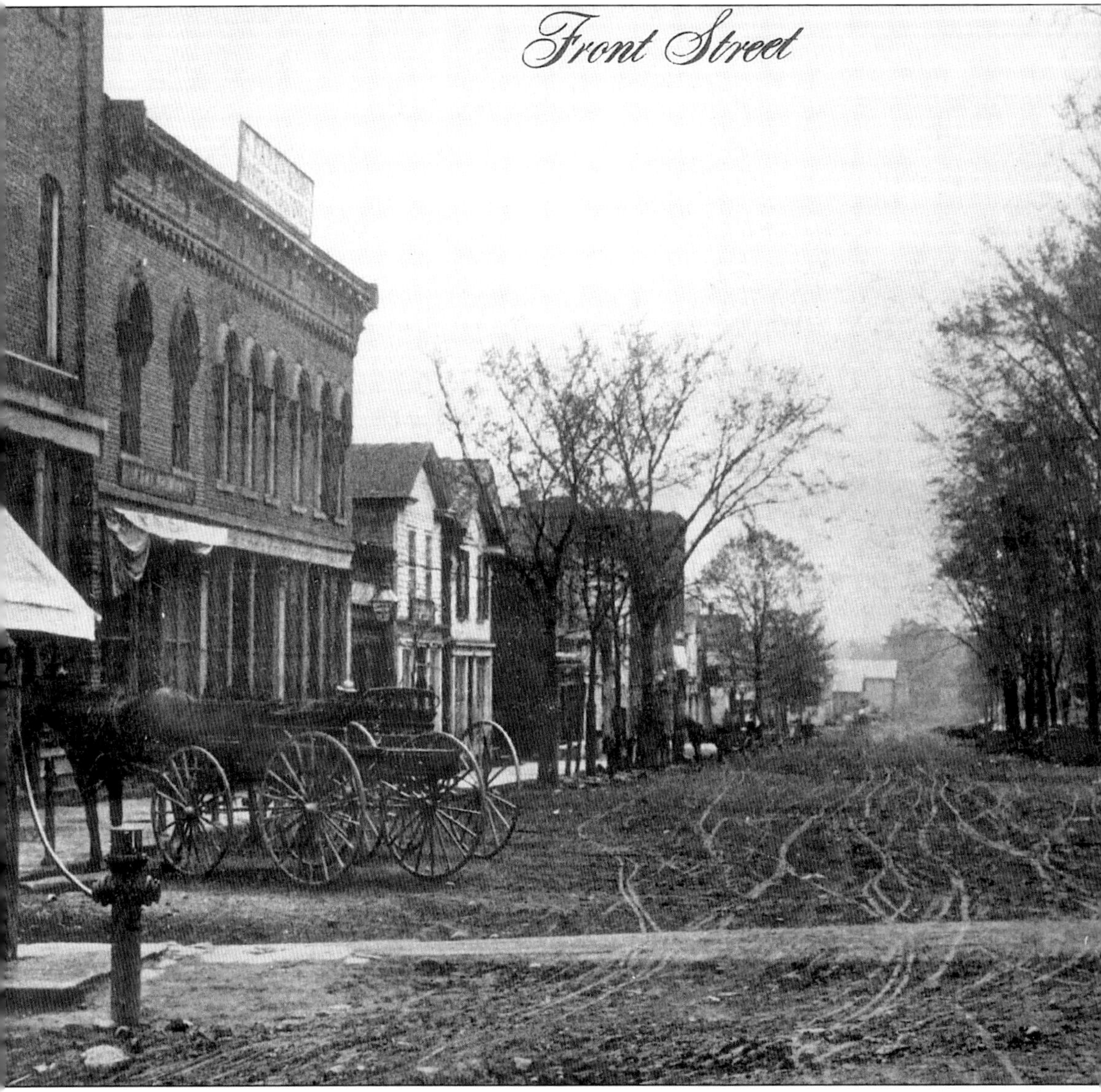

Front Street was once nothing more than a dirt road, as shown in this photo looking south toward Broad Boulevard. The town pump is in the bottom left corner, and the wall of the Edwin Rowland Sill mansion is visible on the right, just behind the tree line. Elkanah Richardson, who lived in a large house just north of Wadsworth on Front Street, laid out the town of Cuyahoga Falls in 1825. The town was later resurveyed, plotted and recorded by Birdseye Booth. When Cuyahoga Falls secured township status in 1851, it encompassed parts of four previously established townships—Stow, Tallmadge, Portage, and Northampton. In 1834, the population of Cuyahoga Falls was 375; by 1890, it was more than 2,500 and growing rapidly.

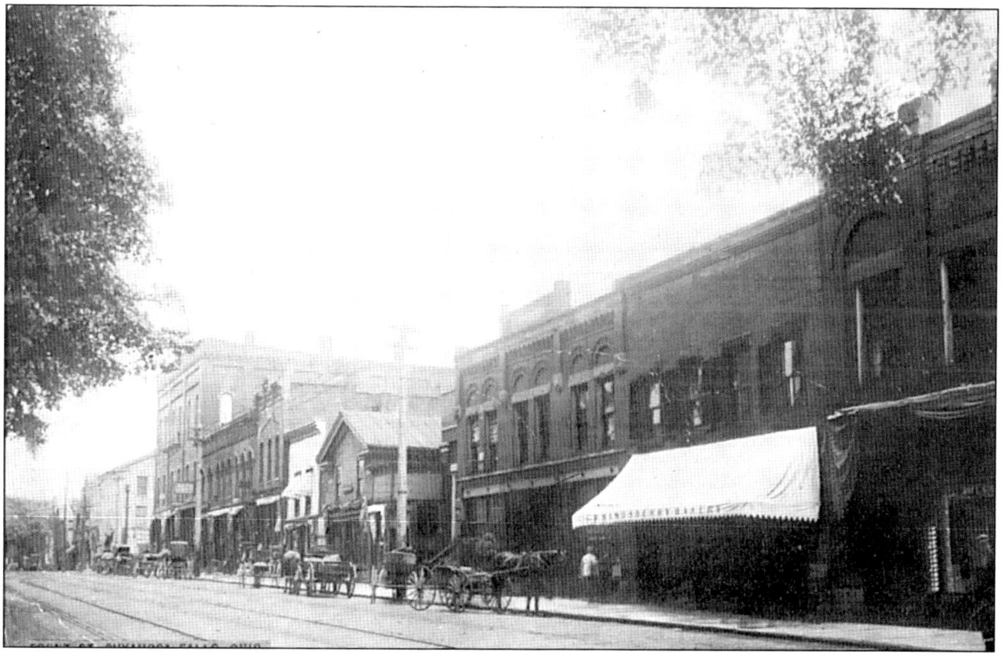

Wagon wheel trails have been replaced with streetcar rails in this postcard view of Front Street. Thomas Walsh constructed electric streetcar lines from Akron to Cuyahoga Falls and Silver Lake Park in the 1890s. The lettering on the awning of the building on the right side of this postcard reads Sandsberry Bakery.

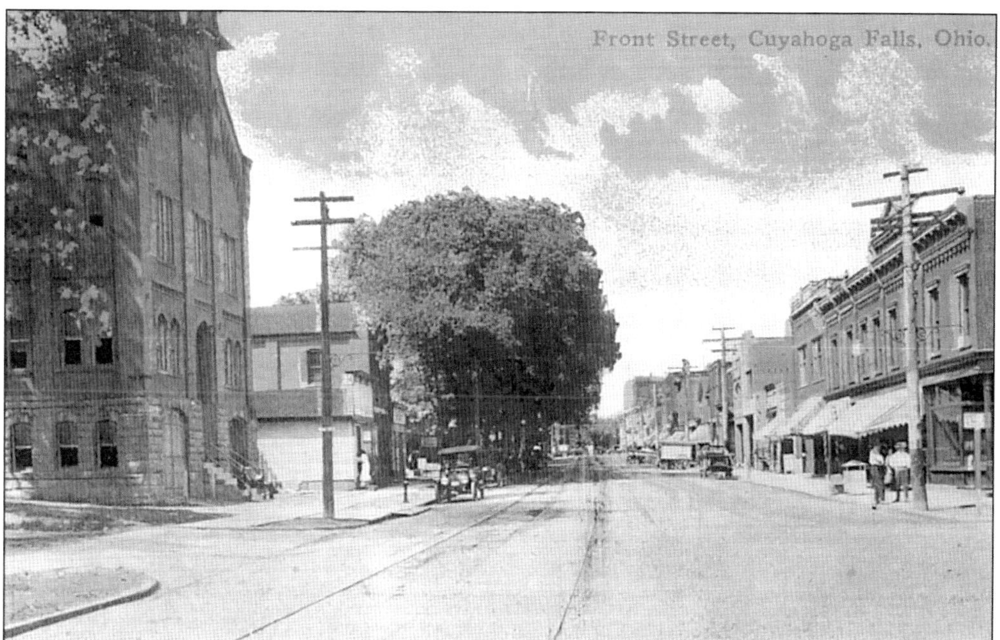

This later postcard view of Front Street shows the city hall building on the left, at the corner of Broad Street. The streetcar rails are still visible, but the horses and wagons have been replaced with automobiles.

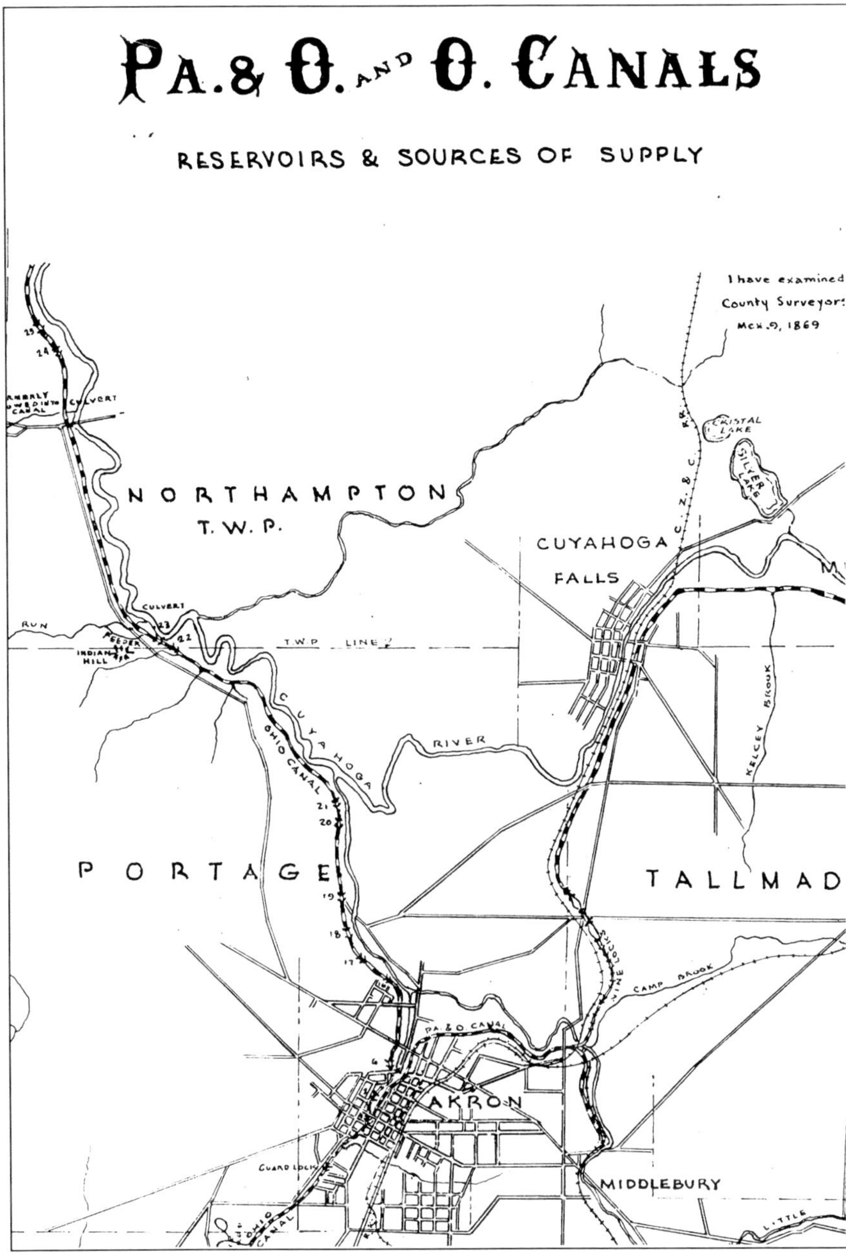

Although the Ohio & Erie Canal bypassed the city, the Pennsylvania & Ohio Canal did dock at Cuyahoga Falls in 1835. Within two years, the population grew to more than 1,200, and the city had two paper mills, a flour mill, two sawmills, a pump-making business, a tool factory, a woolen mill, a stone mill, a chair factory, a planing mill, a furnace foundry, and an engine and machine shop. This map drawn in 1869 shows the route of the P&O Canal, which connected to the O&E Canal at Akron. The P&O Canal was troublesome, because in the summer the canal siphoned off so much Cuyahoga River water that some of the industries had to suspend business for lack of power. Eventually, the canal business was replaced by the Cleveland & Pittsburgh Railroad, which was completed in 1852. Eventually, the canal bed dried up and the water returned to its original Cuyahoga Riverbed.

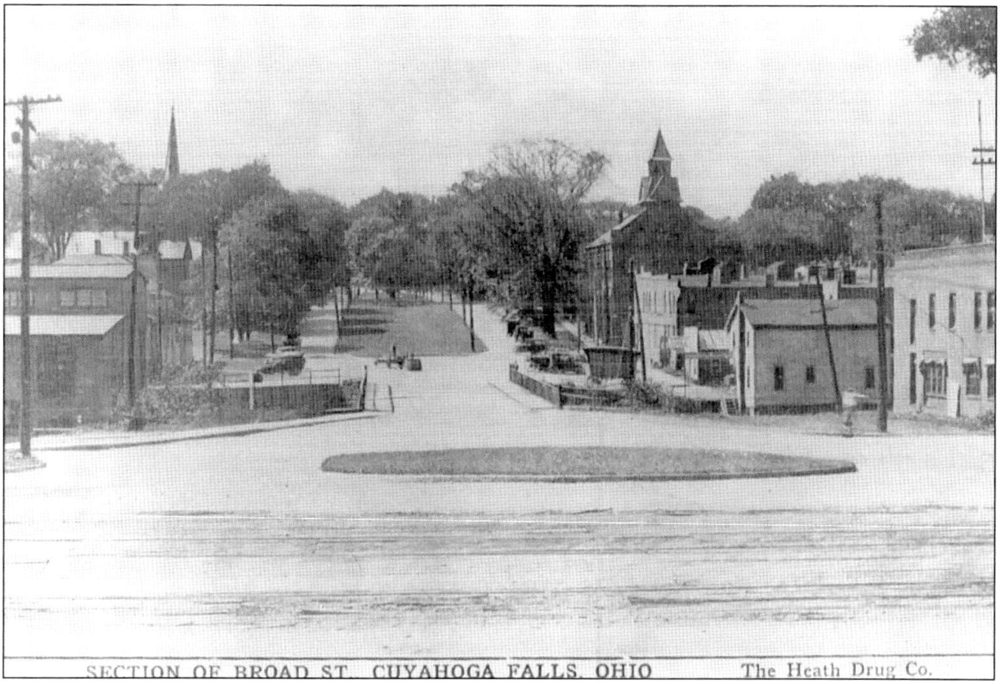

This view facing west shows Broad Street, one of the earliest main routes in the town. Broad Street Park was modeled after the Mall in Washington D.C., which runs from the White House to the Capitol. The original trees in the parkway were elms brought from Connecticut on covered wagons by early settlers.

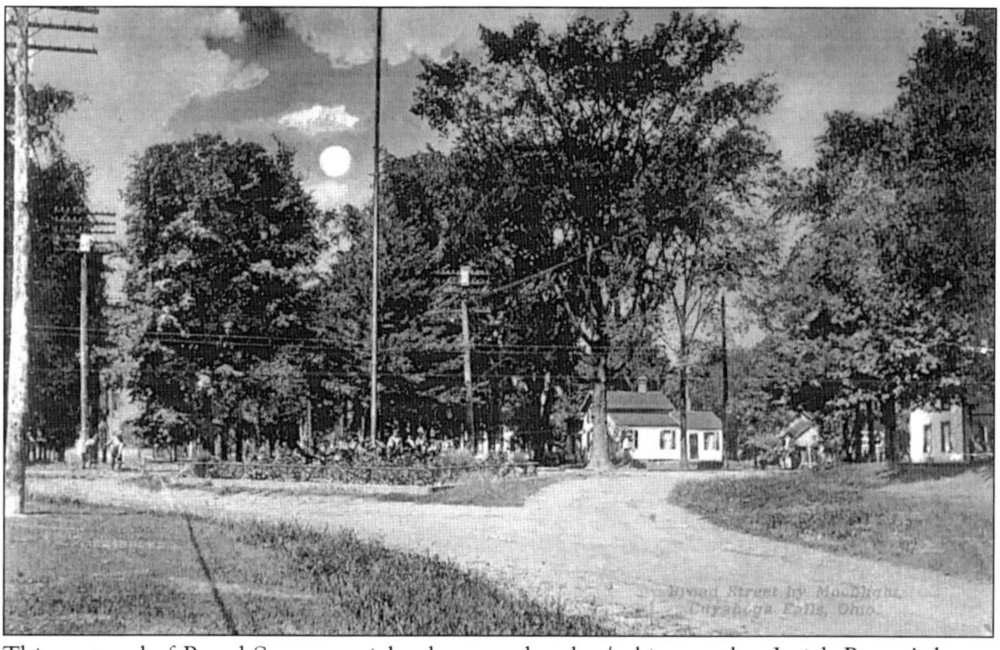

This postcard of Broad Street at night shows undertaker/cabinet-maker Josiah Brown's house on the right. The flagpole in the center was 90 feet high, and erected at a cost of $300 by the women's relief corps. Flowers bloom throughout the summer in Broad Park.

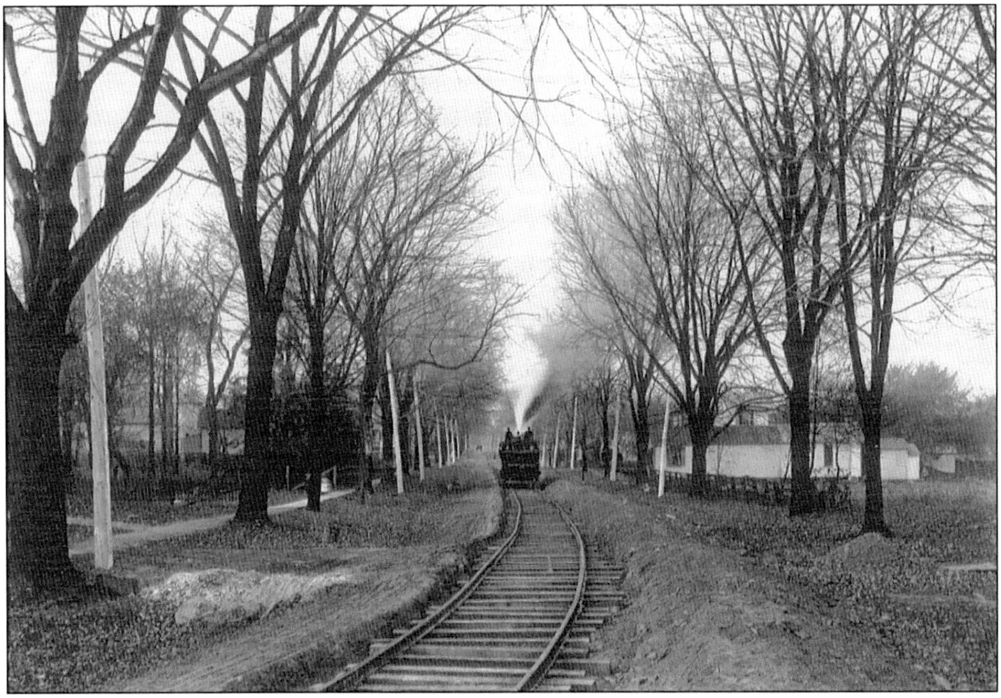

The first rails through Cuyahoga Falls were laid in 1852 when the Cleveland & Pittsburgh Railroad was completed. In 1894, the Akron Bedford & Cleveland Railroad, a high-speed interurban electric system, passed through Cuyahoga Falls. In this 1897 photograph, the rails are laid down the center of Second Street.

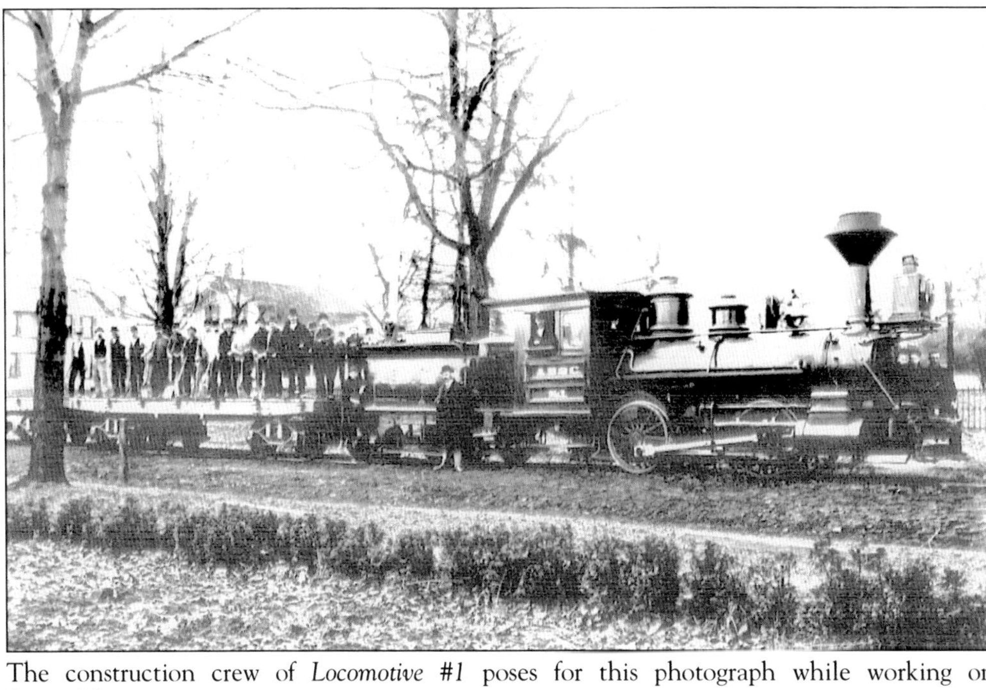

The construction crew of *Locomotive #1* poses for this photograph while working on Second Street.

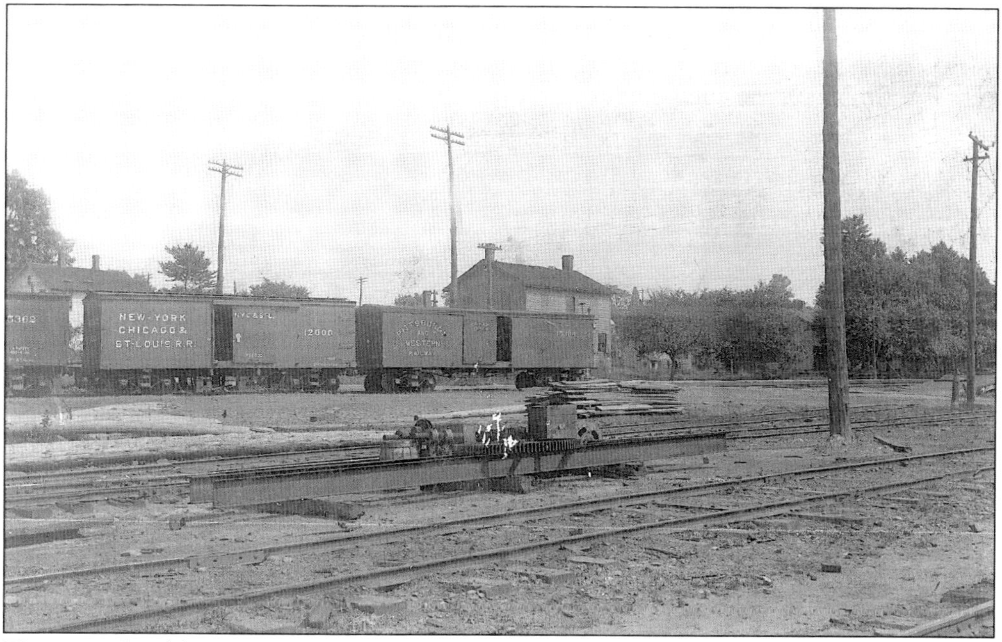

The second rail line to come through Cuyahoga Falls was the Baltimore & Ohio Railroad, which began operation in 1858. The B&O built its depot on Portage Street. They hauled mail, freight, and passengers.

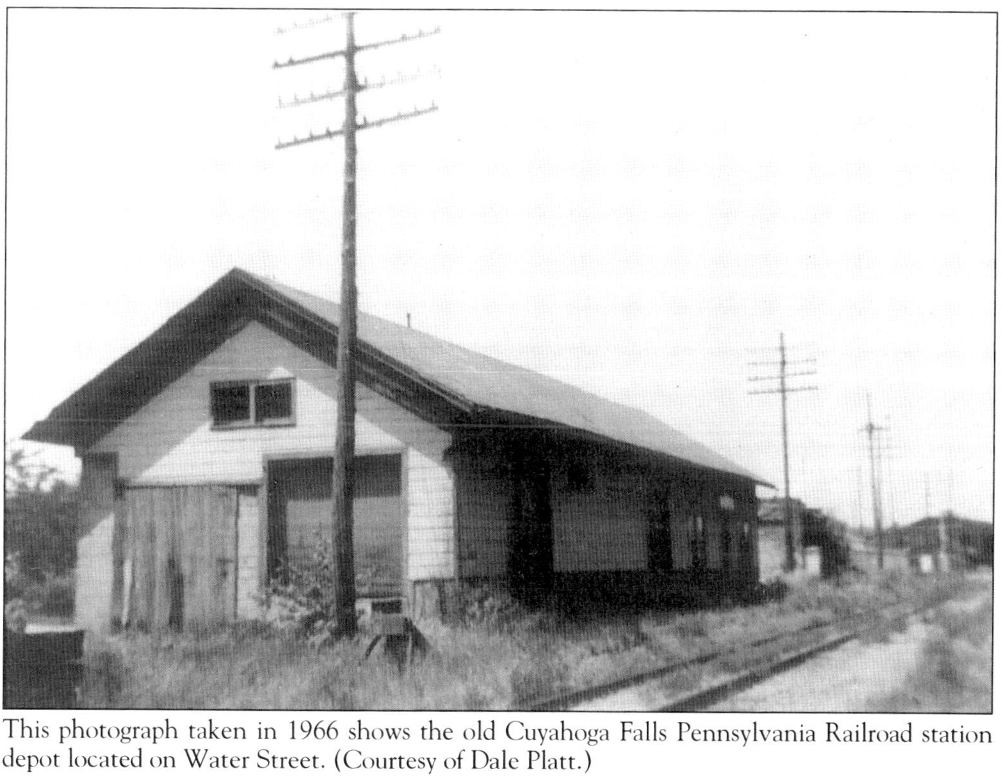

This photograph taken in 1966 shows the old Cuyahoga Falls Pennsylvania Railroad station depot located on Water Street. (Courtesy of Dale Platt.)

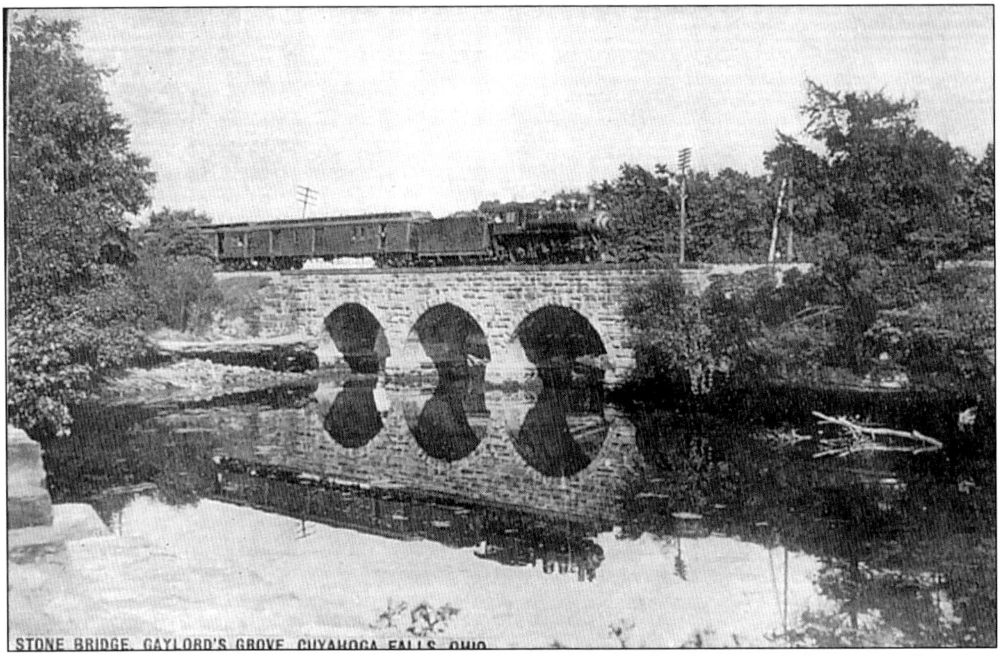

The stone arch bridge, built about 1880, carried the Cleveland, Akron & Columbus rails across the Cuyahoga River. The trains unloaded passengers by the thousands to visit High Bridge Glens Park, Silver Lake Park, and nearby Gaylord Grove picnic grounds.

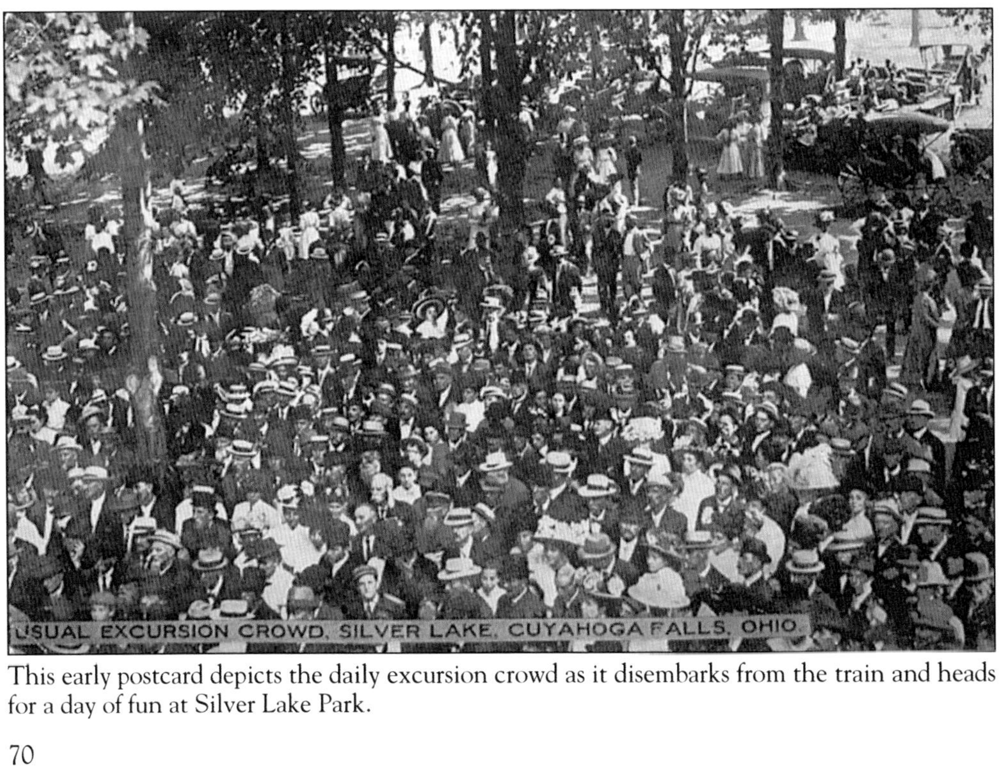

This early postcard depicts the daily excursion crowd as it disembarks from the train and heads for a day of fun at Silver Lake Park.

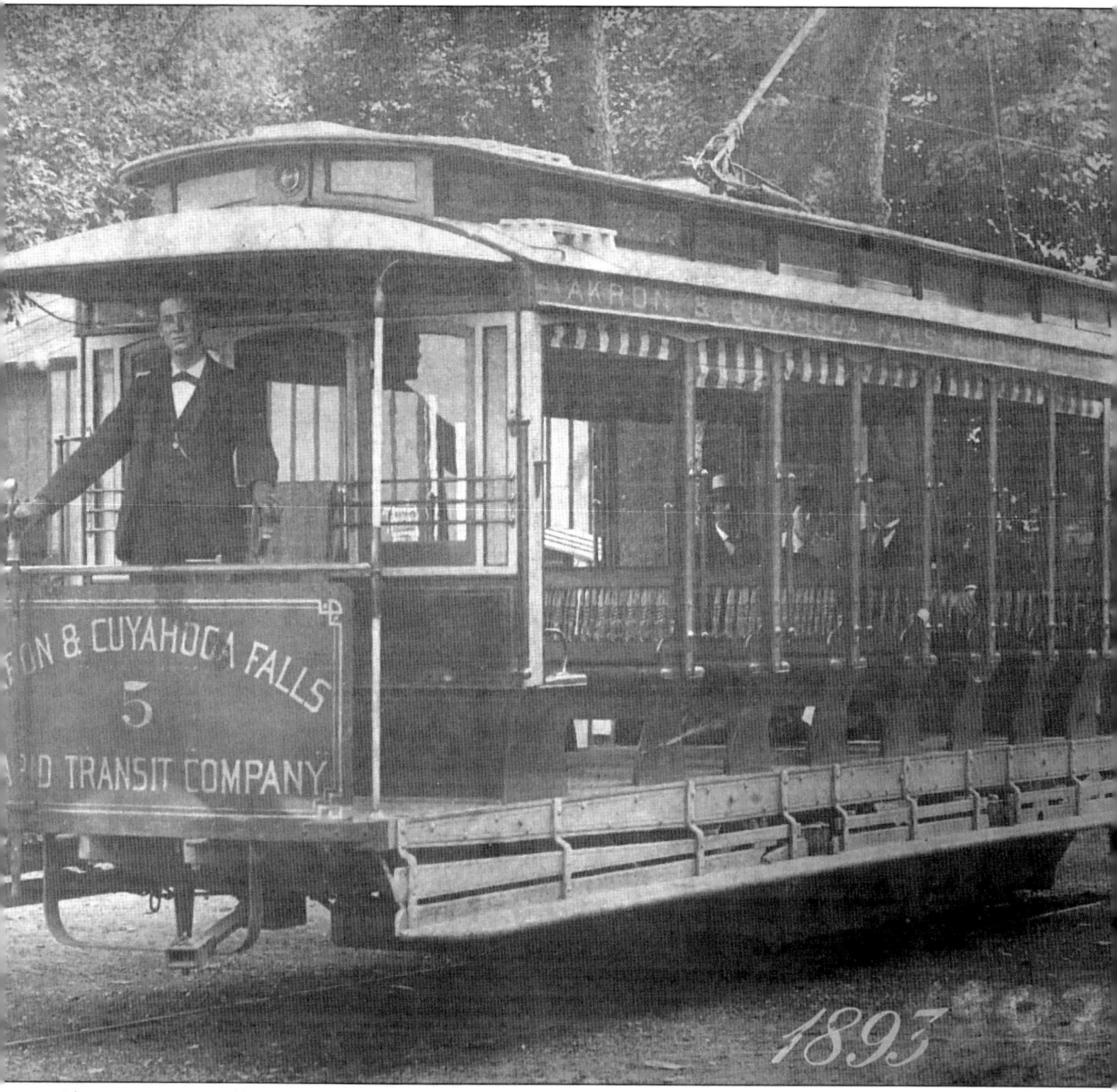

This open-air trolley was operated by the Akron & Cuyahoga Falls Rapid Transit Company, which was owned by Thomas Walsh. After numerous squabbles over the streetcar business with Akron's John F. Seiberling, Walsh received a franchise in 1894 to build a car line from Akron to connect to his Cuyahoga Falls line. Seiberling, however, was determined to beat Walsh and directed his workers to lay lines anyway. By the time Seiberling built a bridge over the Cuyahoga River to carry his tracks, Walsh's streetcar, known as the Mountain Line, was already in business. During the next two years, additional lines were added to connect with the railroads.

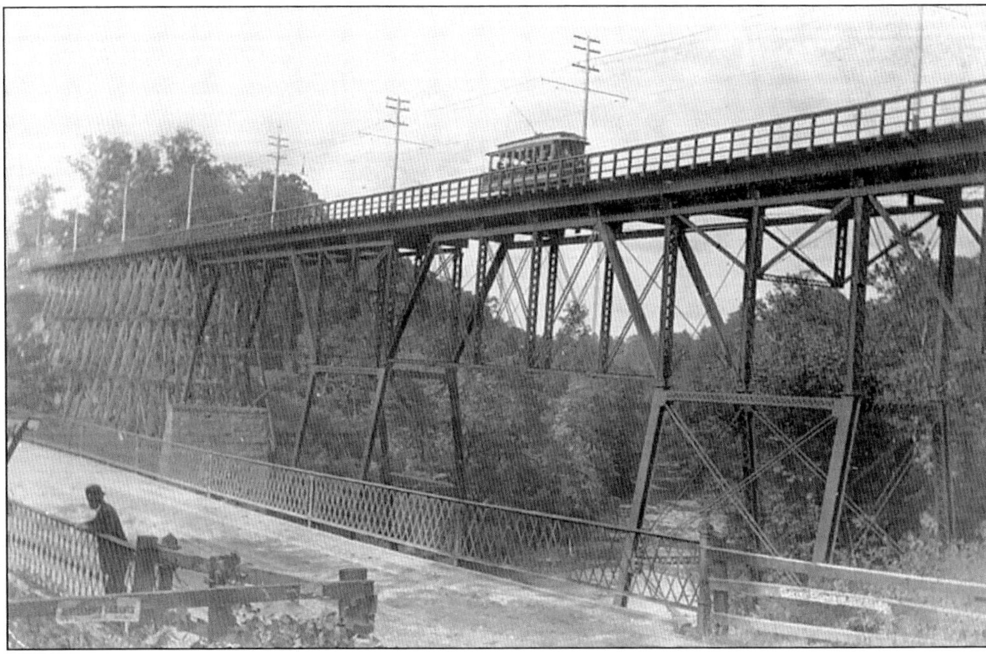

The lower bridge in this postcard scene was built by Frank Seiberling as a streetcar bridge and wagon road. The high trestle was built in 1903 as an electric streetcar line and was believed at the time to be the highest trestle used for this purpose. These bridges were located at the site of the former Ohio Edison power plant.

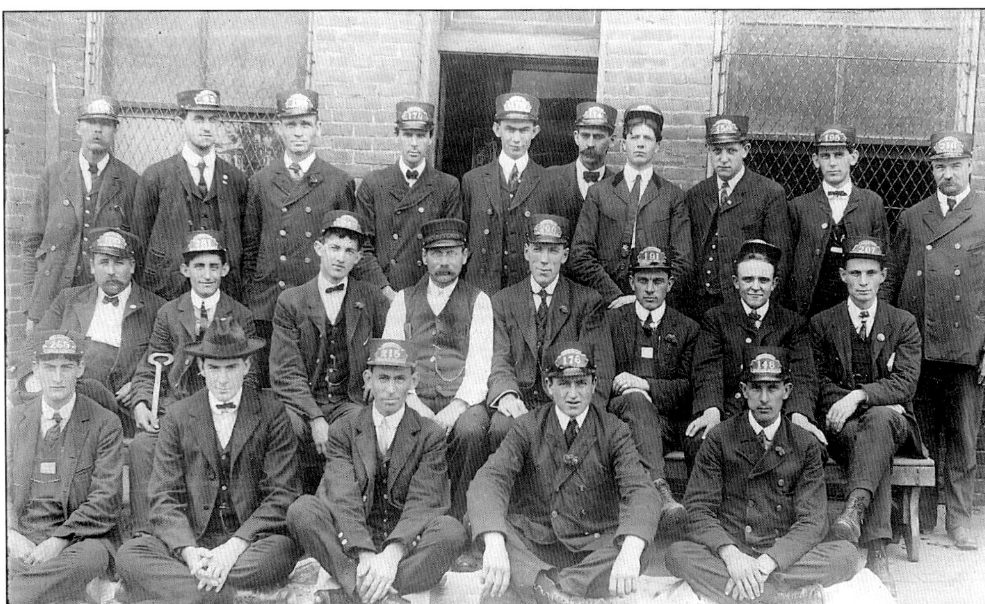

These unidentified streetcar conductors and motormen pose for a formal photograph. Two streetcar companies were operating in Cuyahoga Falls at the turn of the century.

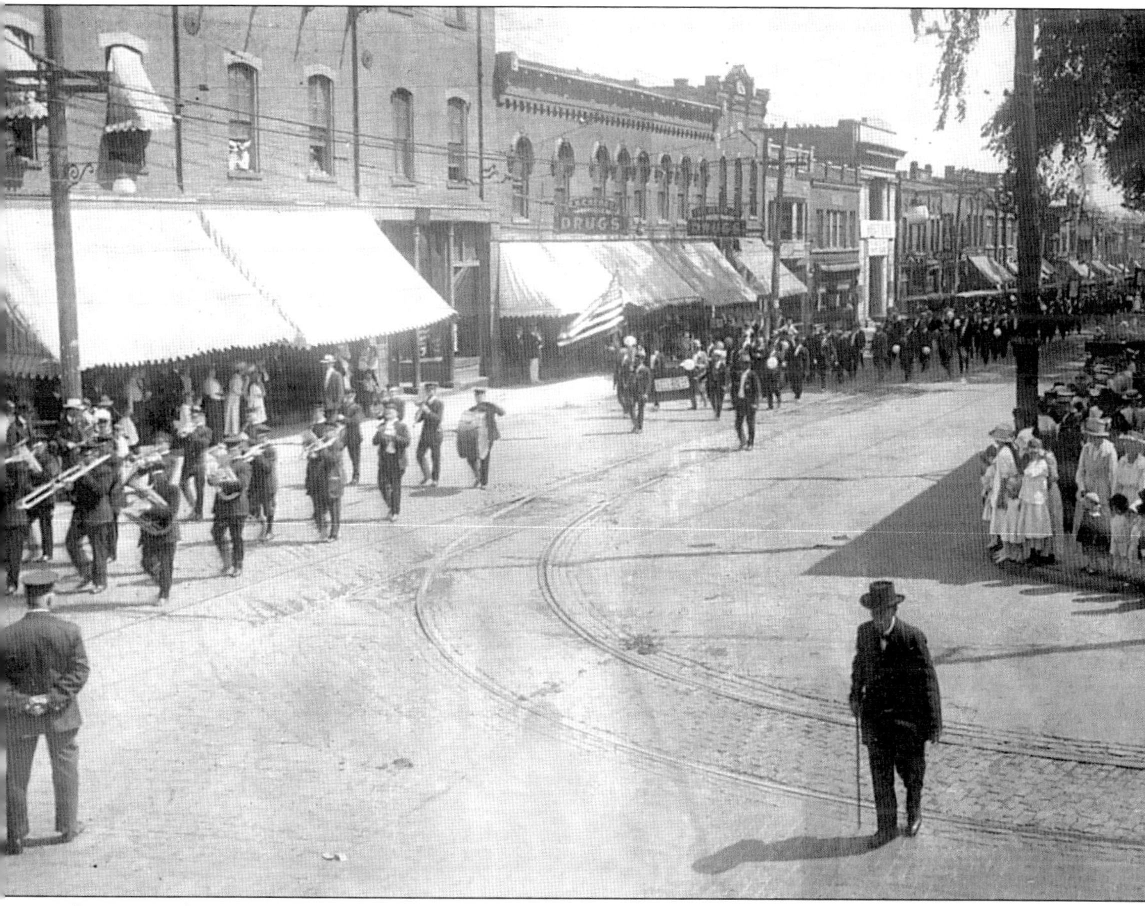

This 1920 photograph shows a parade as it approaches the corner of Front and Portage Streets. The man with the cane crossing the streetcar tracks is Charles Webster, whose granddaughter, Ethel Smith, used the same cane as late as 1993. Notice the brick streets. When Front Street was eventually paved, workers severed a main vein of the public water supply, known as the "Big Spring." Early citizens often went to the spring located on Front Street at the corner of Wadsworth Street. The first piped water came from this spring and was reportedly sent to a holding tank on Portage Street to be distributed throughout Cuyahoga Falls. In 1912, the "Big Spring" produced about 50,000 gallons of water per day. The spring dried up after Front Street was paved.

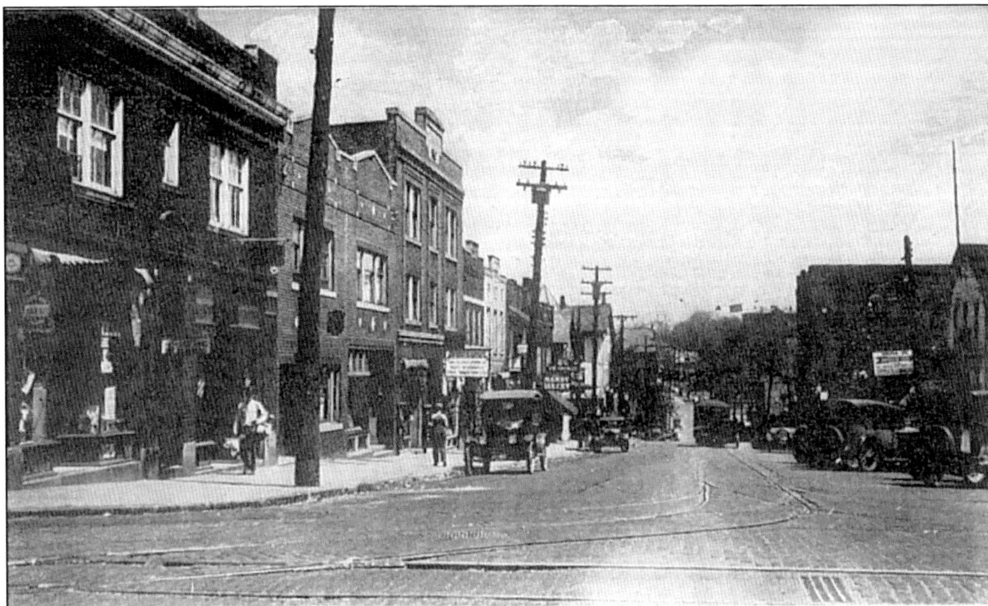

W. Portage Street, Cuyahoga Falls, O.

This is an early postcard view of Portage Street. Notice the electric streetcar lines, or centenary wires, in the sky above the street.

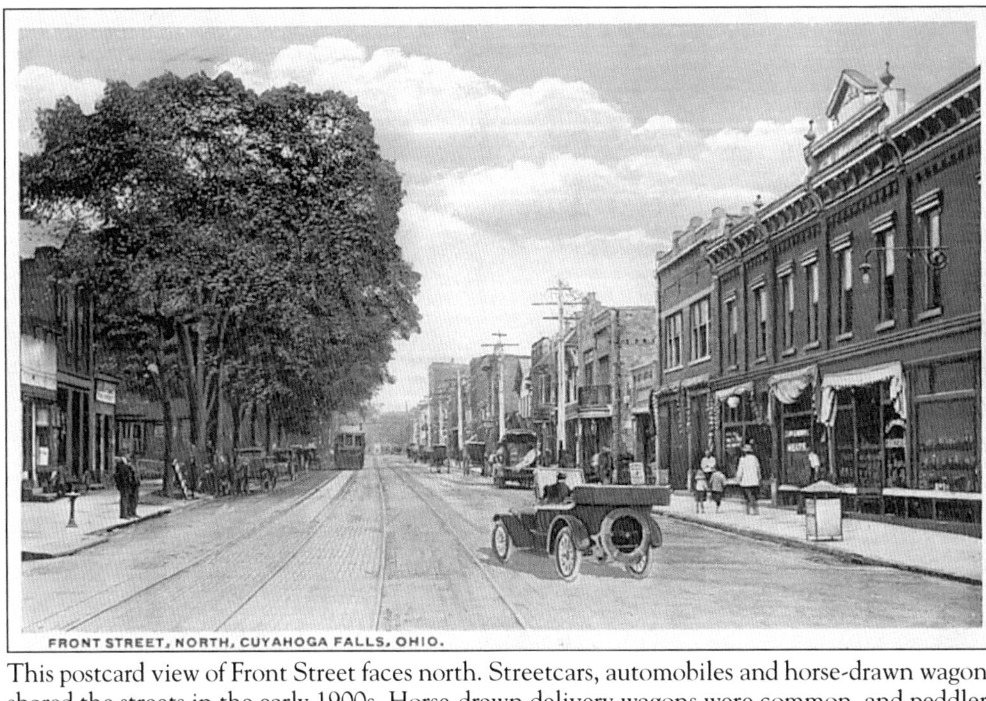

FRONT STREET, NORTH, CUYAHOGA FALLS, OHIO.

This postcard view of Front Street faces north. Streetcars, automobiles and horse-drawn wagons shared the streets in the early 1900s. Horse-drawn delivery wagons were common, and peddlers sold everything from ice cream to produce from these vehicles. One delivery service brought the Sunday newspaper to citizens' doors, and another door-to-door service was the regular pick-up of rags and bottles.

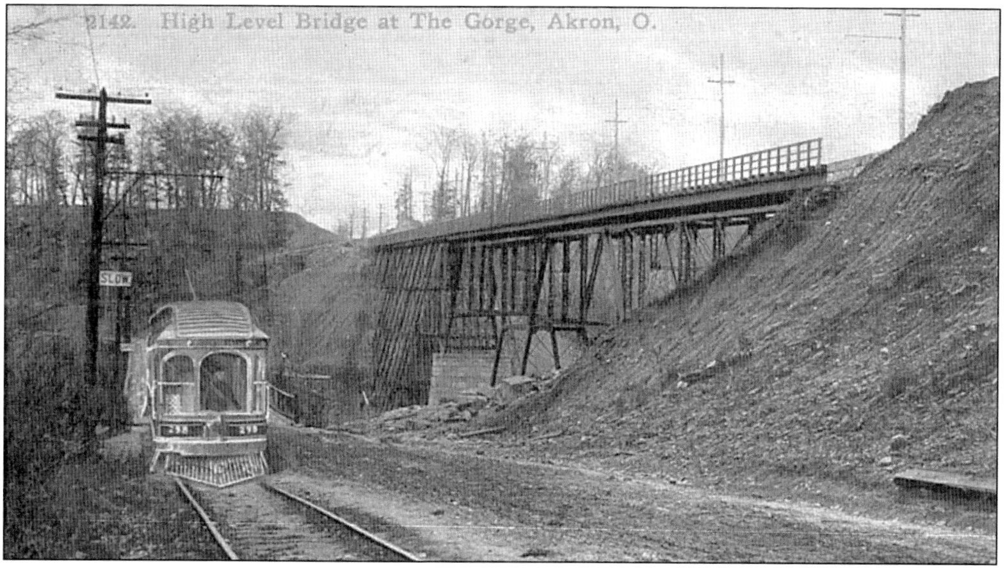

The top postcard shows a streetcar bringing passengers from Cuyahoga Falls into Akron at the Gorge bridge that spanned the Cuyahoga River. The low bridge was also used as a road and the high trestle for electric streetcars. The lower postcard view of the same structures was photographed later. On February 18, 1901, the Northern Ohio Traction Company purchased the Cuyahoga Falls Rapid Transit Company and secured a monopoly of Akron transit operations. The company changed its name to Northern Ohio Traction & Light Company (NOT&L) the following year. The same company also constructed the Gorge power plant, seen in the lower view, which later became Ohio Edison. According to some, the NOT&L was the largest and finest railway system in northeast Ohio. In its heyday, it owned more than 250 route miles that connected Cleveland, Akron, Cuyahoga Falls, Canton, Massillon, New Philadelphia, Kent, Ravenna, and Warren.

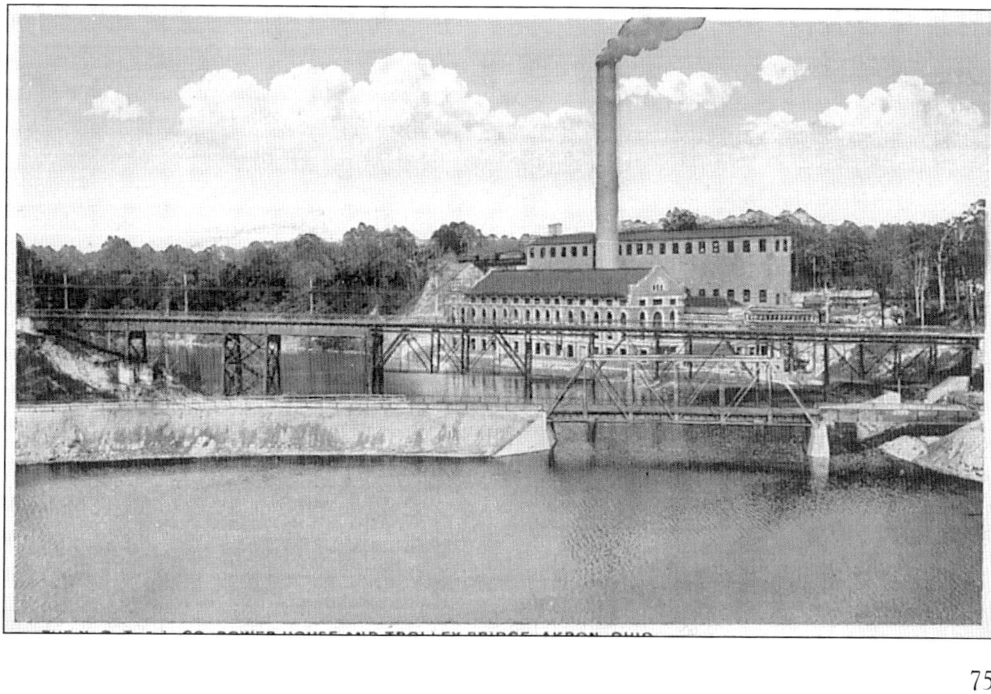

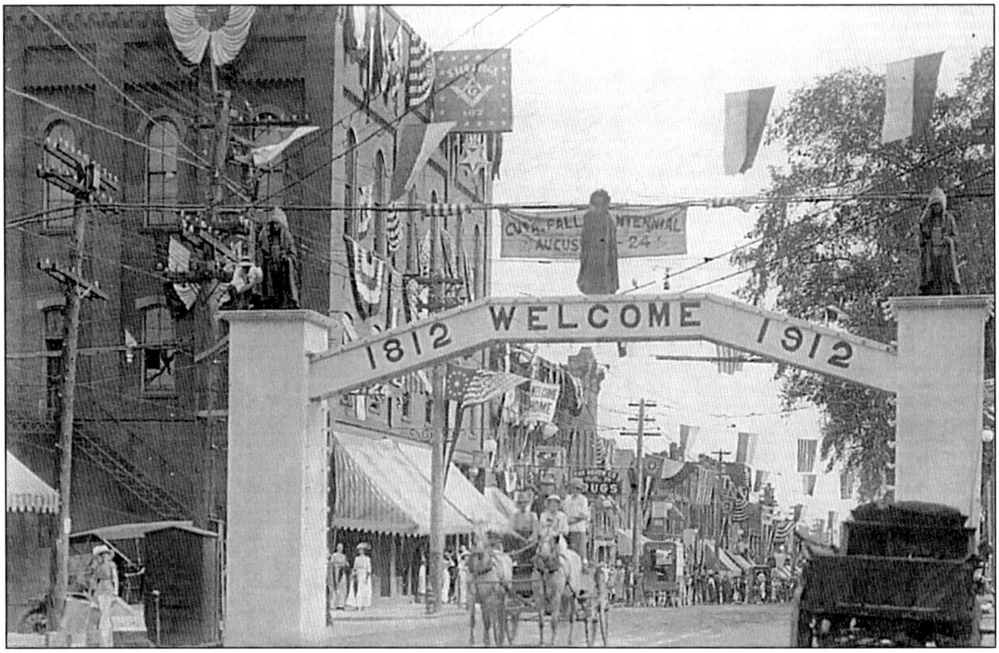

When Cuyahoga Falls celebrated its centennial in 1912, there were few automobiles on the streets. Cornelius Walsh had the first car in town, a Model T he purchased in 1910. In 1912, Joe Babb, whose house still stands on Sackett Avenue, bought a Stanley Steamer from a dealer in Akron. By the spring of 1912, there were only four car owners in Cuyahoga Falls.

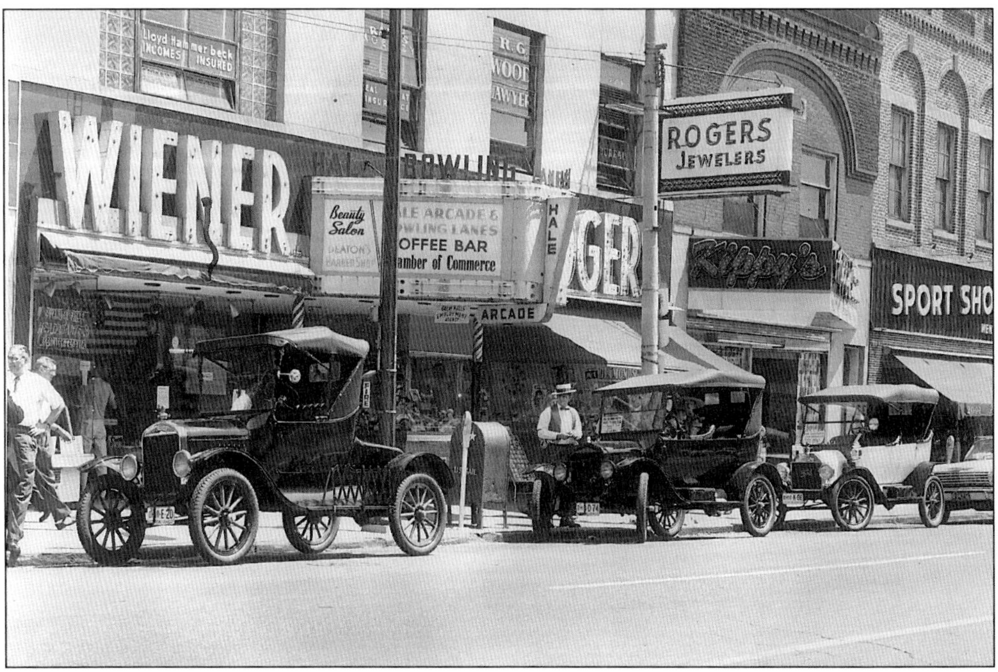

This Front Street view appears dated because of the Model Ts lined up at the curb. The photograph was taken in 1962 when a gathering of antique car owners may have met downtown for a bite to eat at Kippy's.

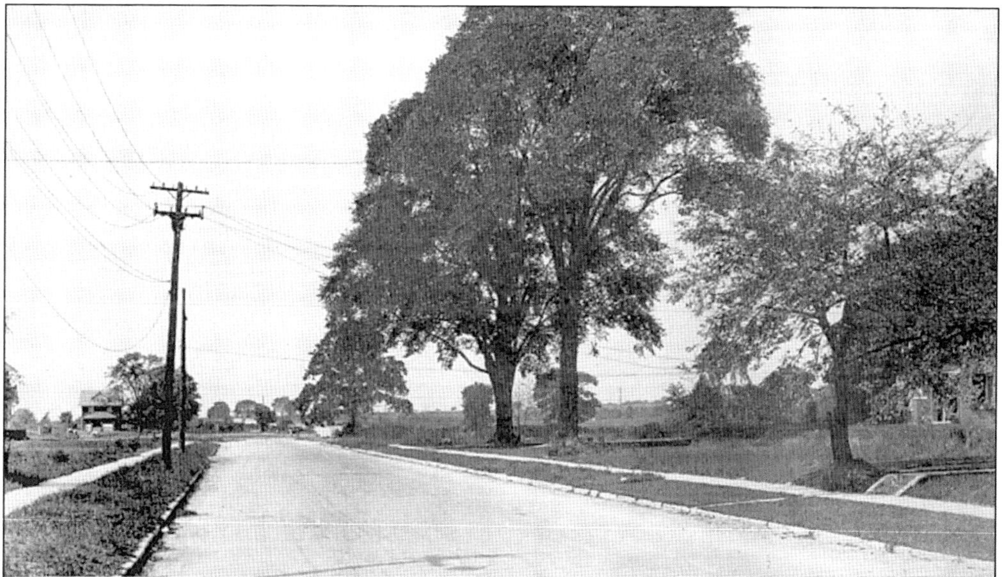

CHESTNUT STREET, CUYAHOGA FALLS, OHIO Published by SHOOK & BELAIR

Until 1920, Chestnut Street (now Chestnut Boulevard) ended at Eleventh Street, pictured here in the distance of this postcard view facing west. The house at the left edge of this photograph is still standing. Eventually, Chestnut Street was extended until it connected with the newly-built State Road.

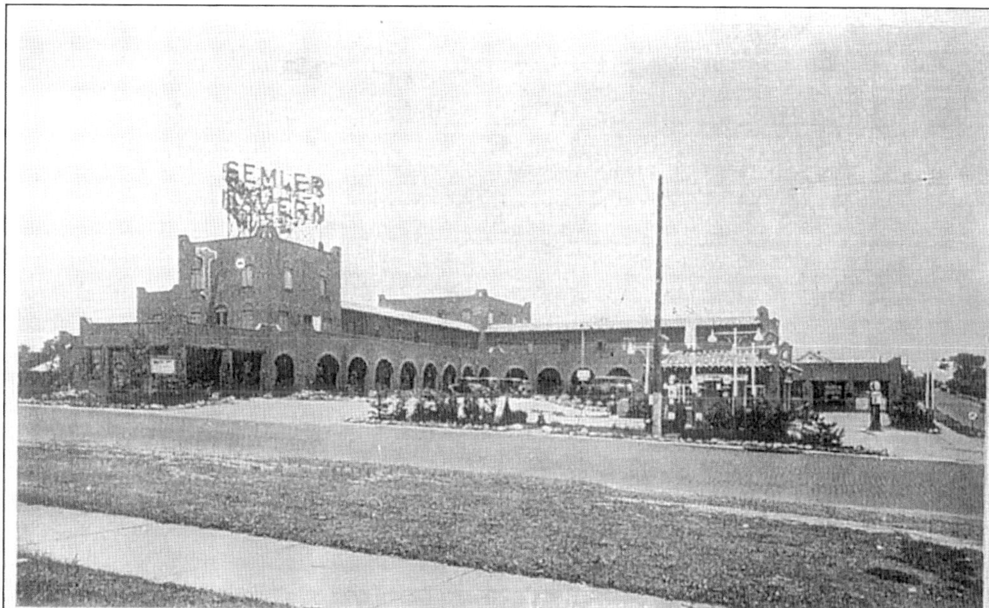

CUYAHOGA FALLS AT CHESTNUT BLVD.
5 MILES FROM DOWNTOWN AKRON—50 ROOMS, TUB, SHOWER, RADIO, GARAGE
B-193

When a young architect named Semler built this tavern in 1926 at the corner of Chestnut and the new State Road, old-timers thought, "he has to be insane." However, the business prospered and new State Road businesses soon sprang up on both sides of the route.

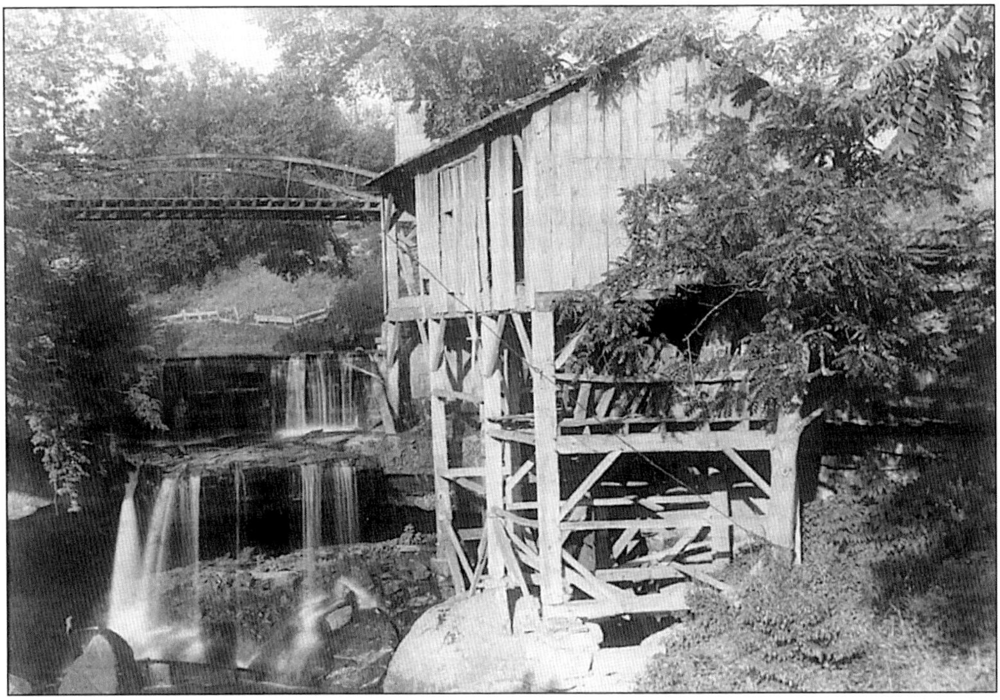

This historic area of Cuyahoga Falls was once known as Iron Bridge, Ohio. The arched bridge in the background, to the left of the old mill, crossed Mud Brook at State Road. (Courtesy of Taylor Memorial Public Library.)

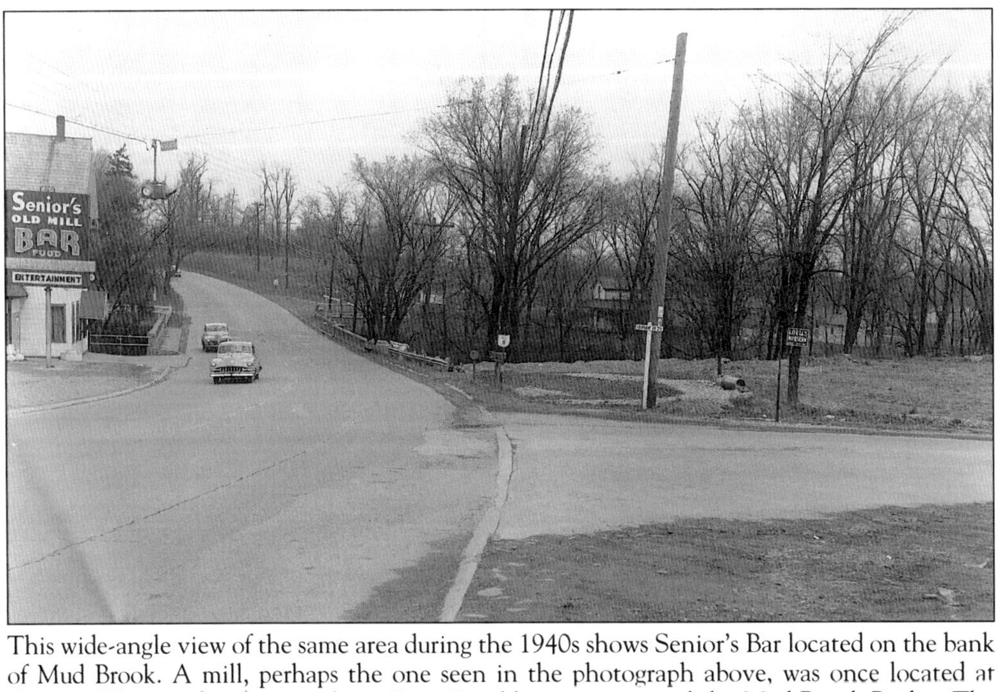

This wide-angle view of the same area during the 1940s shows Senior's Bar located on the bank of Mud Brook. A mill, perhaps the one seen in the photograph above, was once located at this site. The cars heading south on State Road have just crossed the Mud Brook Bridge. The location seen here bears little resemblance to the busy intersection of today.

The Prospect Street bridge, depicted in this 1947 photograph, once connected to Water Street on the other side of the river from Front Street. When the Ackerman Expressway was built, the bridge was preserved as an observation deck. The woman standing on the bridge is Alice Royer. (Courtesy of Earl and Alice Royer.)

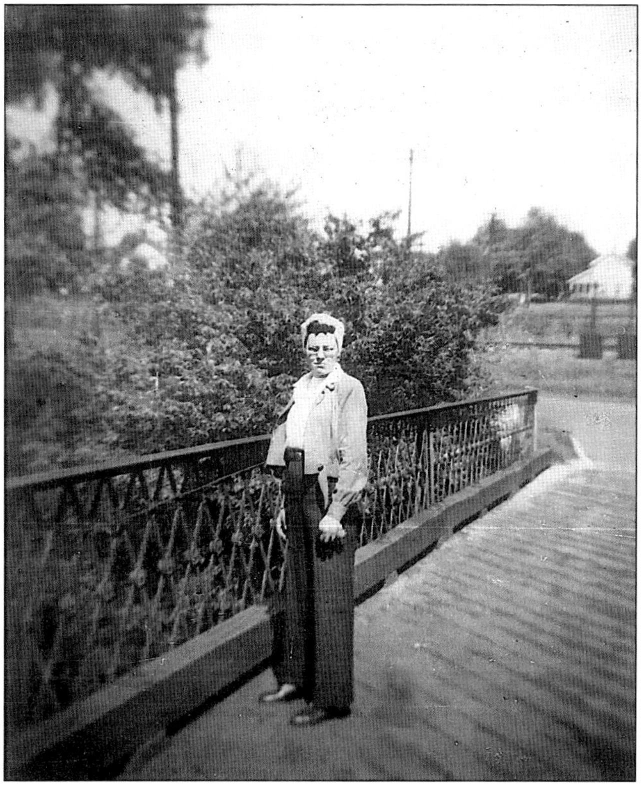

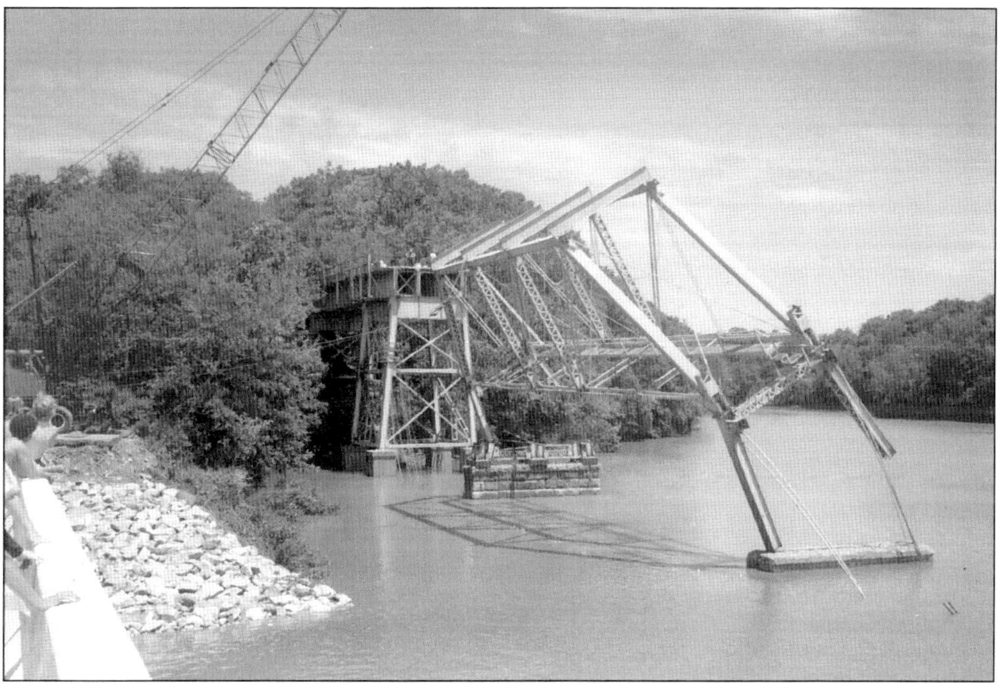

Observers at the left edge of this photograph watch as the old Gorge streetcar trestle is demolished. The observers are standing on the newly-constructed bridge just downriver.

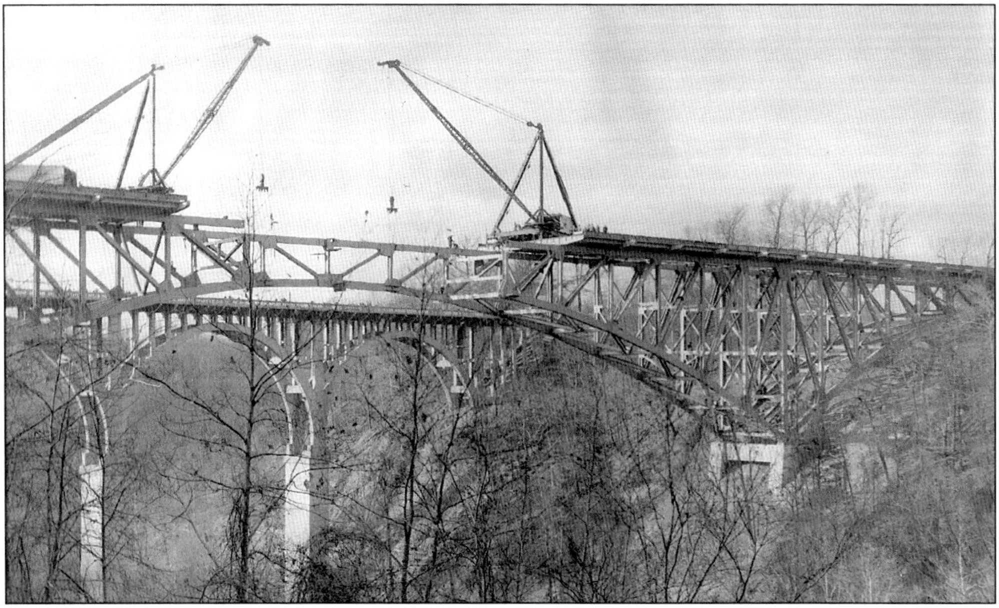

In 1913, the first High Level bridge was built over the Cuyahoga River on the far west side of Cuyahoga Falls. It was believed to be the highest bridge of its construction type in the country. The concrete bridge was 190 feet above the river, 781 feet long, and 26 feet wide. This first bridge is visible in this photograph behind the replacement bridge construction.

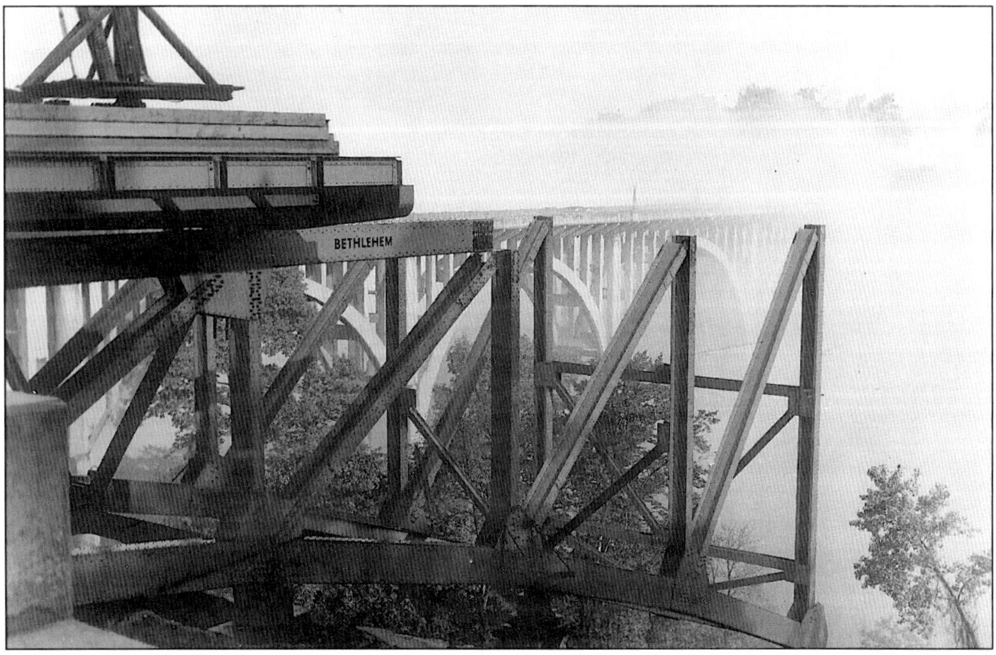

In July of 1950, the Cuyahoga Wrecking Company demolished the old bridge at a cost of $66,600. Amateur photographer Clarence A. Bartlett died when a falling chunk of concrete struck him as the old bridge fell. The new construction is pictured in this photograph by Charles E. Pettit of Cuyahoga Falls. The image, taken in the early morning mist, won third prize in a photography contest.

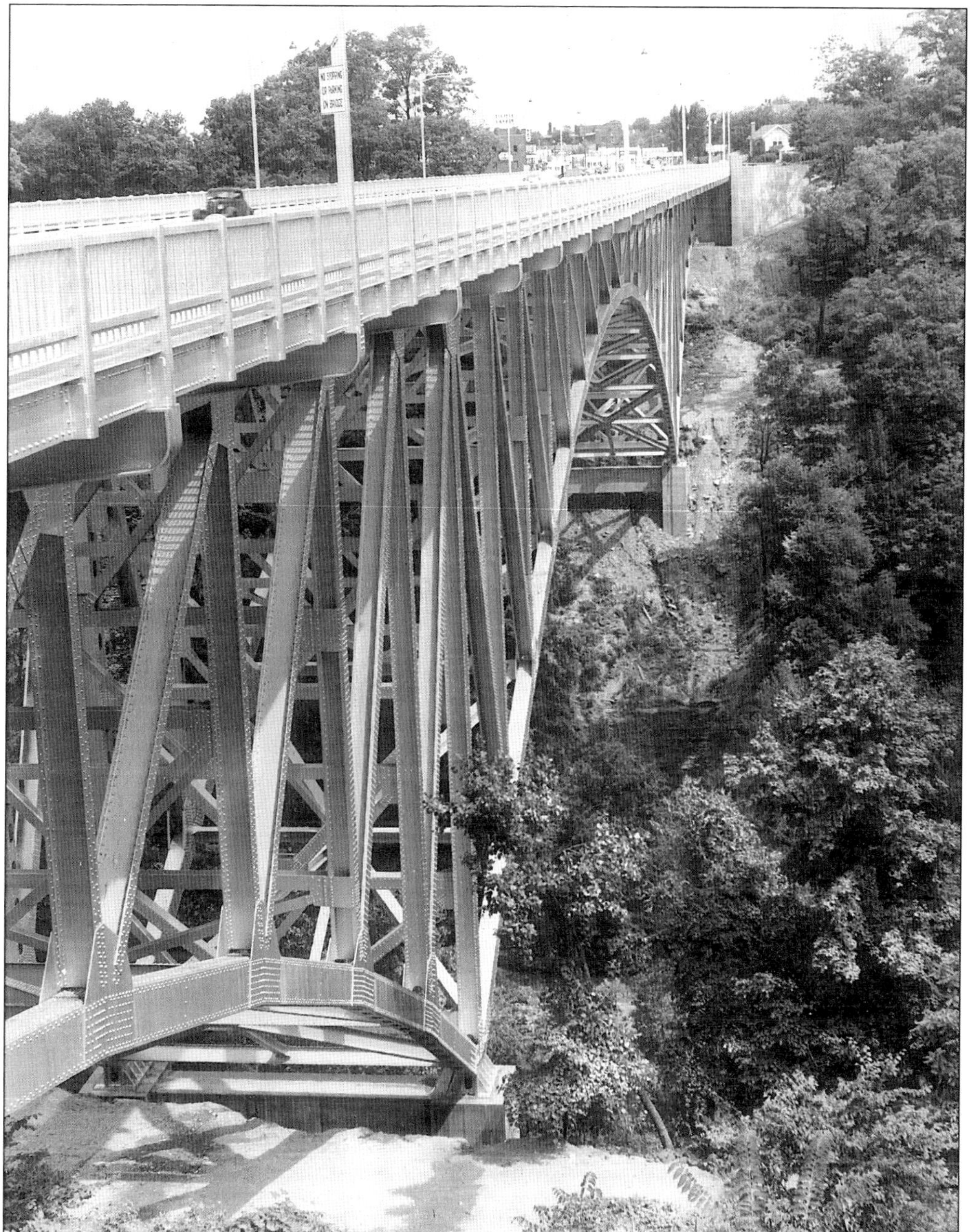

The new High Level bridge pictured here is 220 feet above the riverbed and 15 feet higher than the bridge that it replaced. It is 900 feet long, made up on two 210-foot anchor spans, two 180-foot cantilever spans, with a 120-foot suspended span. The bridge has four lanes of traffic with sidewalks on both sides. Shortly after it opened, it was found to have a serious flaw—the steel grating used on the floor was extremely slippery in rainy and snowy conditions. Accidents were numerous and often fatal. Tire noise and wind blowing through the grate made an eerie sound, giving the bridge its nickname of "the whistling bridge." Eventually, the steel grate was replaced.

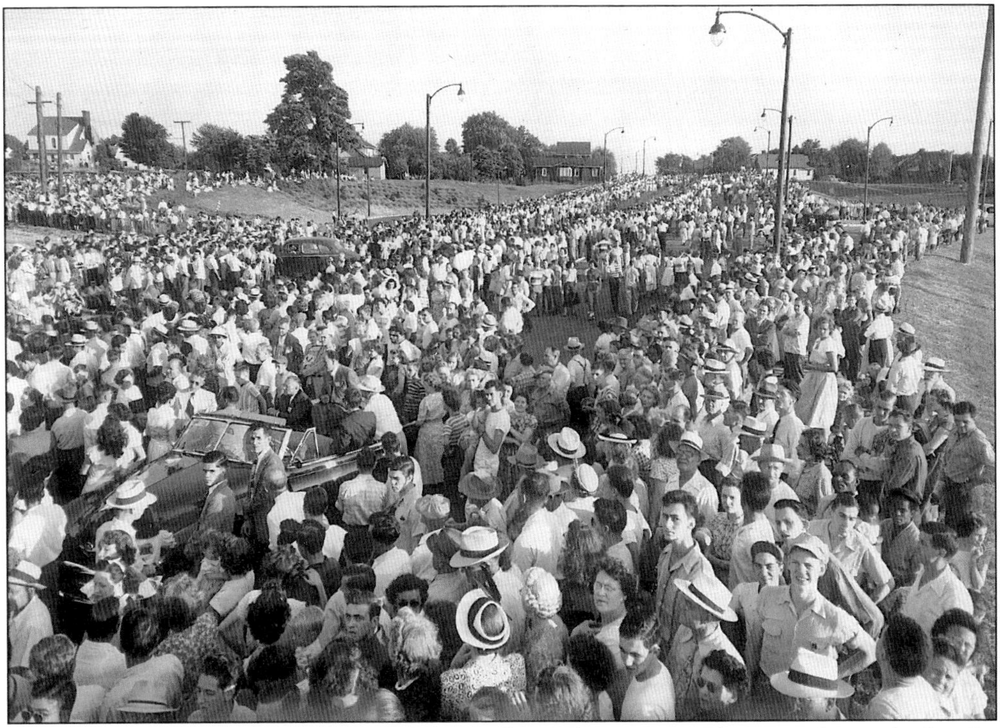

The new High Level bridge was officially opened on July 13, 1949. The event featured a 2-mile-long parade and Governor Frank J. Lausche was on hand for the ribbon cutting. The queen of the celebration was Kent State University student Nancy Crites, who was attended by Nancy McCormish and Marilyn Keiffer.

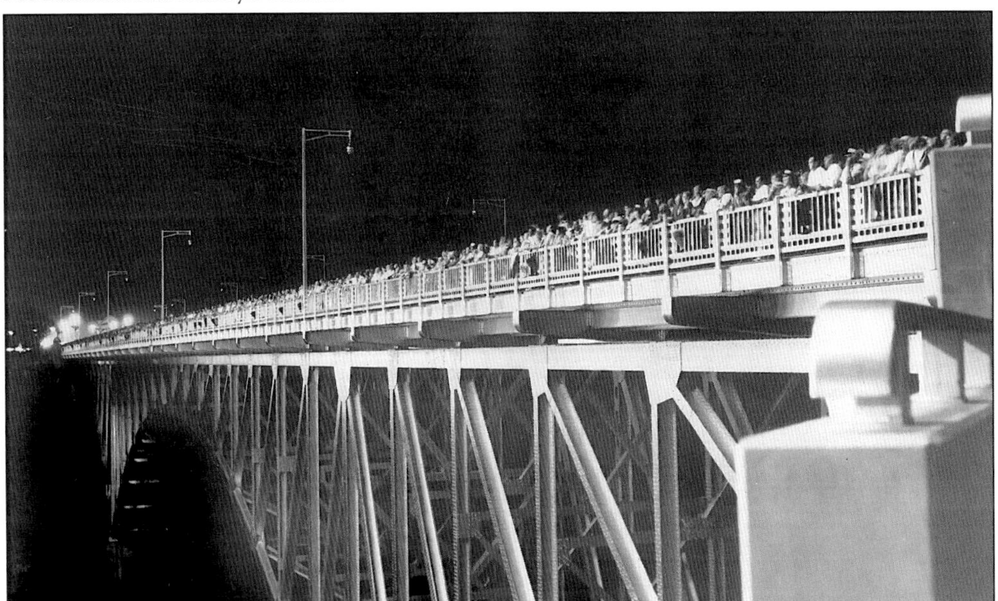

This photograph is an evening view of the 1949 bridge opening, which was attended by approximately 100,000 people. The structure won the annual award of merit as "Most Beautiful Steel Bridge" by the American Institute of Steel Construction in 1949.

Five

TRAGEDIES AND DISASTERS

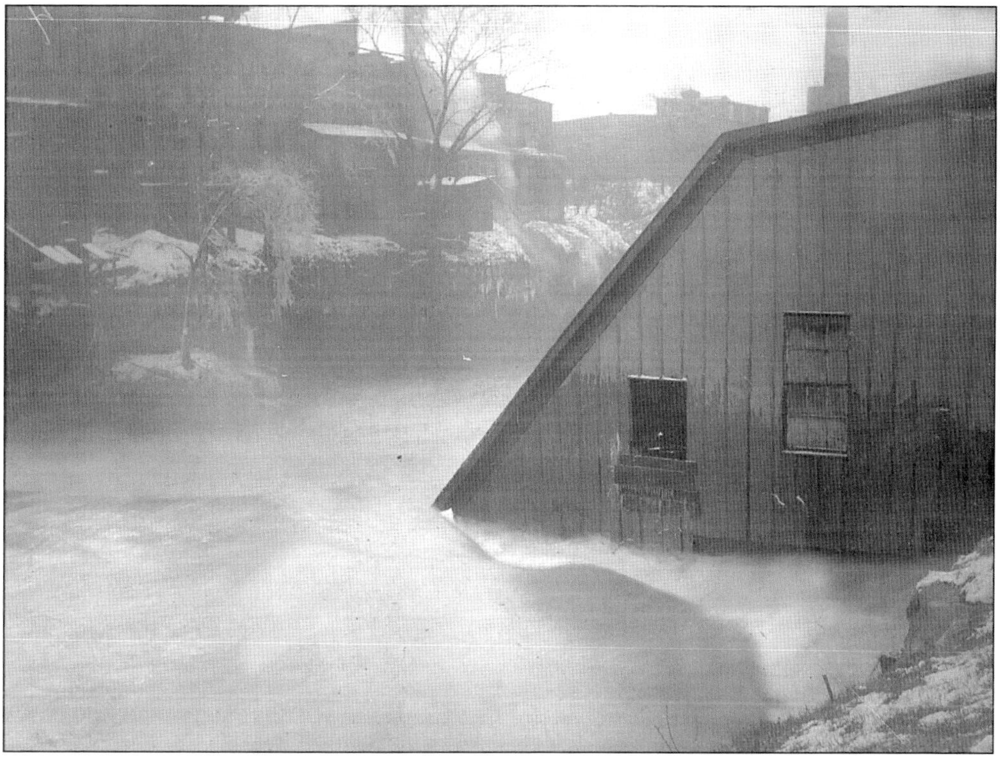

Like any city, Cuyahoga Falls has had its share of disasters and tragedies—both natural and man-made. Fires were a common hazard in the early years when most of the factory buildings along the river were made of wood. Businesses and homes frequently burned to the ground in a matter of hours. On October 24, 1866, several blocks on Front Street were consumed by fire. At that time the town had no fire engine and it would be many years before it did.

Perhaps the worst natural disaster in the history of Cuyahoga Falls was the flood that occurred in late March of 1913. The rain lasted four days, and by the time it was through, 9.55 inches had fallen. Many of the businesses along the river were damaged during the flood, including the Vaughn Machinery building pictured here. Many roads were severely damaged by this storm, which made rescue and repair efforts difficult.

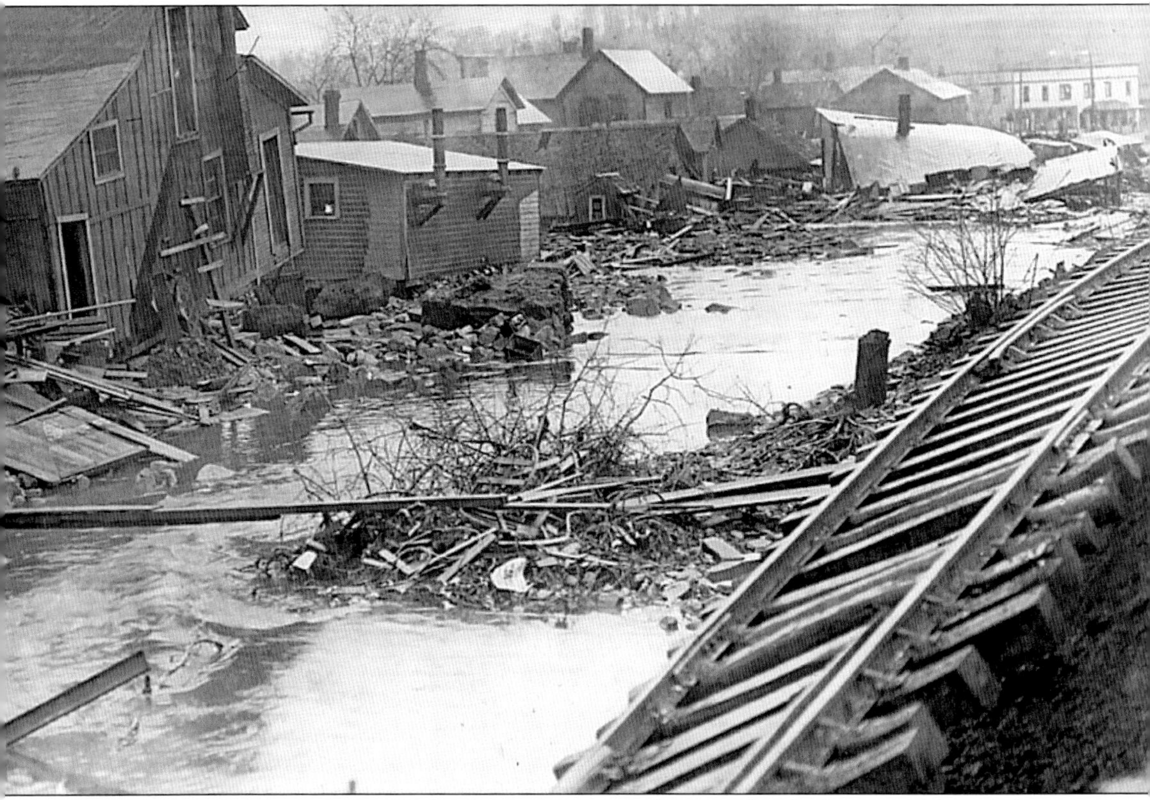

This photo shows a glimpse of the destruction caused by the flood of 1913. Although damage was severe, Cuyahoga Falls was hit less severely than other areas in Ohio. In Dayton, 1,500 people were killed during the same four-day period, and in Akron, five people were killed and over 500 people were driven from their homes. No deaths were reported in Cuyahoga Falls. (Courtesy of Pete Mellinger.)

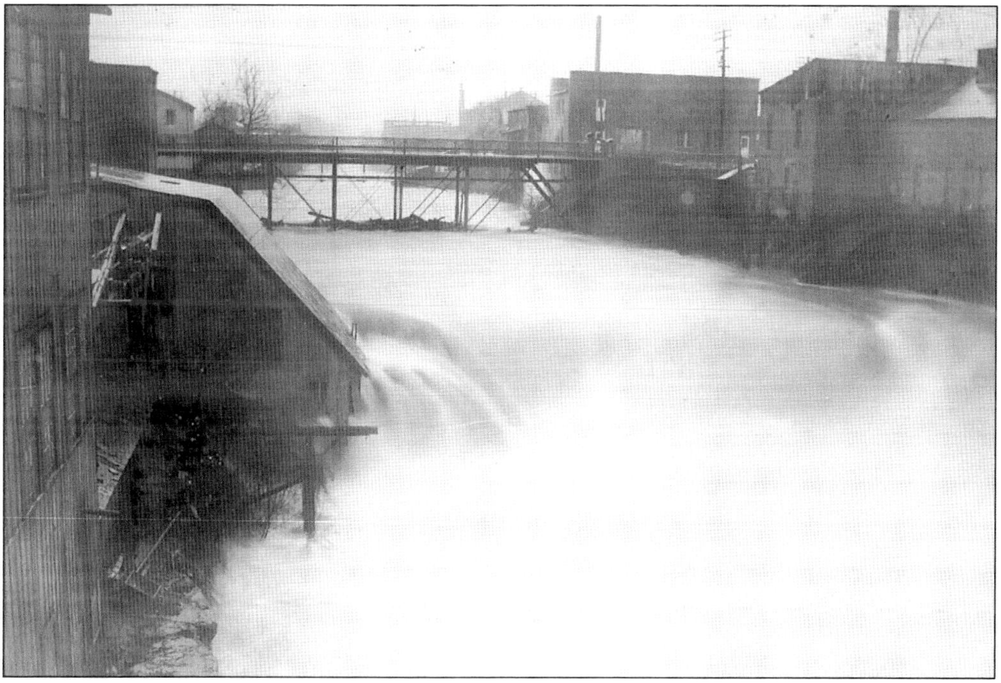

This image shows another view of the rampaging Cuyahoga River during the flood of 1913. At the height of the flooding, water reached the girders below the Broad Street bridge shown in the background. (Courtesy of Pete Mellinger.)

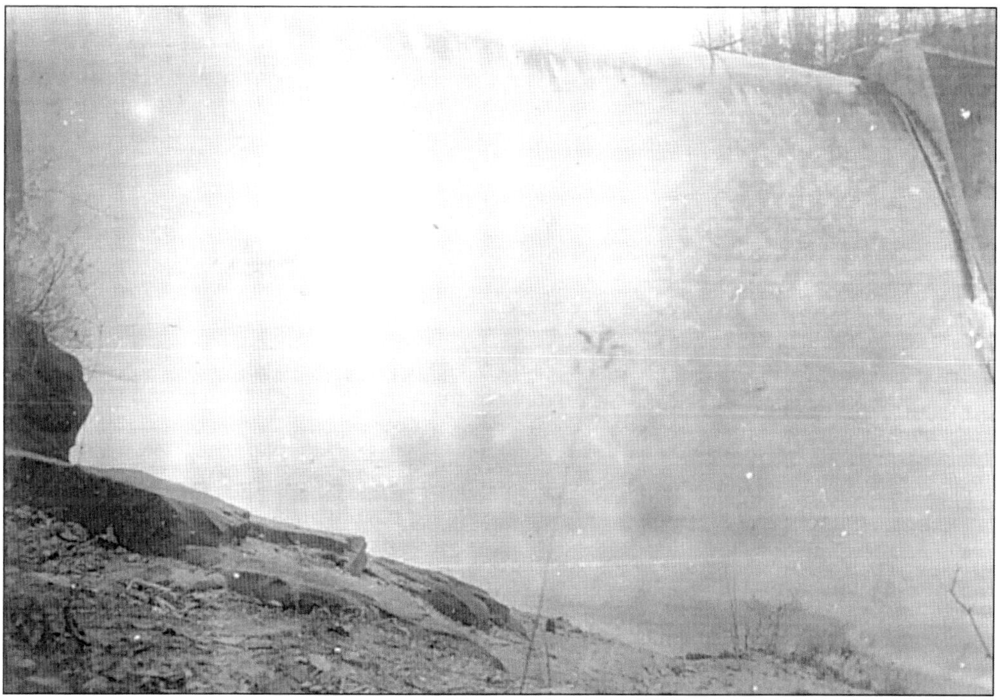

Not even the newly-constructed big dam in the gorge could contain the rains as water rushed over, flooding the powerhouse and cutting off power to the city for several days. (Courtesy of Dale Platt.)

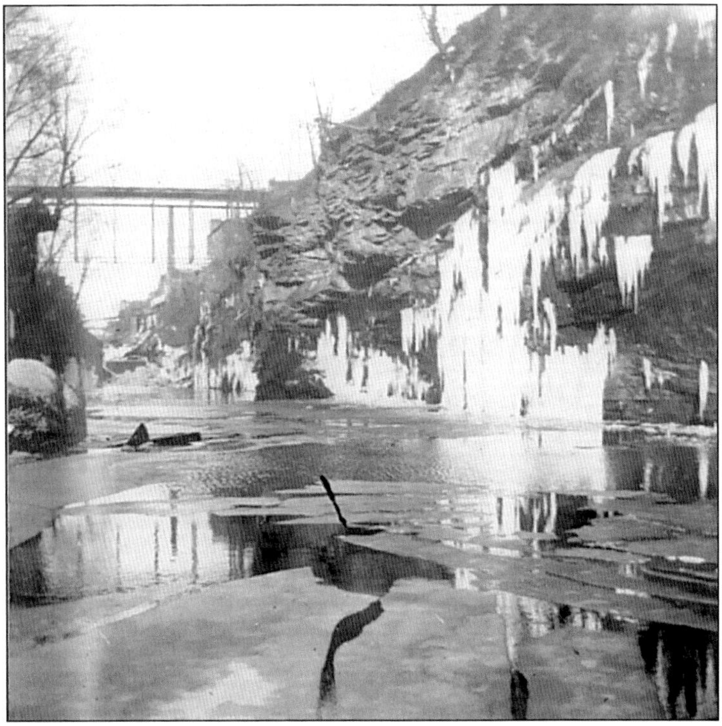

The Glens bridge shown here in winter seems serene amidst its beautiful surroundings, but this area was once the site of one of Cuyahoga Falls' worst disasters—the *Mountain Line* wreck—which took the lives of four people. The accident occurred June 11, 1918.

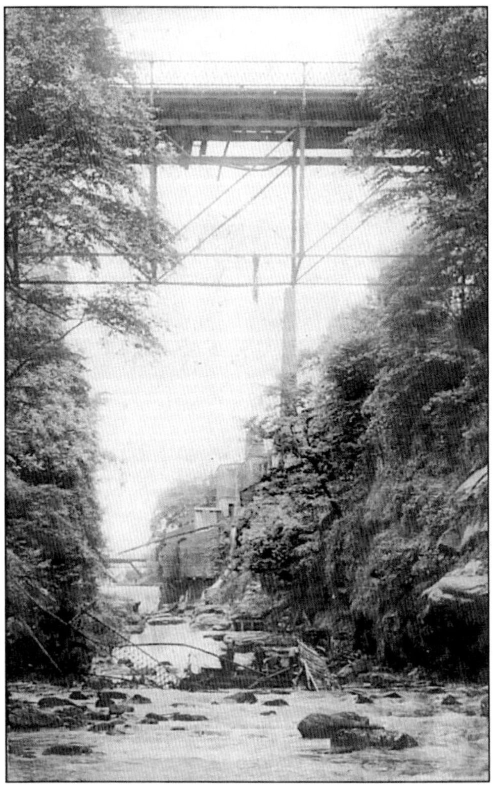

When the *Mountain Line* train jumped the rails of the Glens bridge, it fell more than 98 feet into the river—killing four people. The motorman and the machinist were the only survivors. Both men had fractured skulls and broken legs but recovered fully from their injuries. This photo of the accident site shows the wreckage in the river.

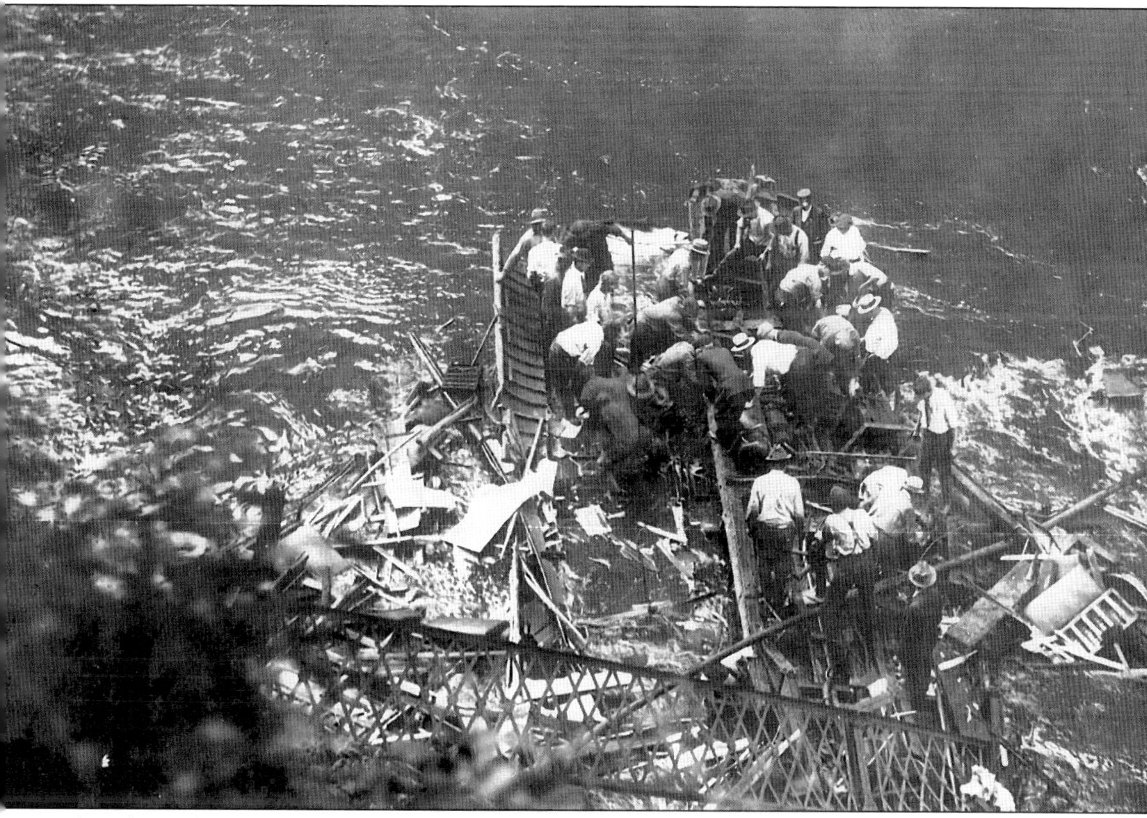

This photo shows the wreckage of the *Mountain Line* at the bottom of the Glens. The men are working to clean up the debris. The *Mountain Line* tragedy was the second disaster to occur at the same site. Years earlier a horse was pulling a carriage carrying a man and woman across the bridge, which was undergoing repairs. The horse walked through the barricade and the animal and both human passengers fell through the floor. The horse landed on its feet on a rock ledge, but the man and woman were killed. The next morning when the horse was discovered, a rescuer was lowered down to fasten a harness to the animal. High above the ledge, 20 men and one small boy pulled the horse back up to safety.

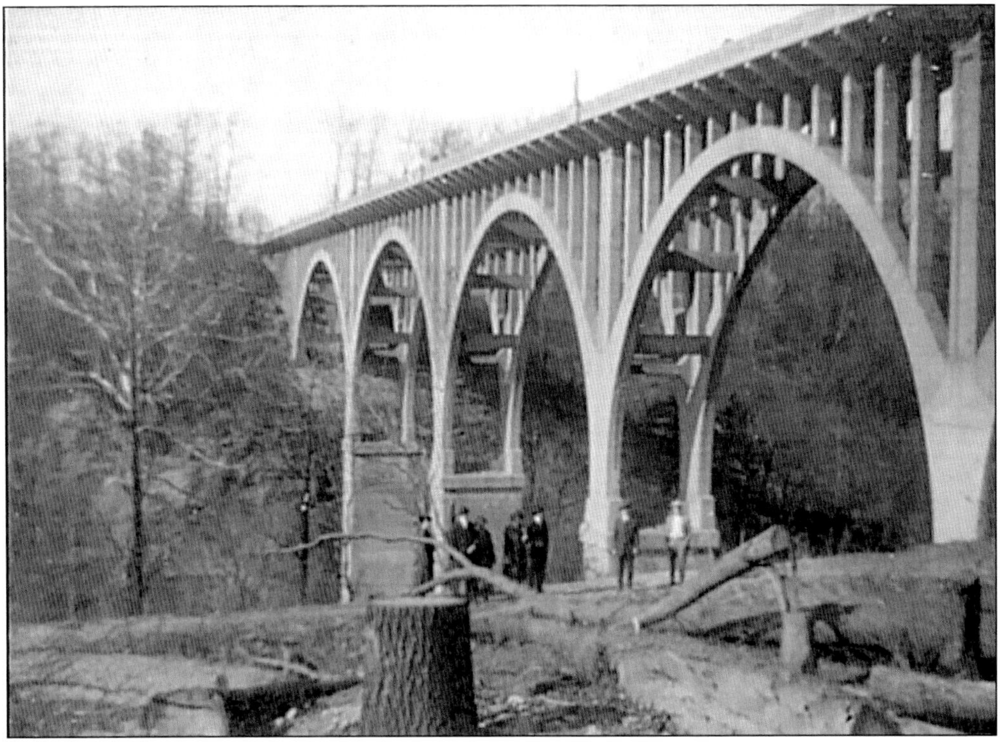

In May of 1924, another natural disaster hit Cuyahoga Falls when a powerful tornado tore through the city, causing extensive damage. This photo was taken next to the old High Level bridge. Notice the many trees snapped in half by the storm.

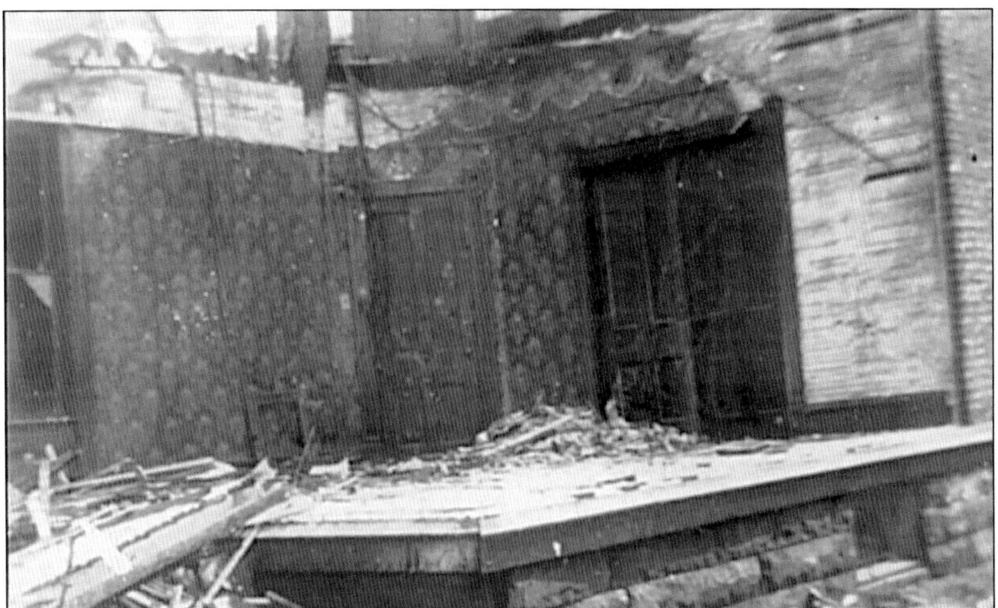

This home was destroyed in the tornado of 1924. The outside walls have been completely ripped apart.

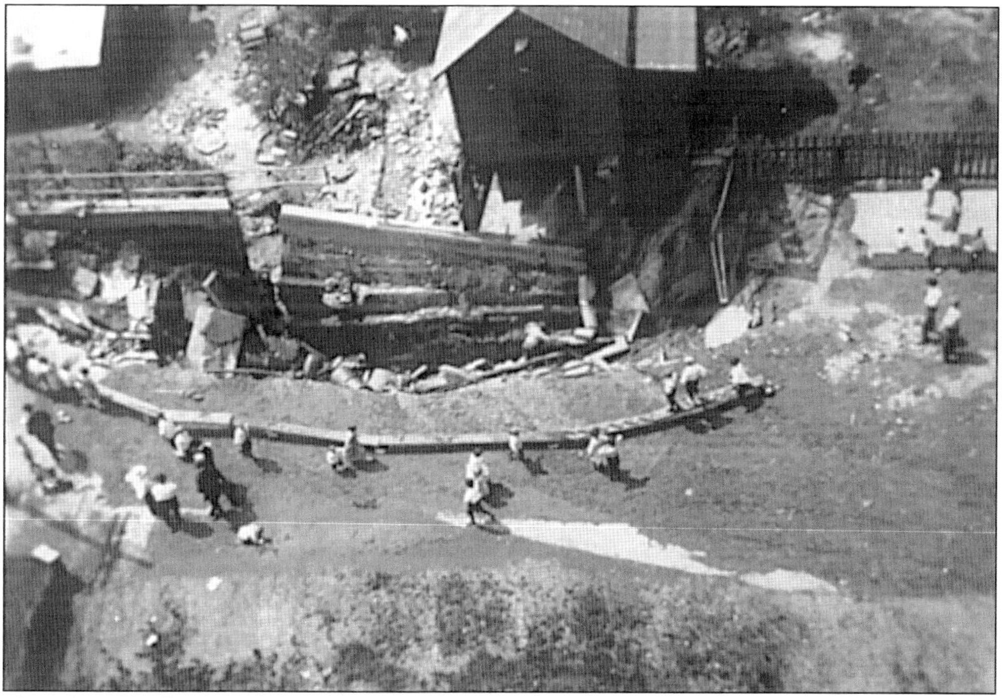

This photograph shows people looking at a concrete retaining wall that was ripped in half by the tornado of 1924.

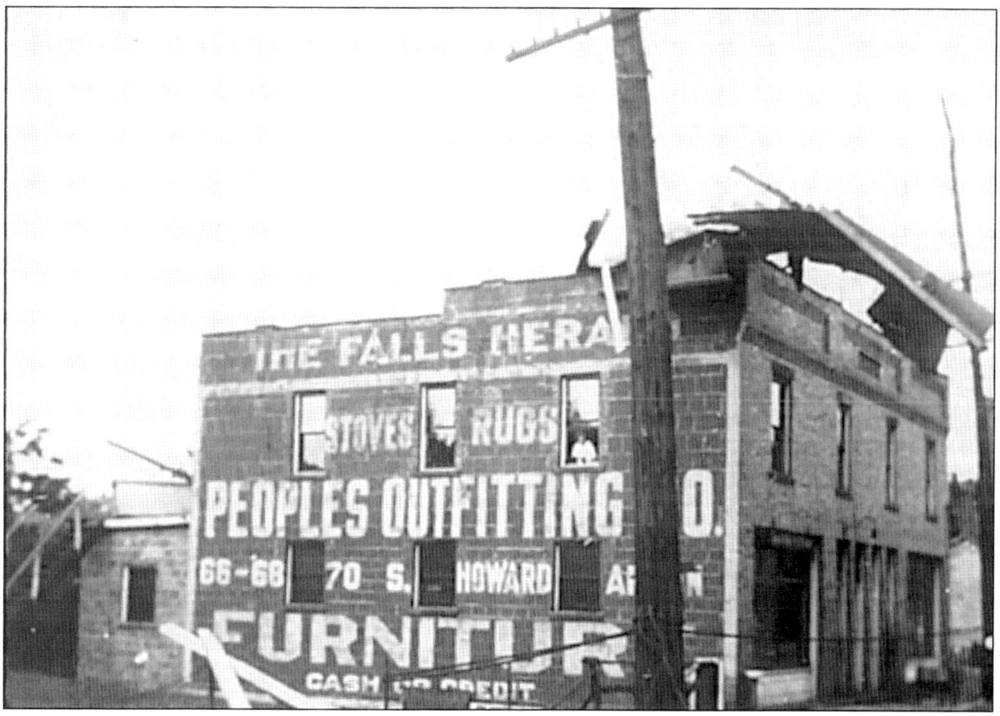

The roof of this building was torn off by the tornado of 1924.

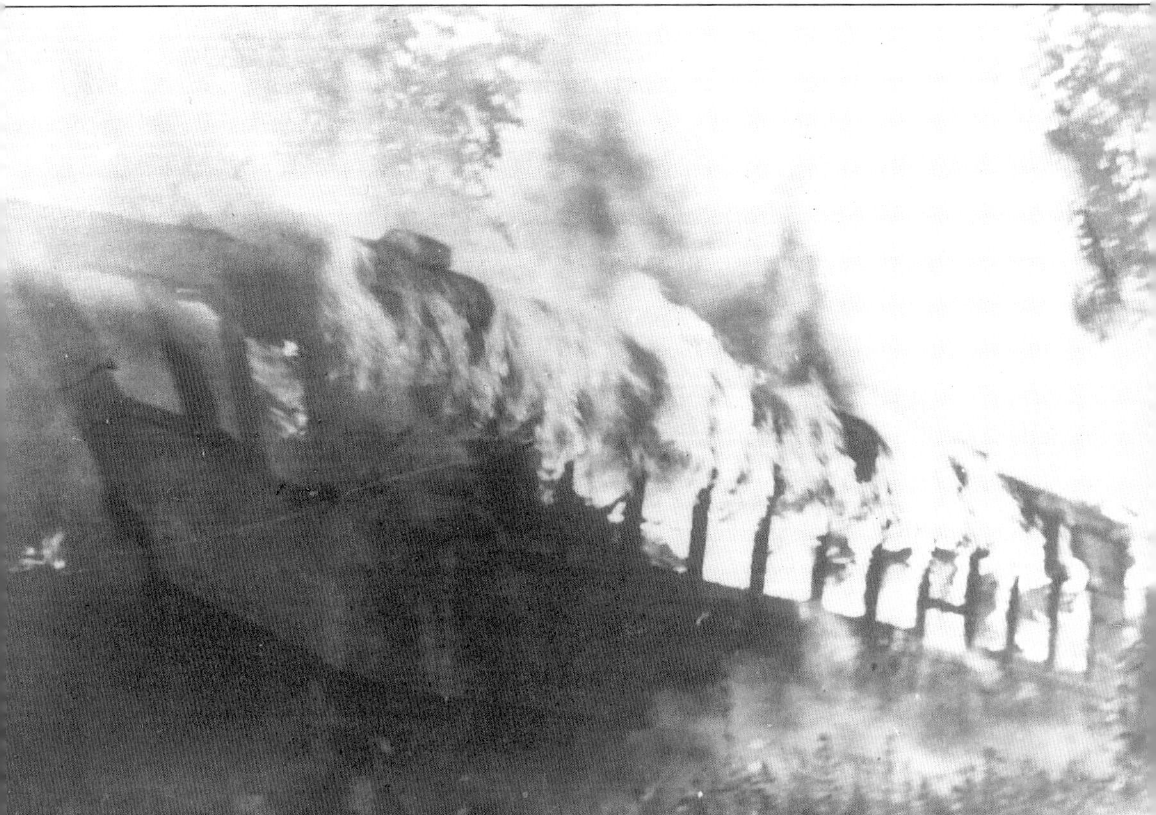

The most well-known tragedy in the history of Cuyahoga Falls is the *Doodlebug* disaster. In the early evening of July 31, 1940, the *Doodlebug*, a commuter train, collided with a freight train. Forty-three people were killed. Before the crash, the *Doodlebug's* engineer, Thomas Murtaugh, had opened the throttle and had the train speeding along at 55 miles an hour as it barreled through Silver Lake. Murtaugh's orders were to pull the train off to a side rail in order to let a freight train pass. Unfortunately for the passengers, Murtaugh failed to adhere to his orders. Shortly after passing Hudson Drive, the *Doodlebug* came face-to-face with the freight train headed for Cleveland. The two-car *Doodlebug* was no match for the 73-car freight, and it was pushed backwards over 200 yards before coming to a complete stop.

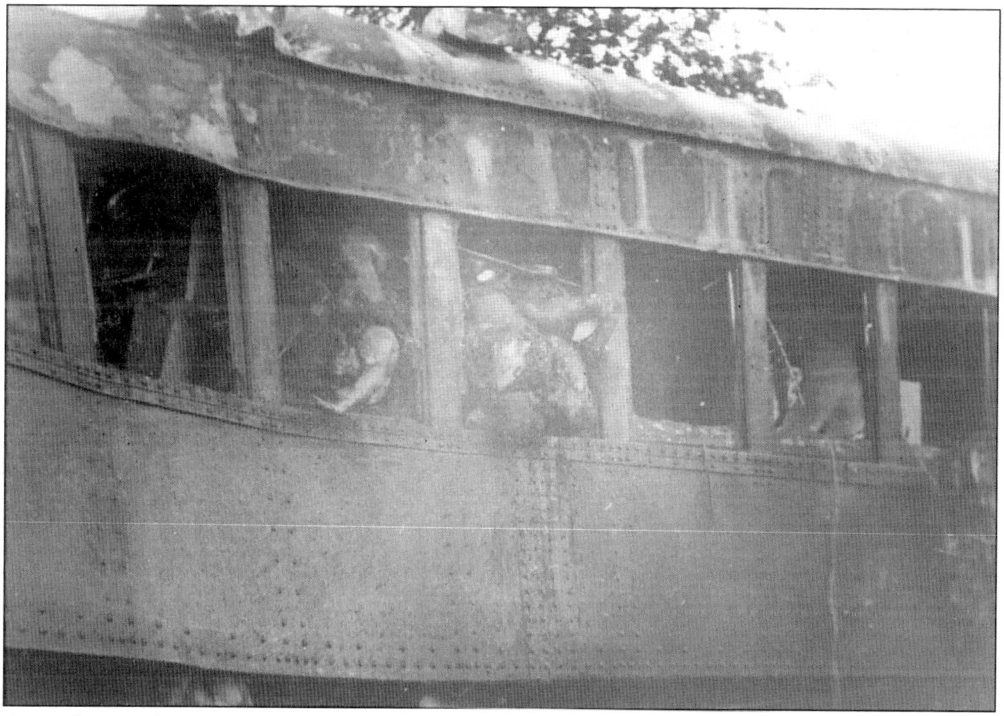

According to the coroner's report, only nine people died on impact when the *Doodlebug* crashed. The remaining 34 were burned to death when the 200-gallon gasoline tank exploded. The only survivors were Murtaugh and his two crewmen who jumped off before the collision. This photo shows the charred remains of the *Doodlebug*. Firemen had to spray the train with water for 45 minutes before they could approach it, and workers struggled late into the night cleaning up the debris and identifying the bodies.

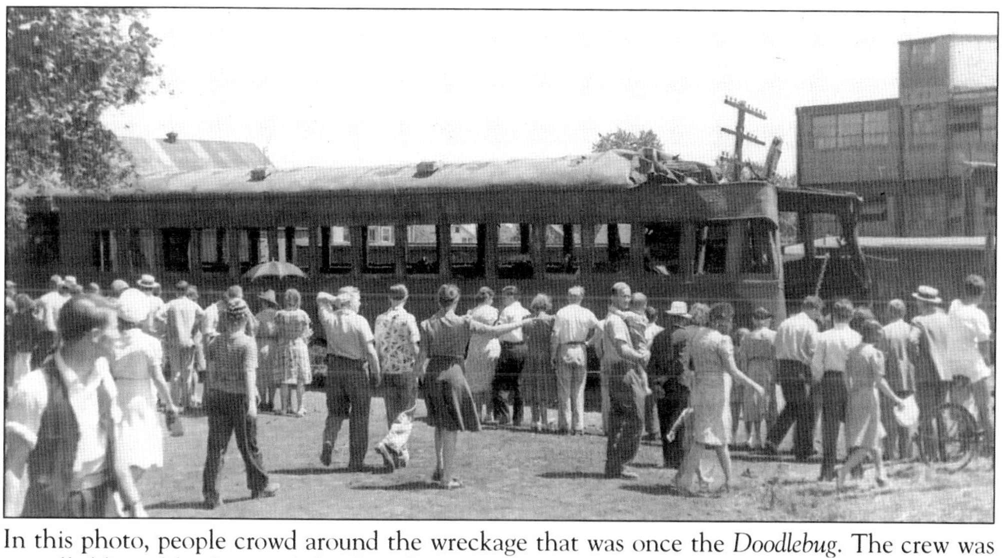

In this photo, people crowd around the wreckage that was once the *Doodlebug*. The crew was initially blamed for the wreck, but later hearings determined that the orders were wrongly worded and the crew was exonerated. Lawsuits lasted for several years after, and at least $600,000 was awarded to victims' families. (Courtesy of Dale Platt.)

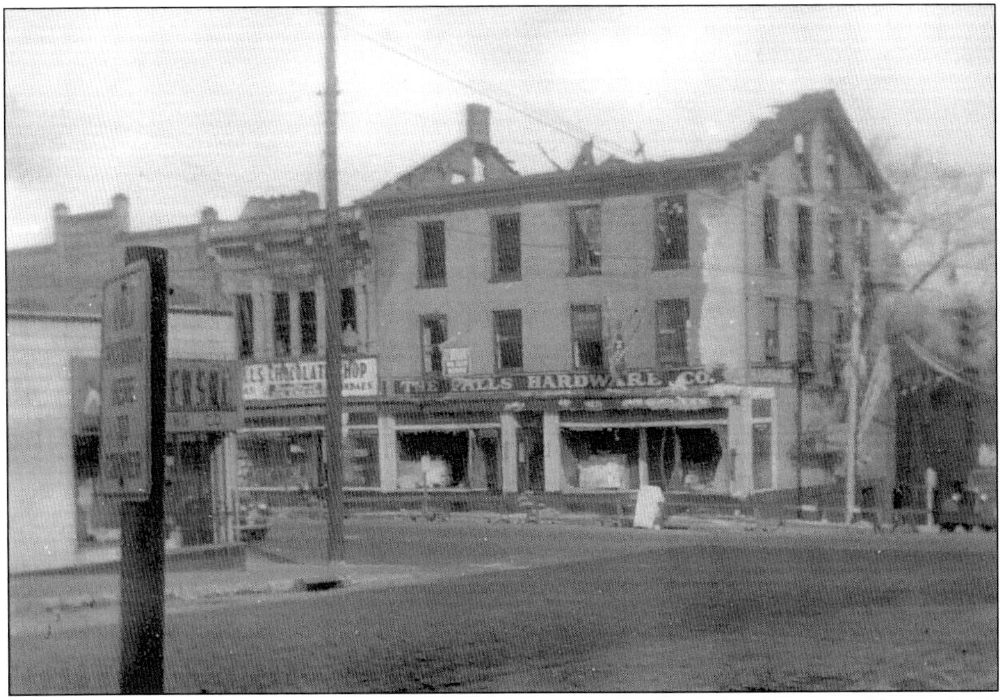

In 1948, a fire destroyed the Falls Hardware Company and the Falls Chocolate Shop, which were located on the corner of Front Street and Portage Trail.

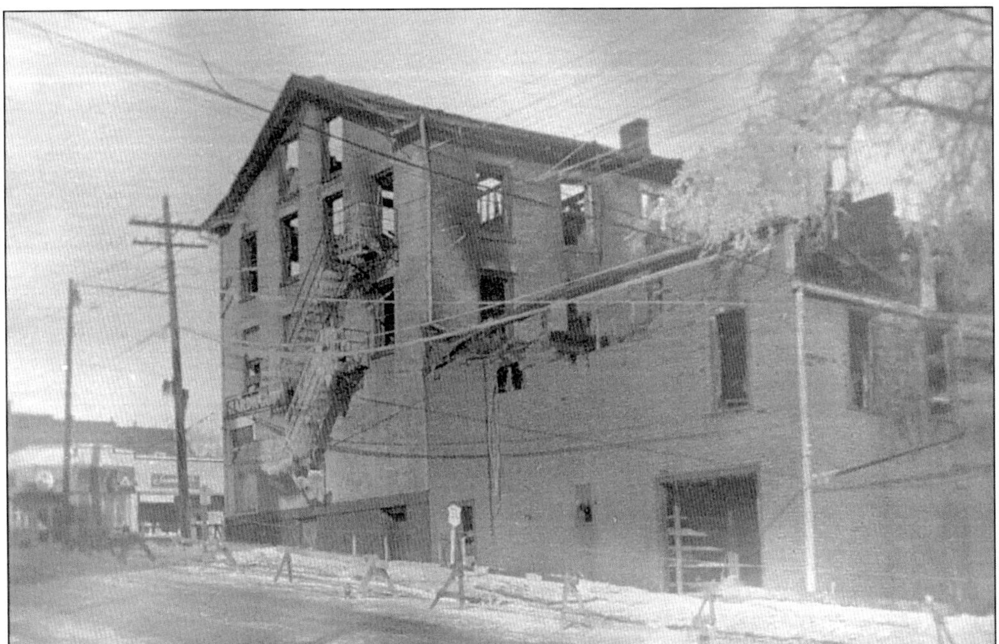

This view, as pictured from Portage Trail, shows the side of the Falls Hardware Company building that was gutted by the flames.

The Falls Chocolate Shop was a casualty of the fire of 1948.

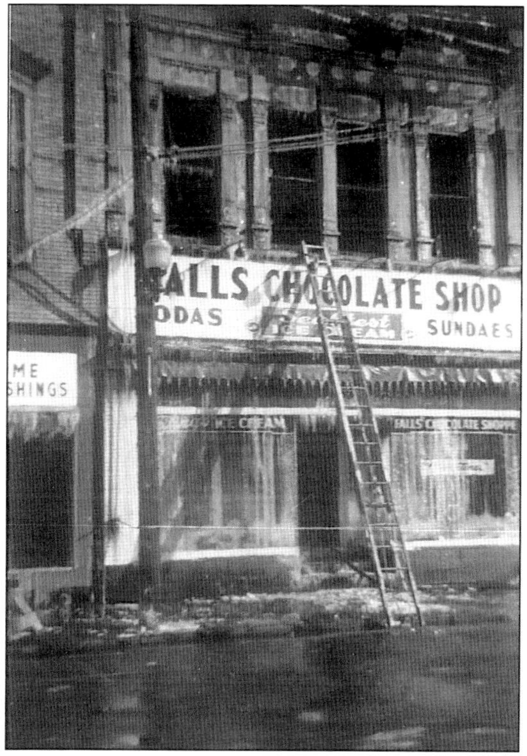

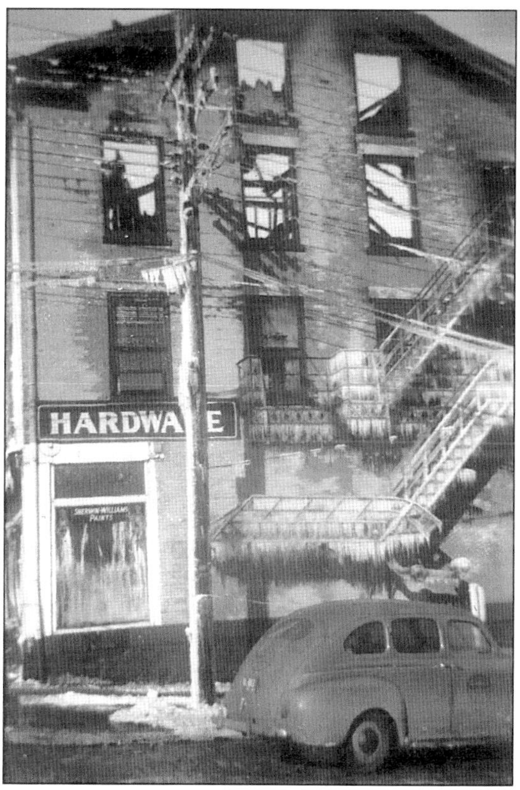

Icicles hang from the fire escape stairs of the Falls Hardware Company building in the aftermath of the 1948 fire.

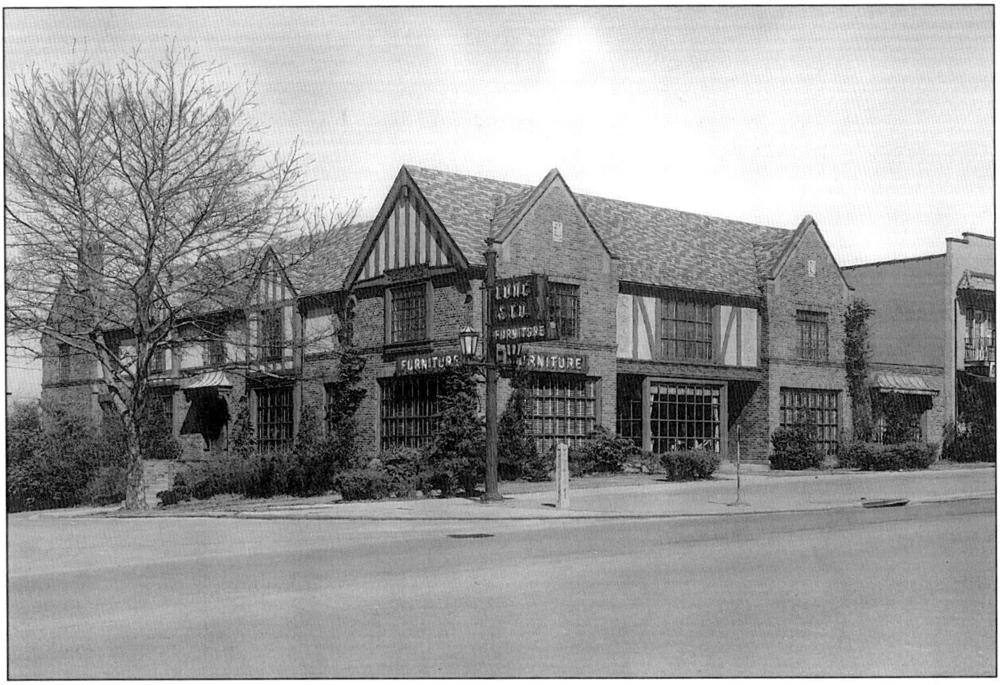

Long Furniture was established in this beautiful building formerly located at the corner of State Road and Chestnut Boulevard. The store occupied this space from 1930 to 1980. During the Depression years, the Long family lived in a third-floor apartment in this building. The business was known as Tom's Carpet & Antiques from 1980 to 1995 when it was sold to the proprietor of Abbey Ann's.

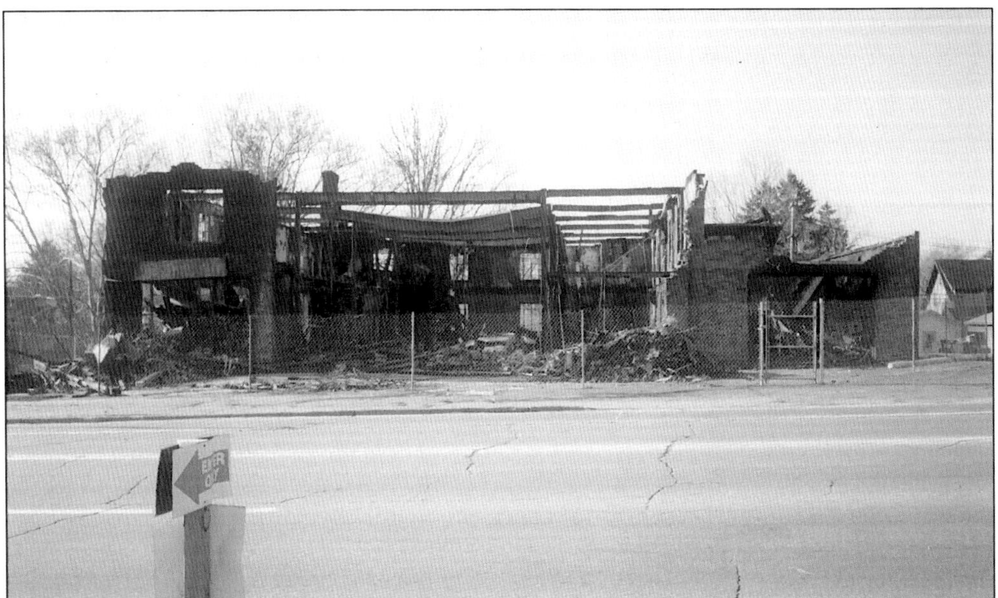
Residents of Cuyahoga Falls were saddened by the loss of a beautiful landmark building when Abbey Ann's (formerly Long Furniture) burned in December of 1995. The building was completely destroyed in the blaze.

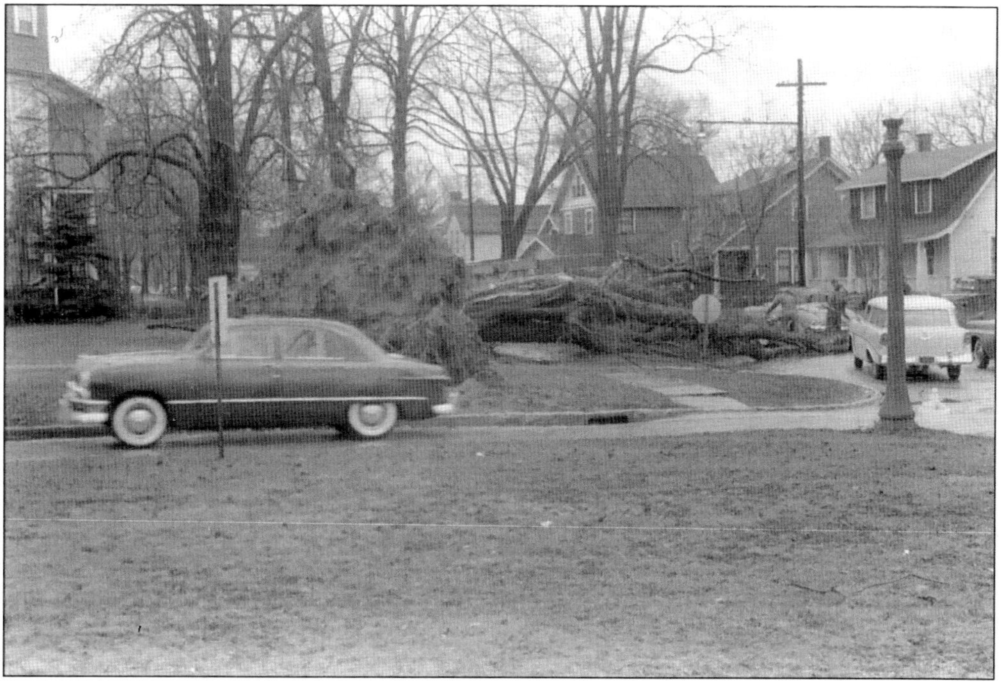

This tree, located near the corner of Broad Boulevard and Third Street, was another casualty as the tornado passed through the center of town.

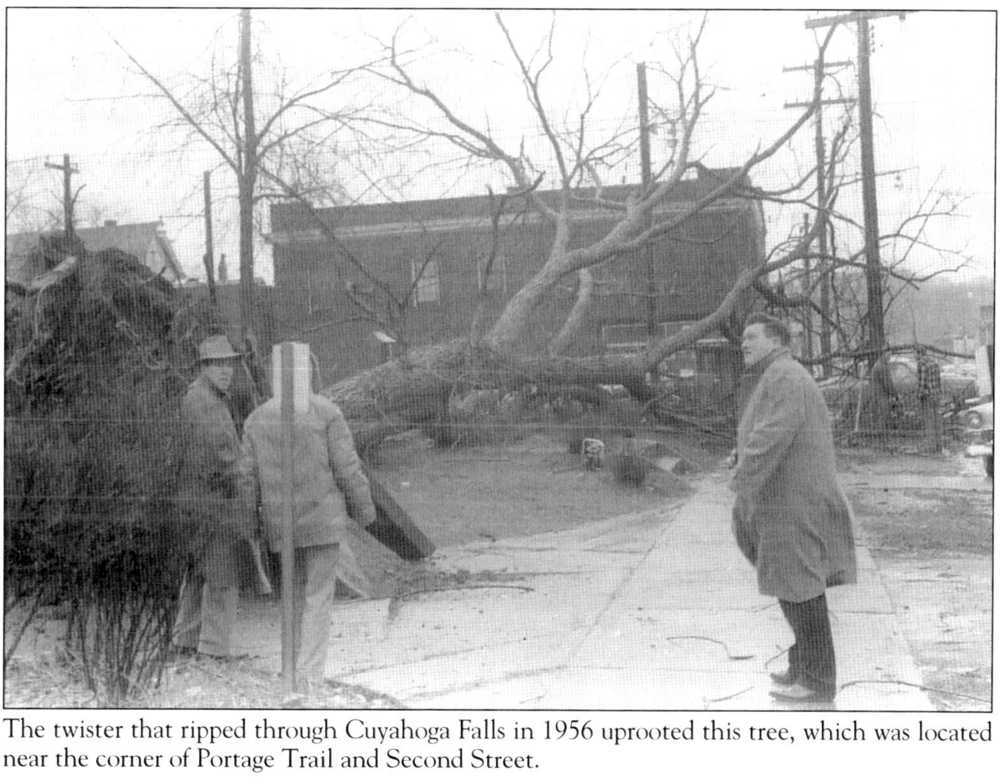

The twister that ripped through Cuyahoga Falls in 1956 uprooted this tree, which was located near the corner of Portage Trail and Second Street.

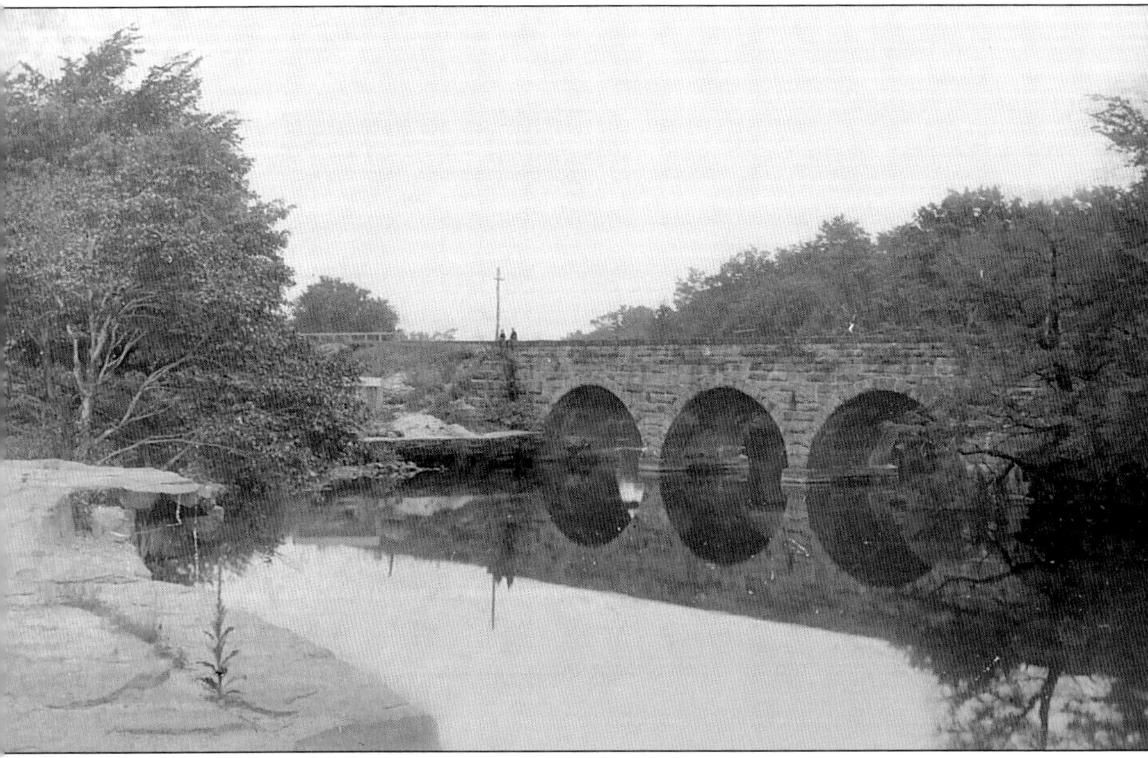

The historic and beautiful Bailey Road bridge pictured here was located near the scene of a grisly murder. In April of 1853, James Parks and William Beatsom set out on a trip to Pittsburgh to buy beef cattle. Beatsom was a butcher, and the two had become friends when they were in Buffalo a month earlier. Leaving from Cleveland, the two men began drinking heavily. They arrived in Hudson and got off the train to stretch their legs, and then—by mistake—boarded a train for Akron. When the conductor figured out they were on the wrong train, he let them off in Cuyahoga Falls. The next morning a passerby noticed a trail of blood that disappeared into the canal beneath a bridge on Bailey Road. Following a short search, they found the headless body of Beatsom. After a more extensive search, Parks was arrested and charged with murder. Park's defense was simple—he claimed that he found Beatsom dead in the bushes near the canal. Afraid that he would be held responsible, he cut off Beatsom's head so Beatsom could not be identified. This defense did not hold up, and Parks was convicted of murder and sentenced to death. In the week prior to his execution, Parks made three unsuccessful suicide attempts, and was eventually hanged for his crime.

Six

NURTURING MIND, BODY, AND SPIRIT

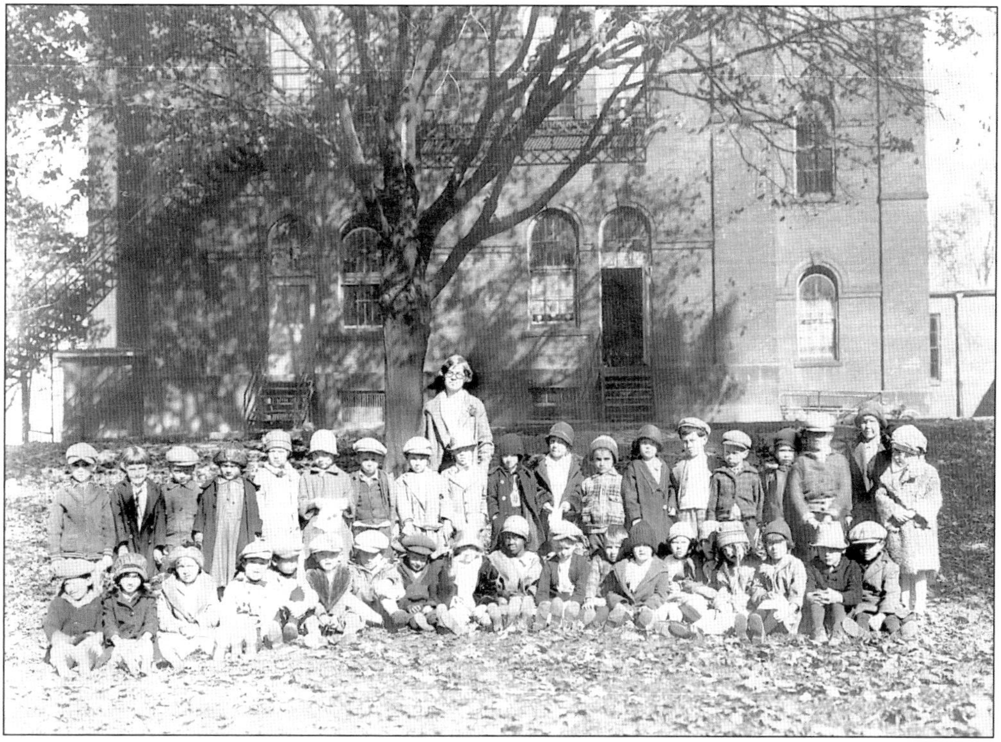

Cuyahoga Falls had long been recognized as a prosperous industrial city, but by 1925 the city also became noted for its fine homes, good schools, and many churches. Entertainment and recreational facilities were established and expanded. In the February 21st edition of the *Falls News Reporter*, Marion Repass, a junior high school student, wrote: ". . . it (Cuyahoga Falls) has many attractions for home life, such as low tax rates, good educational advantages, beautiful modern homes, low cost of living and nearness to 'The City of Opportunity,' Akron. It is also the cleanest, healthiest, and fastest growing city in the state of Ohio, and I think it has the best school teachers in the U—S—of A." Presumably, Marion received an A for her essay.

The photo above depicts the 1927-1928 first grade class of the East School, which was built in 1871. At first, the school housed elementary to high school students. The high school was removed in 1922 when the present one was completed. The East School continued to be used as an elementary school until 1938.

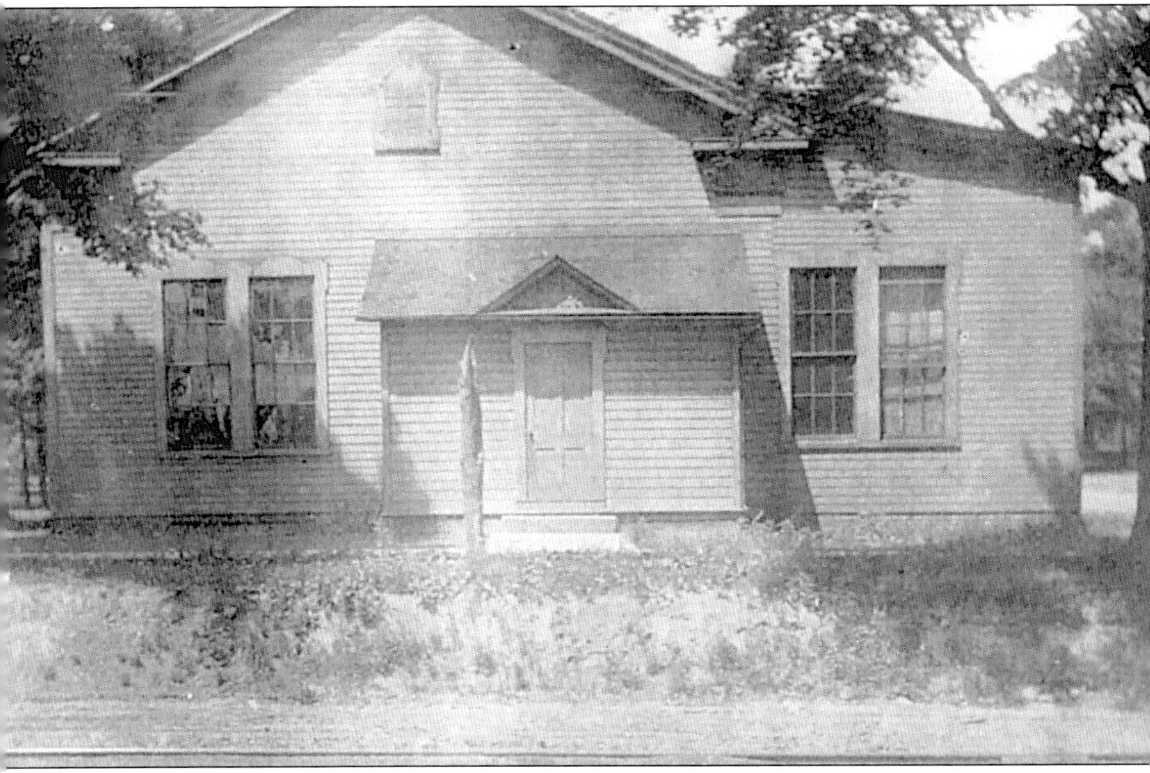

The first school in Cuyahoga Falls was a log building located at the corner of Broad and Front Streets. A private boy's school was opened in 1834 and led by J.H. Reynolds. Two years later, Miss Sarah Carpenter established a seminary for girls. After the organization of Cuyahoga Falls Township, the Cuyahoga Falls school district was established, and Mr. H.K. Taylor was employed as principal. Taylor was the head of the Lyceum organization, which established the high school program in 1855. Classes were held in the Lyceum building, pictured above, which was probably located just north of St. John's Episcopal Church. By 1857, there were a total of 482 students and seven teachers—six women and one man. The Lyceum served as the primary school in Cuyahoga Falls until the completion of East School in 1871.

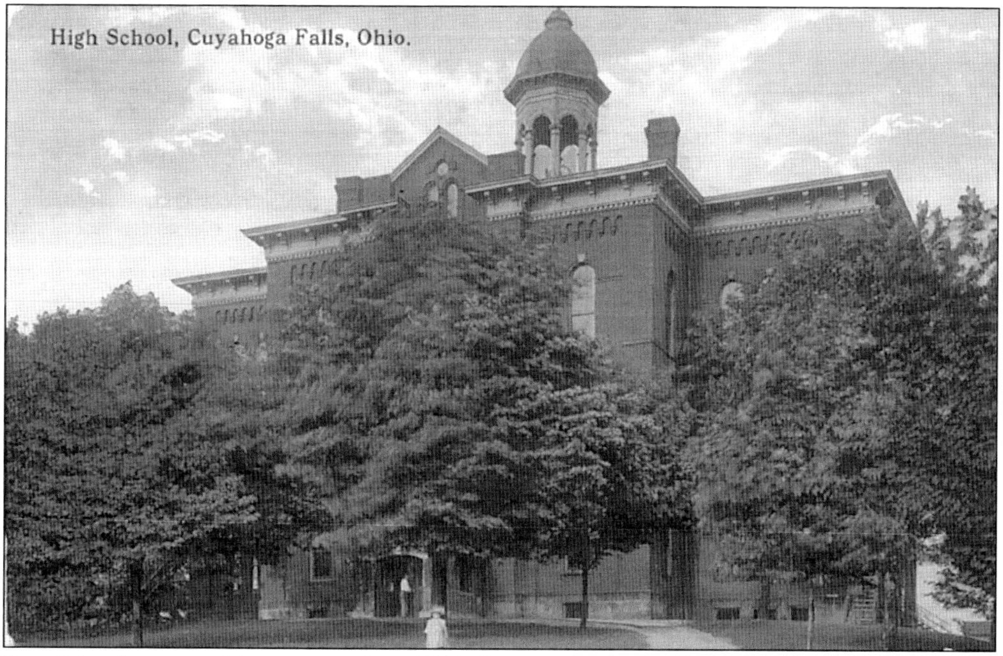

East School, pictured here, opened in 1871. Primary grades on the east side of town attended school here with high school students until 1922 when the present high school was completed.

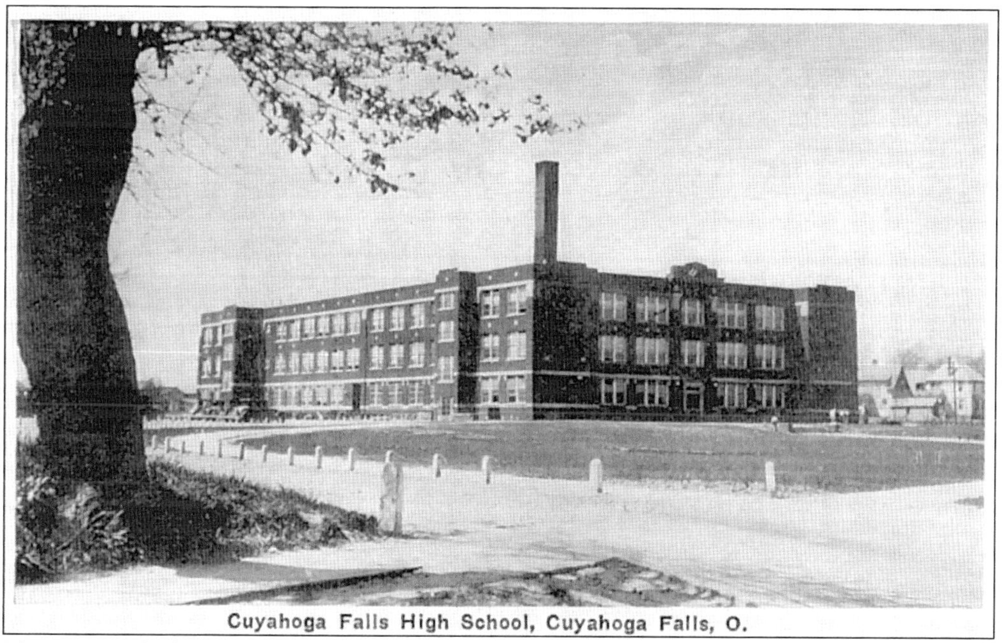

The present high school building was opened in September of 1922 at the corner of Fourth and Stow Streets. The school cost $306,131 to build and had an enrollment of 650 students. Students from Cuyahoga Falls, Tallmadge, Northhampton, and Silver Lake attended the new high school.

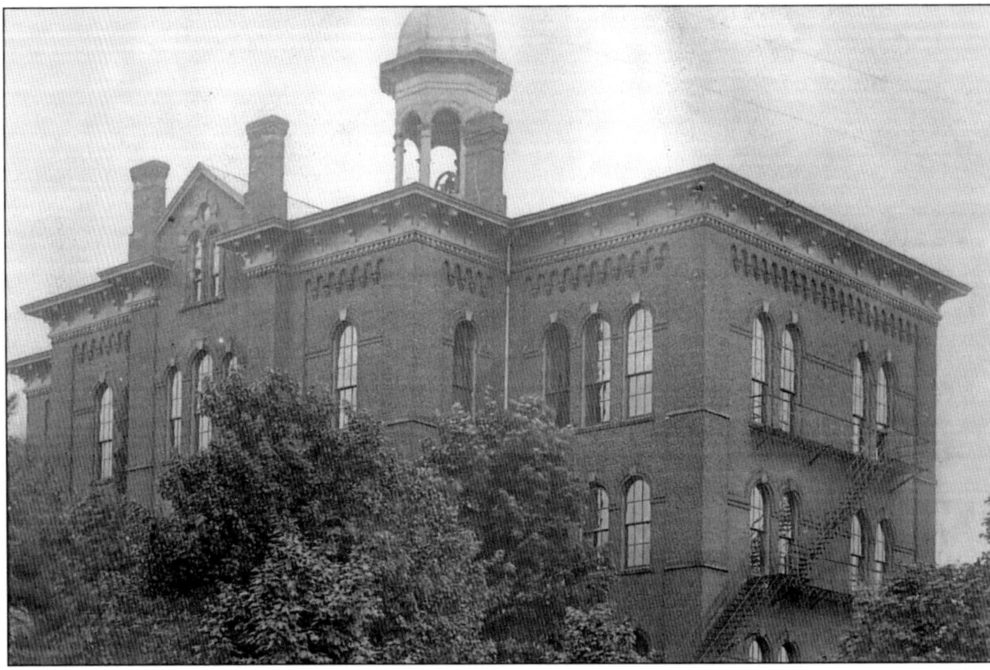

When the East School—pictured in this eerie view—closed in 1938, the building was used as a warehouse for the Cuyahoga Falls school system until it was torn down to make room for an apartment complex.

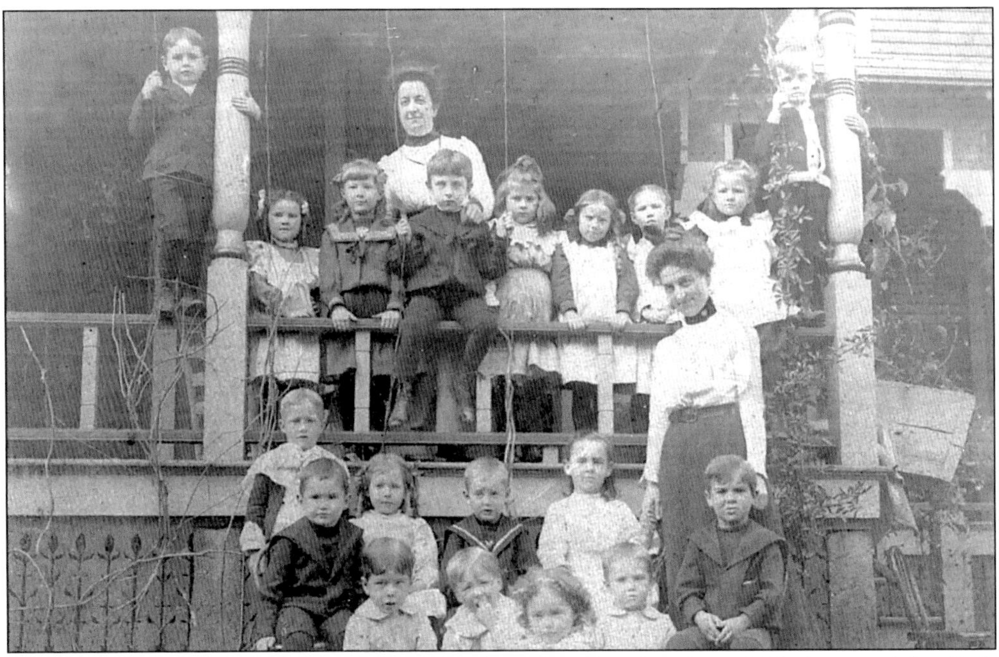

This photo depicts a kindergarten class conducted at the Cuyahoga Falls home of the Park sisters. Words written on the back of the photo give a clue to what it was like to attend the Parks' school: "They picked us up in horse-drawn surrey—blew whistle, we came out with our little baskets of jelly sandwiches."

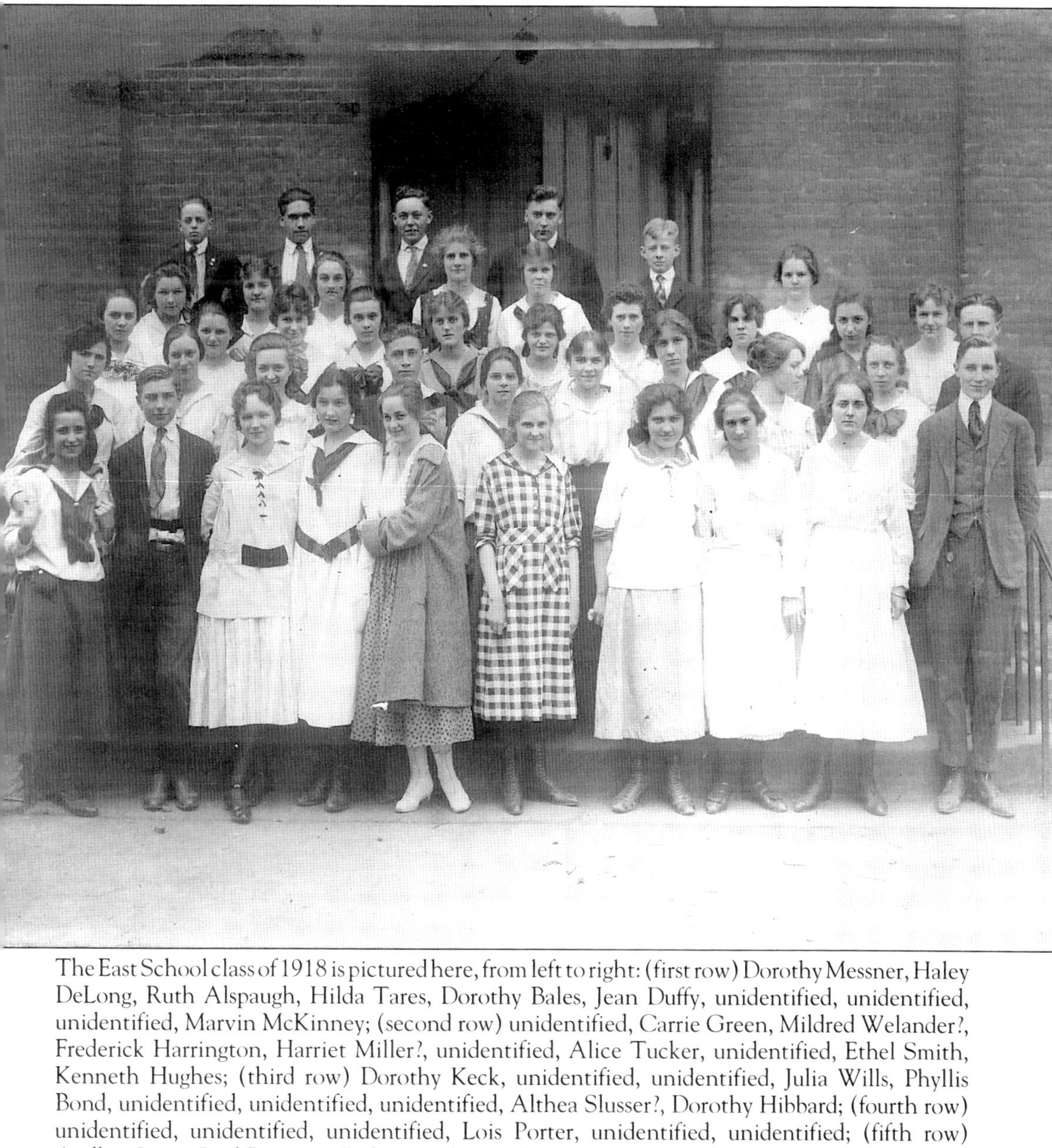

The East School class of 1918 is pictured here, from left to right: (first row) Dorothy Messner, Haley DeLong, Ruth Alspaugh, Hilda Tares, Dorothy Bales, Jean Duffy, unidentified, unidentified, unidentified, Marvin McKinney; (second row) unidentified, Carrie Green, Mildred Welander?, Frederick Harrington, Harriet Miller?, unidentified, Alice Tucker, unidentified, Ethel Smith, Kenneth Hughes; (third row) Dorothy Keck, unidentified, unidentified, Julia Wills, Phyllis Bond, unidentified, unidentified, unidentified, Althea Slusser?, Dorothy Hibbard; (fourth row) unidentified, unidentified, unidentified, Lois Porter, unidentified, unidentified; (fifth row) Audley Gray?, Paul Benway?, Robert Jordan, Aubrey Boltz, and John Sabin.

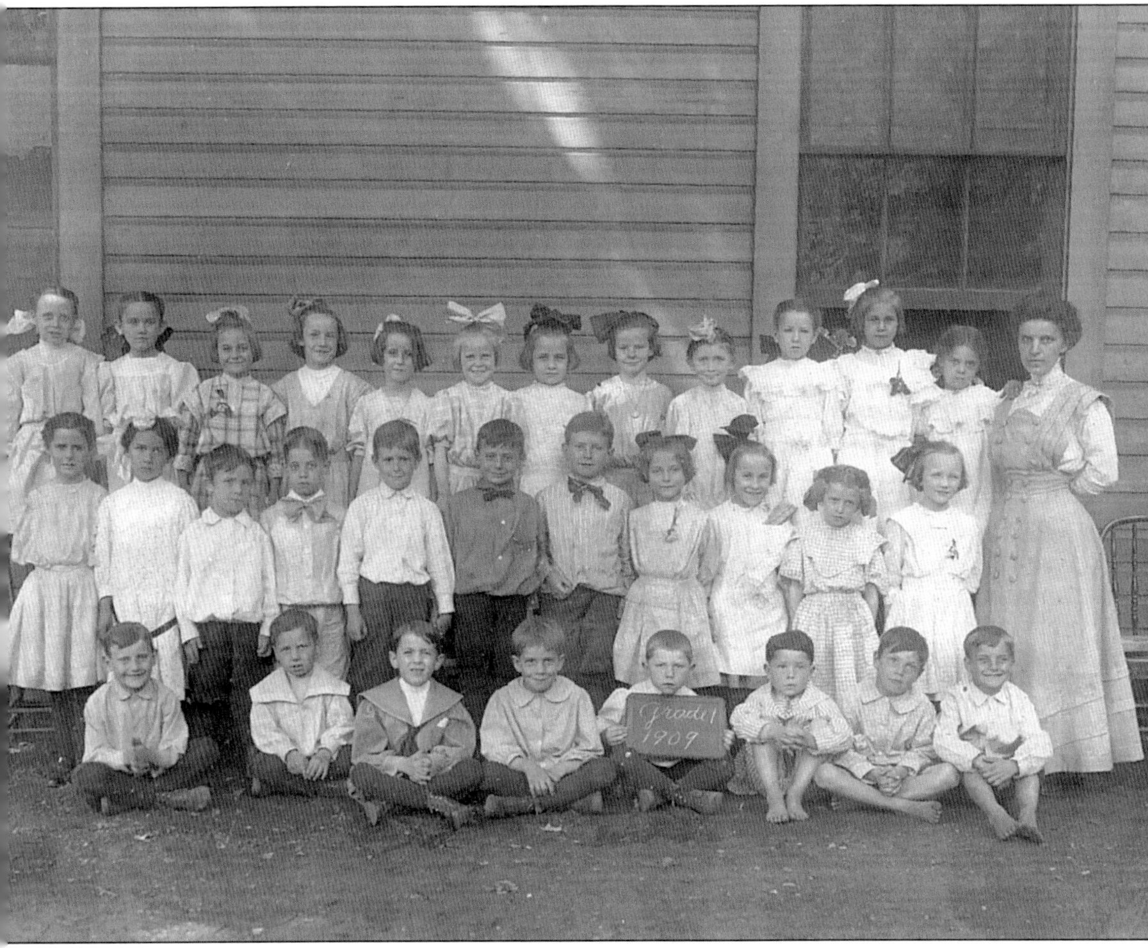

Pictured here is the first grade class of the Lyceum school in 1909, taught by Miss Hinkle. During this time many changes were taking place in the educational system of Cuyahoga Falls. W.H. Richardson was elected superintendent in 1908 and implemented his philosophy of "work-study-play" in the school. Richardson adopted the Gary Plan, which emphasized the importance of "doing and learning." Starting in the fourth grade, students had daily periods in shop, music, art, home economics, and supervised play. Students were also released for one hour each week, upon parental consent, to attend classes in religion. Cuyahoga Falls was only the third community in the nation to implement the Gary Plan and the first in Ohio. This was considered a revolutionary method of education at the time. Unfortunately, Falls was forced to return to a traditional method of education during the Great Depression because of financial problems.

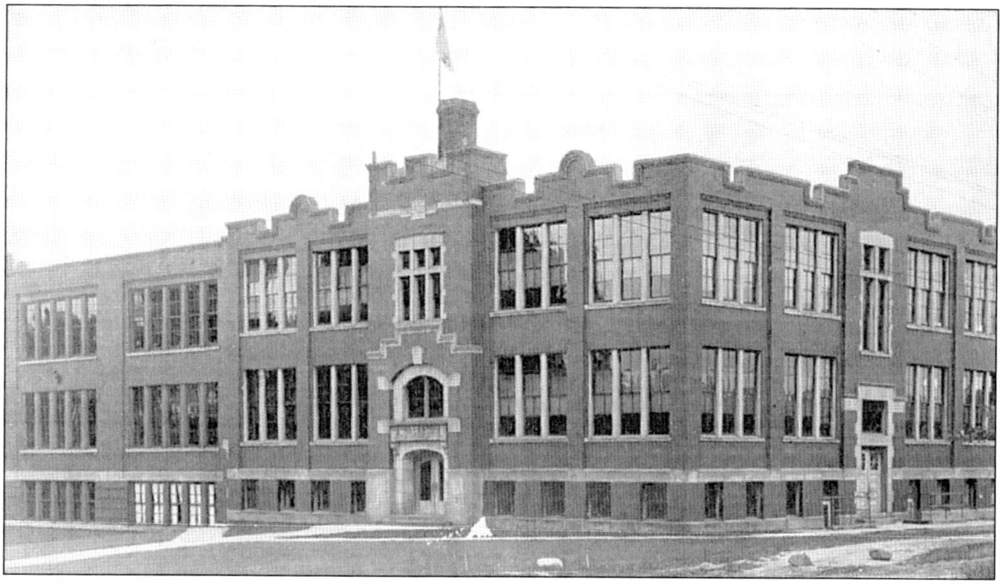

Broad Street School was located at the corner of Broad and Fourth Streets. It was built in 1909, and was remodeled in 1913 to meet the requirements of the Gary System. It was used as an elementary school, but the Falls High varsity basketball team played their home games in the Broad Street School gym until the new high school was completed. In 1968, Broad Street School was torn down and replaced by DeWitt School.

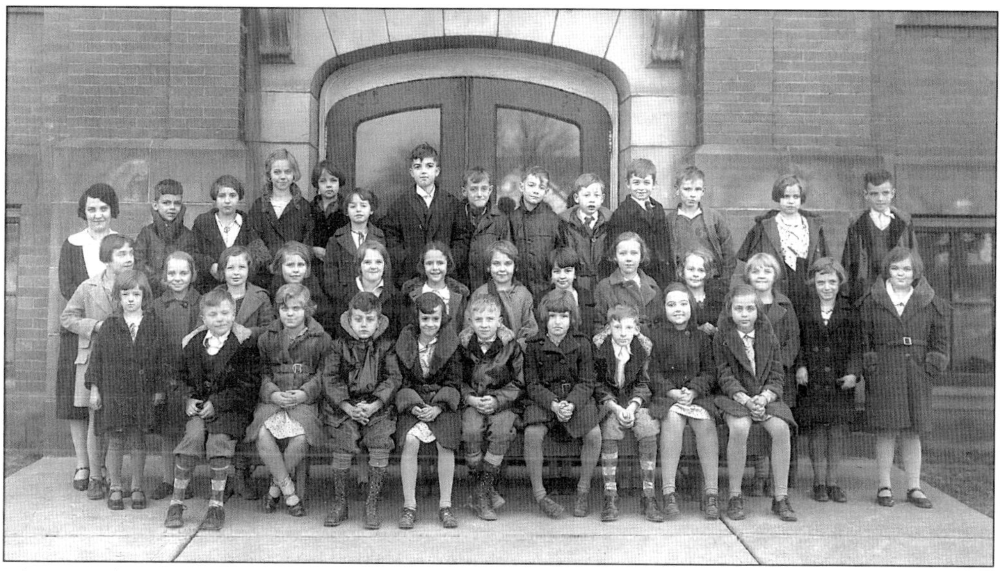

The Broad Street School class of 1933-1934 is pictured here, from left to right: (first row) Vera Ocker, Harold Robinson, Virginia Walker, Bruce Rothmann, Virginia Phillips, Wilmer Jones, Marjorie Burt, John Hilston, Joan Halpin, Verna Lee Wilson; (second row) Marjorie Elliott, Mary Hammaker, unidentified, Peggie Evans, Alice Prevost, Sally Shafer, Marjorie Reese, Audray McCullough, Nancy Rice, Margaret Turner, Betty Pizer, Elizabeth Janess, Gloria Degnon; (third row) Frank Barwell, unidentified, Eleanor Ritchie, Betty Radcliff, Phyllis Lybarger, unidentified, Don Meredith, Dean Meredith, unidentified, unidentified, Bill Lund, Colleen Pilliod, and Donald Wright.

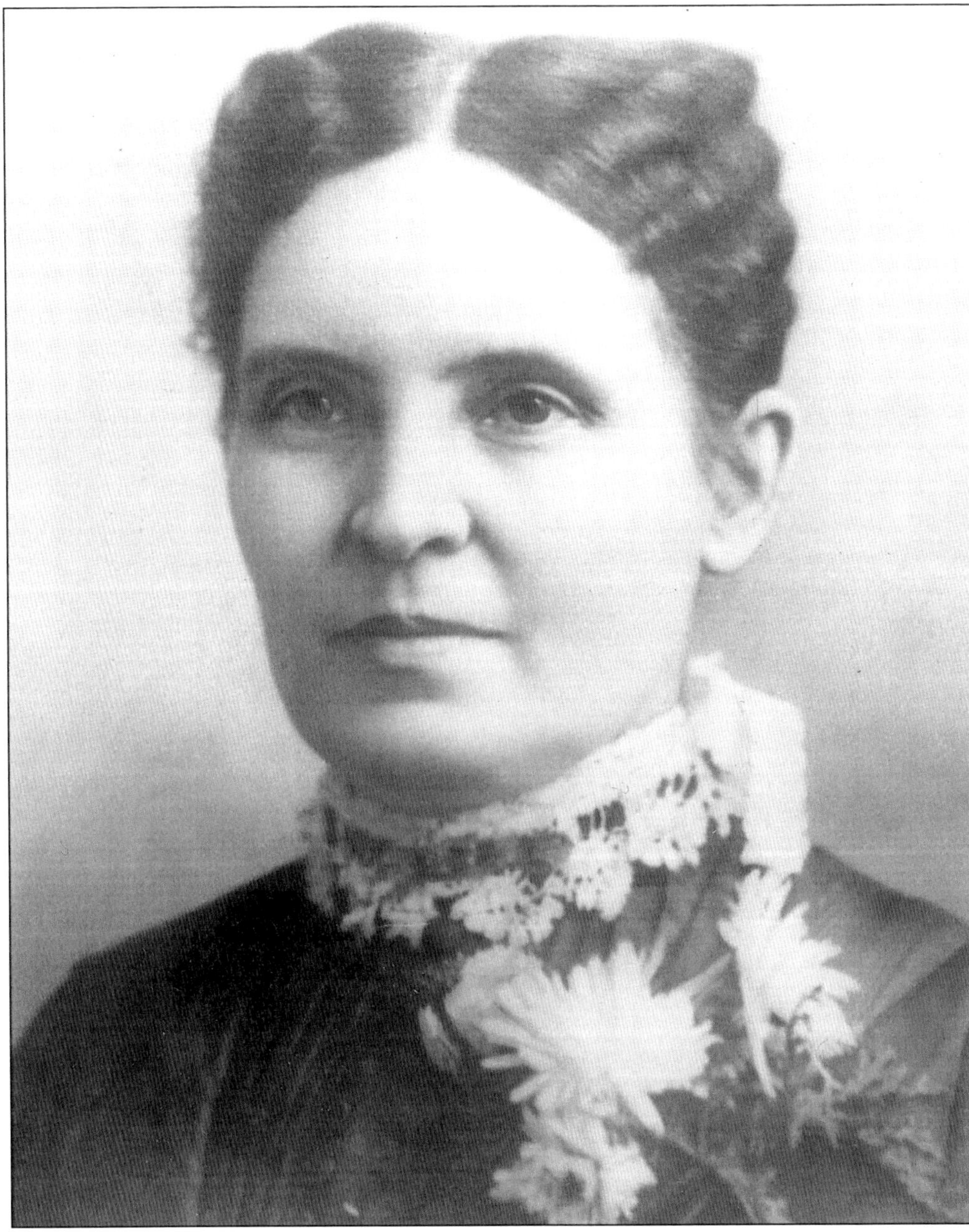

Ellen Knight was born in East Cleveland on October 2, 1840. In 1865, she was married to Mathew Crawford, a well-known horticulturist, and the couple moved to Cuyahoga Falls, where they operated a bulb and berry plant company. In 1870, Ellen Knight Crawford began teaching in the Cuyahoga Falls school system, and she continued teaching until 1890. She was beloved by her students. Mrs. Crawford reportedly had a saying that no student of hers ever forgot: "For every evil under the sun, there is a remedy or there is none. If there is, try to find it. If there is not, never mind it." She also served on the board of education from 1914 to 1916, before her tragic death. Mrs. Crawford was on her way to a board of education meeting on March 2, 1916, walking through a late snowstorm. A southbound streetcar hit her as she attempted to cross Second Street at Broad Street. She was then carried into the Congregational Church, where she died.

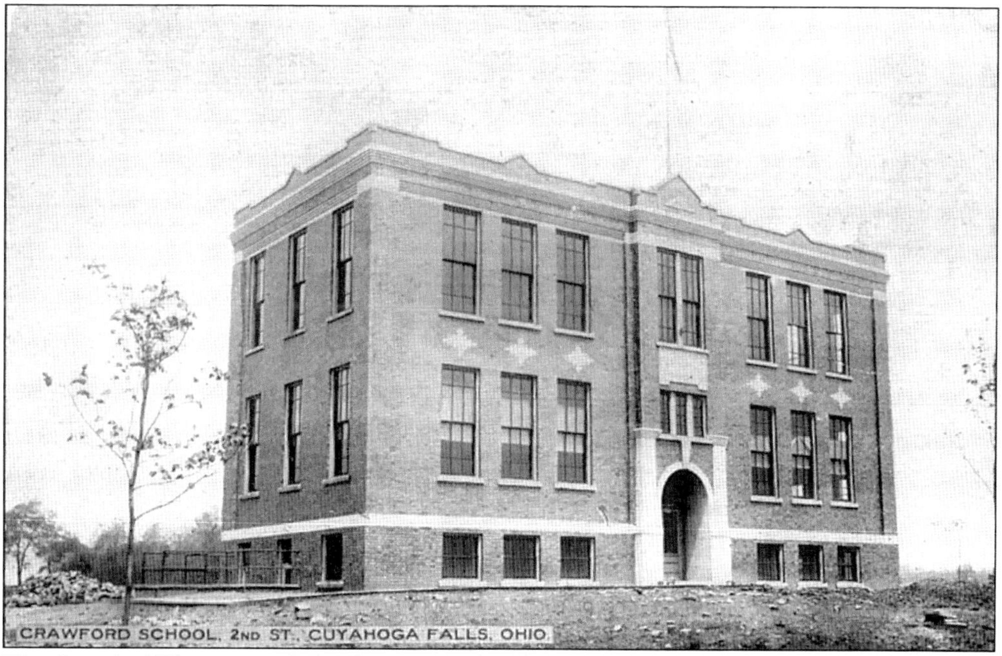

The Crawford Elementary School was named in honor of Ellen Knight Crawford. The school was located between Second and Third Streets on the north side of Tifft. Mrs. Crawford was so well-liked that for many years, her former students held a reunion every July to honor her. In 1924, several of her students paid tribute to her by building a memorial fountain in the Broad Boulevard parkway.

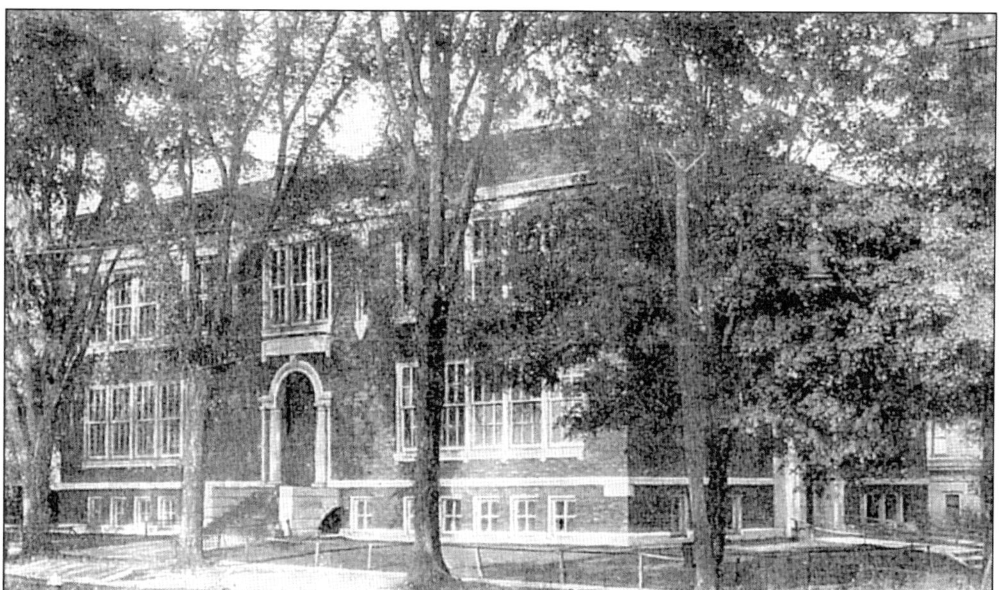

In 1923 the four-room St. Joseph's School was constructed. The facility has since expanded to the present building pictured here, which is located at 1909 Third Street.

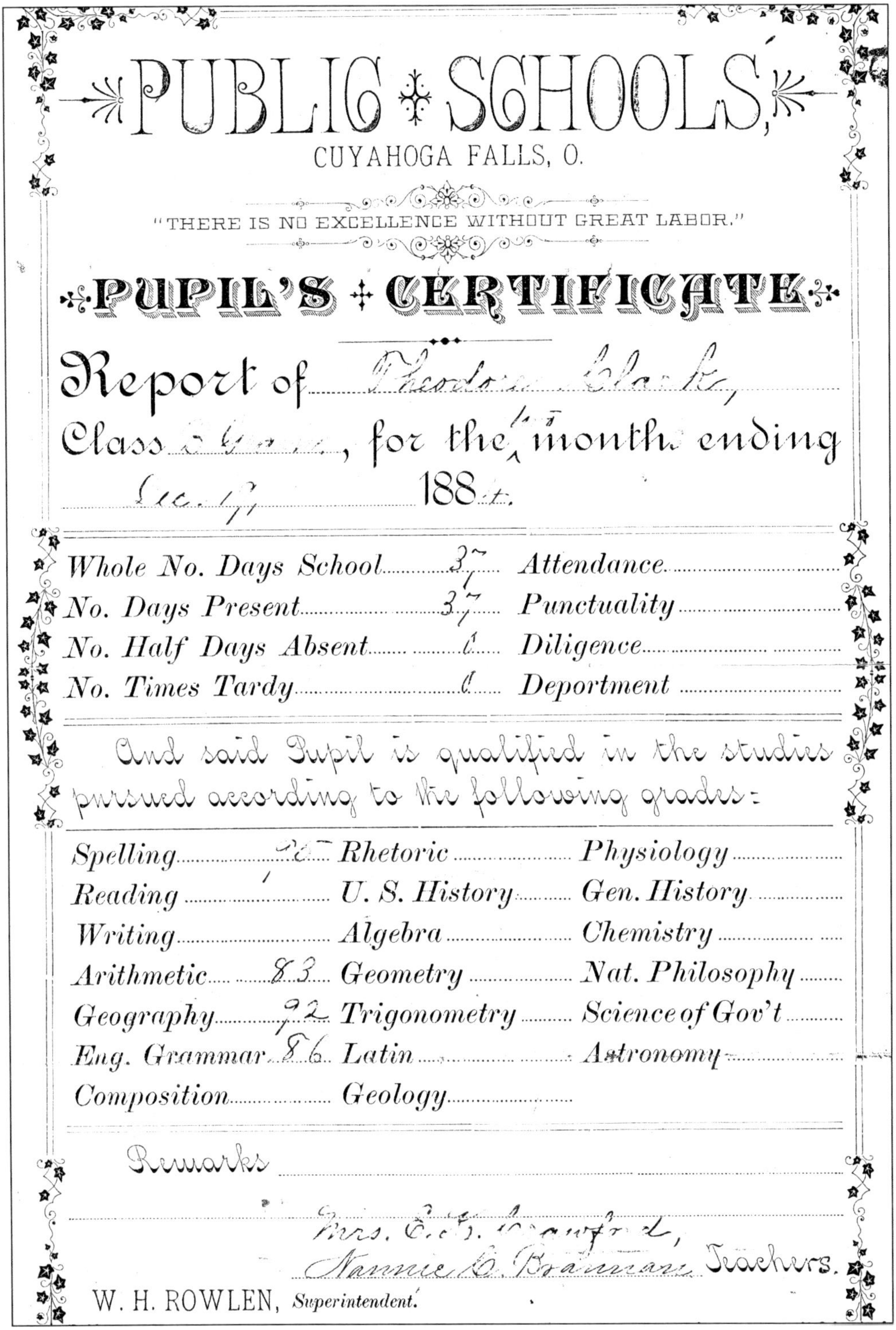

PUBLIC SCHOOLS,
CUYAHOGA FALLS, O.

"THERE IS NO EXCELLENCE WITHOUT GREAT LABOR."

PUPIL'S CERTIFICATE

Report of Theodore Clark,
Class 2 Gram., for the month ending
188

Whole No. Days School	37	*Attendance*	
No. Days Present	37	*Punctuality*	
No. Half Days Absent	0	*Diligence*	
No. Times Tardy	0	*Deportment*	

And said Pupil is qualified in the studies pursued according to the following grades:

Spelling	98	*Rhetoric*		*Physiology*	
Reading		*U. S. History*		*Gen. History*	
Writing		*Algebra*		*Chemistry*	
Arithmetic	83	*Geometry*		*Nat. Philosophy*	
Geography	92	*Trigonometry*		*Science of Gov't*	
Eng. Grammar	86	*Latin*		*Astronomy*	
Composition		*Geology*			

Remarks

Mrs. E. K. Crawford,
Nannie B. Brannan, Teachers.

W. H. ROWLEN, *Superintendent.*

Long before computers printed out report cards, grade reports were done by hand. This is Theodore Clark's report card from 1884. Notice the teacher's name on the bottom—Ellen Knight Crawford.

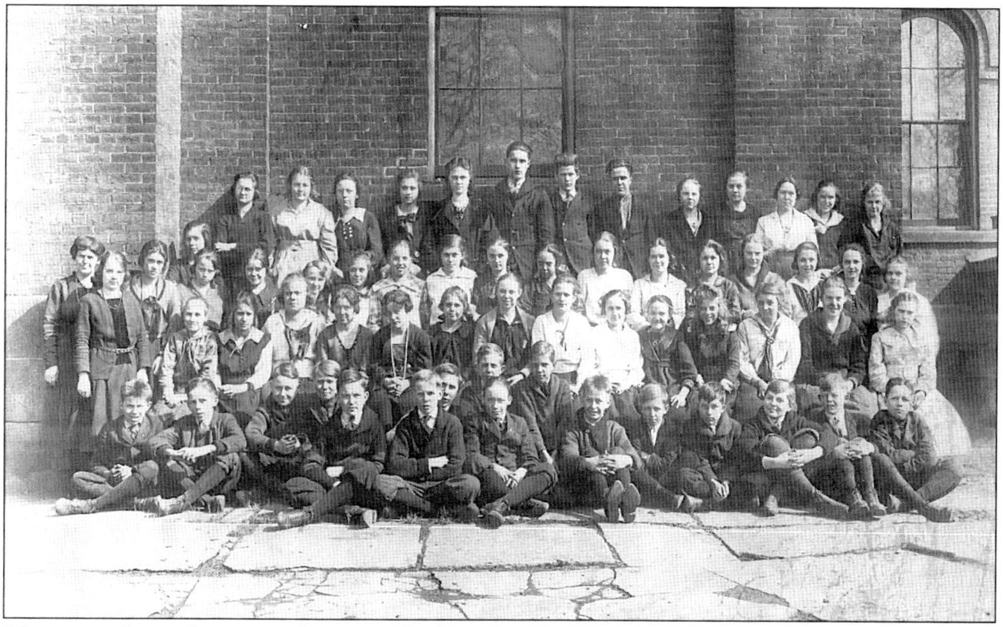

This is a photo depicting the 1919 freshman class at East School. This same group would eventually become the first graduating class at the new high school on Fourth Street in 1923. (Courtesy of Pete Mellinger.)

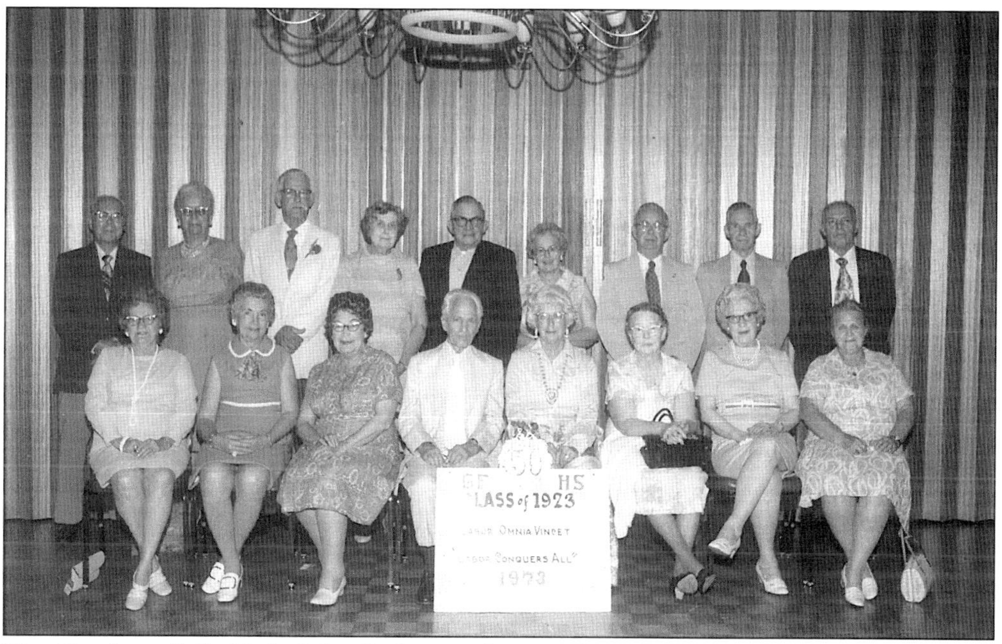

The Cuyahoga Falls High School's first graduating class of 1923 at their 50th year reunion is pictured here, from left to right: (front row) Josephine Reid Cropley, Lillian Barker Karl, Donna Babb Pack, David Felmly, Ida Mae Taylor Blankenship, Edith Creswell Hawley, Lillian Harrington Broske, Della LeClere Hughes; (back row) Lysle Miller, Ruth Mason Williams, Roland Burroughs, Violet Theiss Lange, Alfred Barker, Vera Barber Eddy, Alphonse Lindquist, Lester Cochran, and Donald Orth. (Courtesy of Pete Mellinger.)

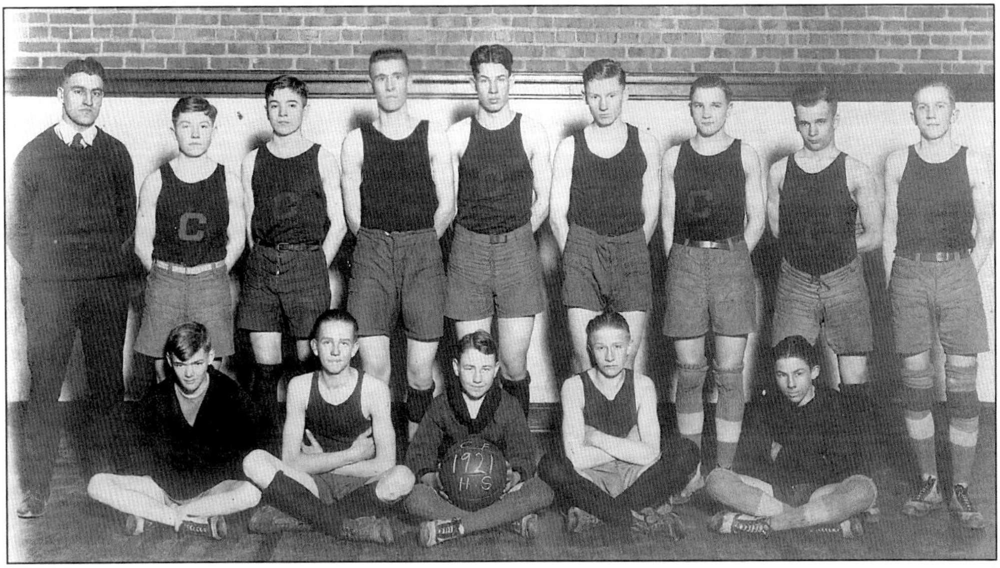

Basketball has an extensive history in Cuyahoga Falls. At East School, chairs were removed from a classroom, windows were boarded up, and the first basketball courts were formed in 1913. In 1917, a gym was added to the Broad Street School where the high school teams played for two years until a gym was added to East School in 1919. The team of 1921, pictured here, was the last team to play in East School before moving to the new high school.

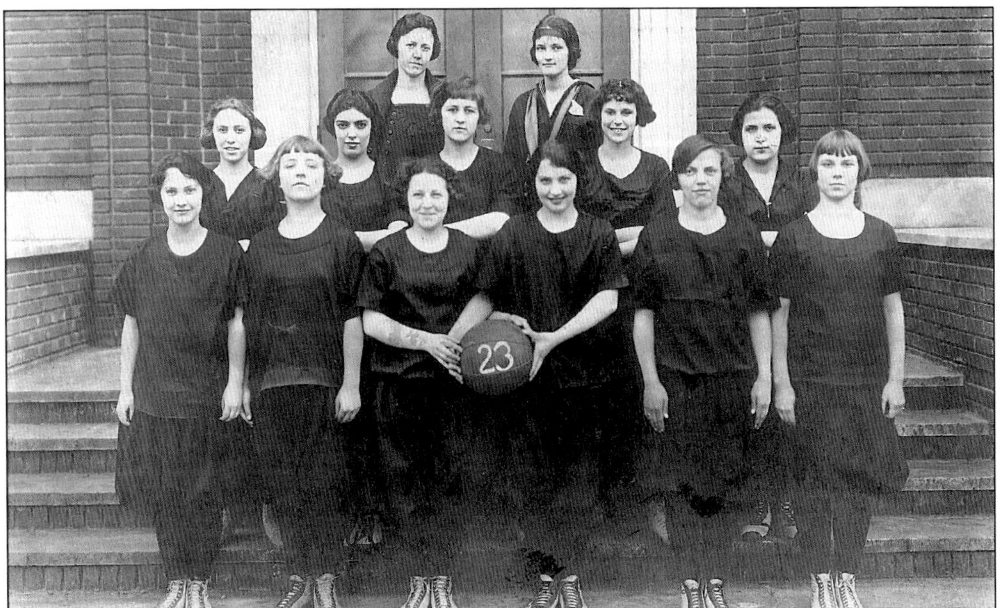

The 1923 Cuyahoga Falls High School girls basketball team nicknamed themselves "the 23 girls," according to the message written on the back of this photo. They are pictured here, from left to right: (first row) Margery Richardson Snyder, Alma Wood Fisher, Margaret Gross, Edith Richardson Thompson, Sue Spindls, Peg McCorkle; (second row) Ida Mae Taylor Blankenship, unidentified, Ada Shaffer, Edna Spooner, Lillian "Wim" Harrington; (third row) unidentified, Van Benschoten, and ? McElwain.

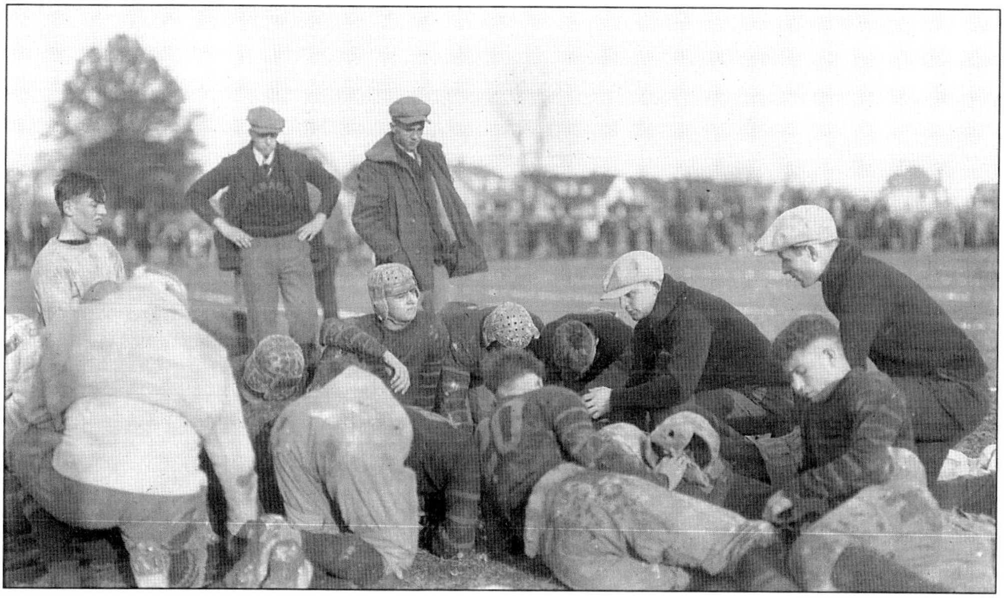

This action photo was taken in 1924, the first year that the football squad played on the new high school field. The field included a grandstand that held 300 people and changed the way fans were able to view Falls High football games. Before the grandstand was built, spectators had to watch the games from ground level. The stadium was later dedicated to Earl C. Clifford, board of education president, who died in the July 1940 *Doodlebug* commuter train crash.

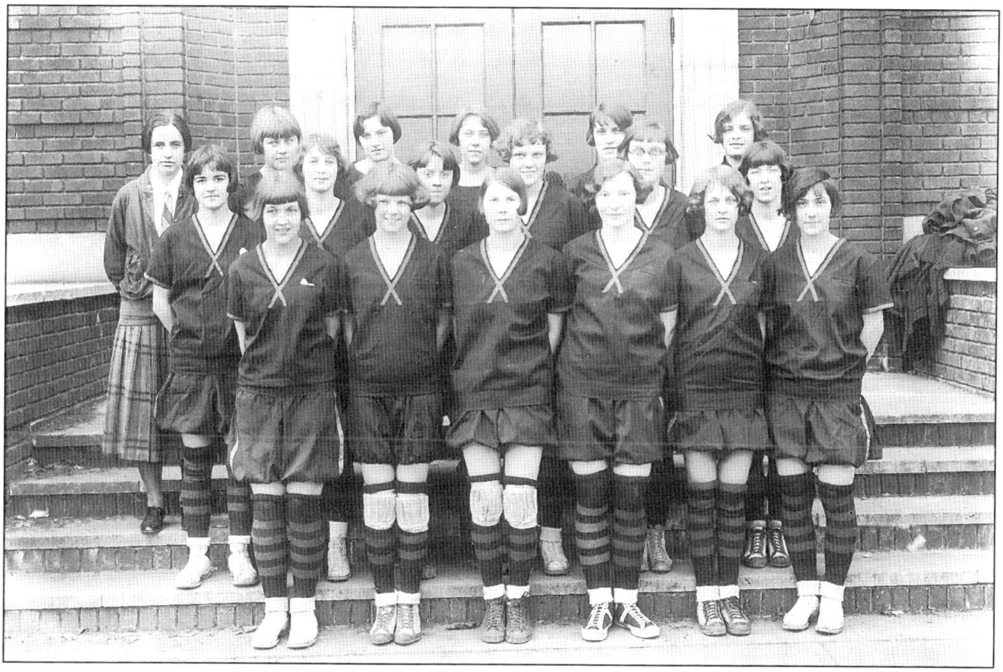

The 1924 Cuyahoga Falls girls basketball team is pictured here, from left to right: (first row) Thelma Salmon, Una Crane, unidentified, Ruth Read; (second row) unidentified, Ethel Lewis?, unidentified, unidentified, Mildred Brothers, unidentified; (third row) unidentified, Dorothy Wittington, Mildred De Musey, ? Dotson, and Ruth McElwain.

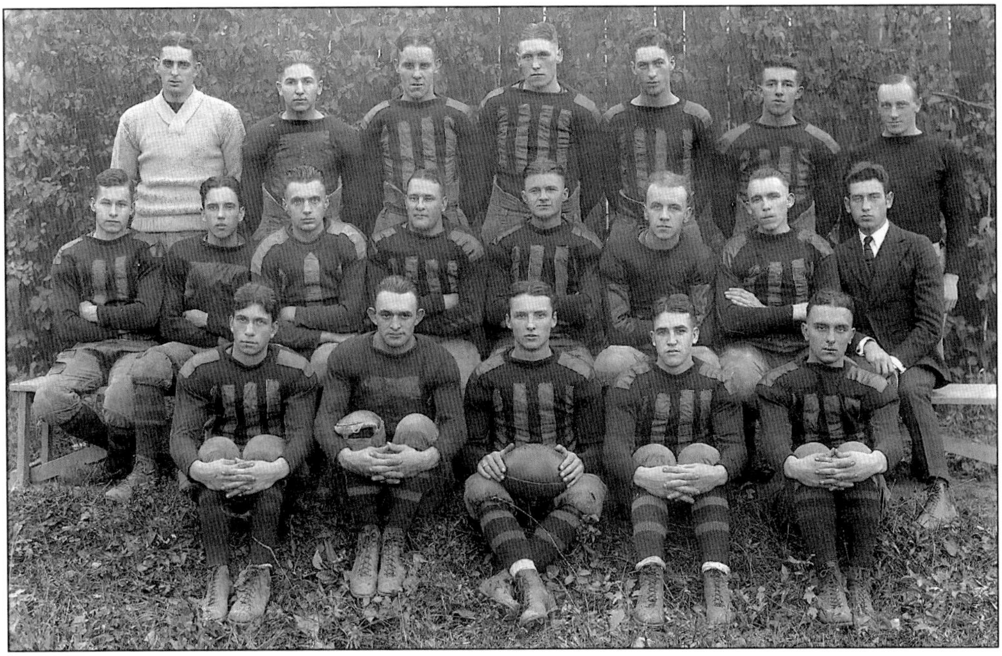

Pictured here is the team photo of the 1924 Cuyahoga Falls High School football team. The following year, however, was perhaps the greatest year Falls High football ever had. Coached by Paul Yost, the Falls High team went undefeated, winning nine games and scoring 251 points, while holding its opponents scoreless for the entire season.

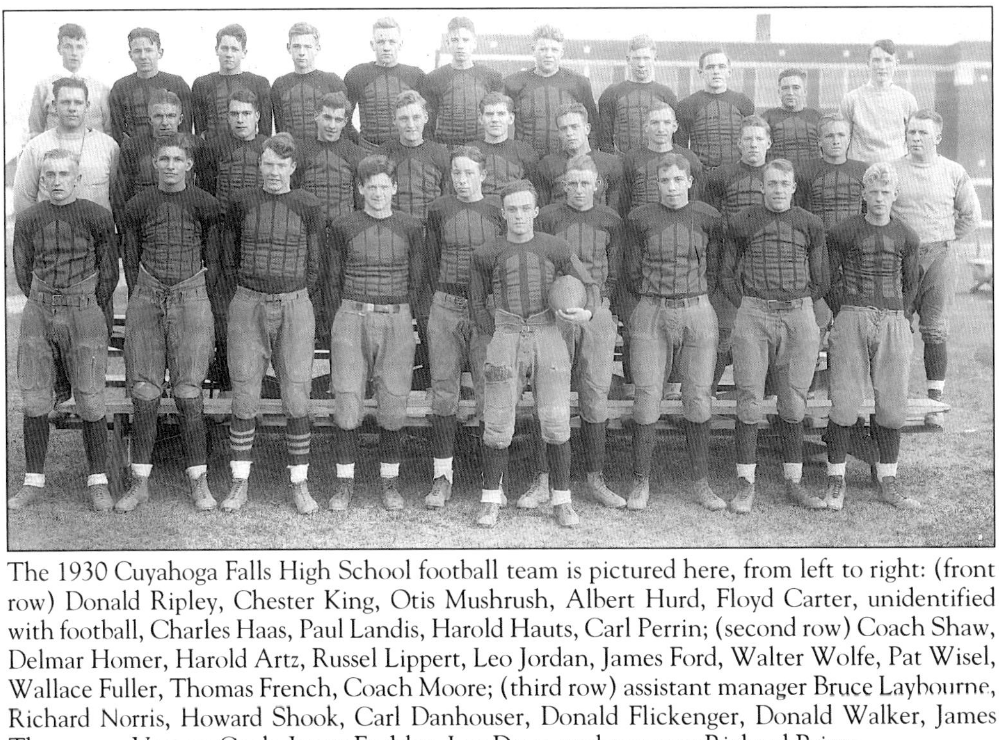

The 1930 Cuyahoga Falls High School football team is pictured here, from left to right: (front row) Donald Ripley, Chester King, Otis Mushrush, Albert Hurd, Floyd Carter, unidentified with football, Charles Haas, Paul Landis, Harold Hauts, Carl Perrin; (second row) Coach Shaw, Delmar Homer, Harold Artz, Russel Lippert, Leo Jordan, James Ford, Walter Wolfe, Pat Wisel, Wallace Fuller, Thomas French, Coach Moore; (third row) assistant manager Bruce Laybourne, Richard Norris, Howard Shook, Carl Danhouser, Donald Flickenger, Donald Walker, James Thompson, Vernon Cook, James Endsley, Leo Dean, and manager Richard Briggs.

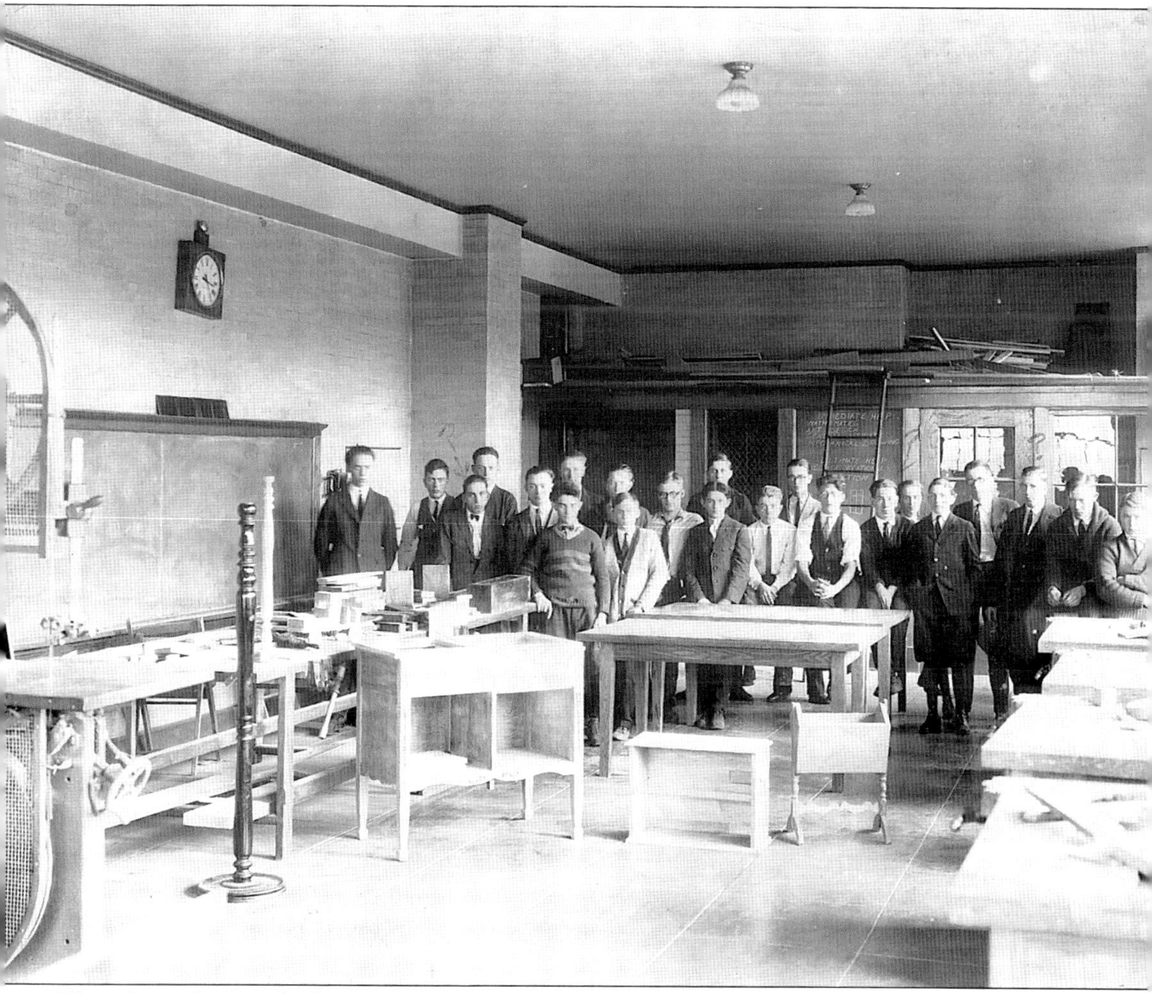

This photo depicts the boys industrial arts class at East School in 1924. Students named on the back of this photo include: Herman Robinson, Henry Sechrist, ? Murry, Harry Hoots, Al Romito, Charles Deviss, Roy Benway, Stan Zebo, Eric Thompson, Harold Mellinger, Ralph Yountz, Clark Johnson, Walter Mellinger, Kenneth Hill, Ben Cooper, B. Bordenker, and Tuffy Smith. Eric Thompson would later become Cuyahoga Falls' historian and *Falls News Press* columnist. Much of the information in this book can be credited to the writings of the late Mr. Thompson. (Courtesy of Pete Mellinger.)

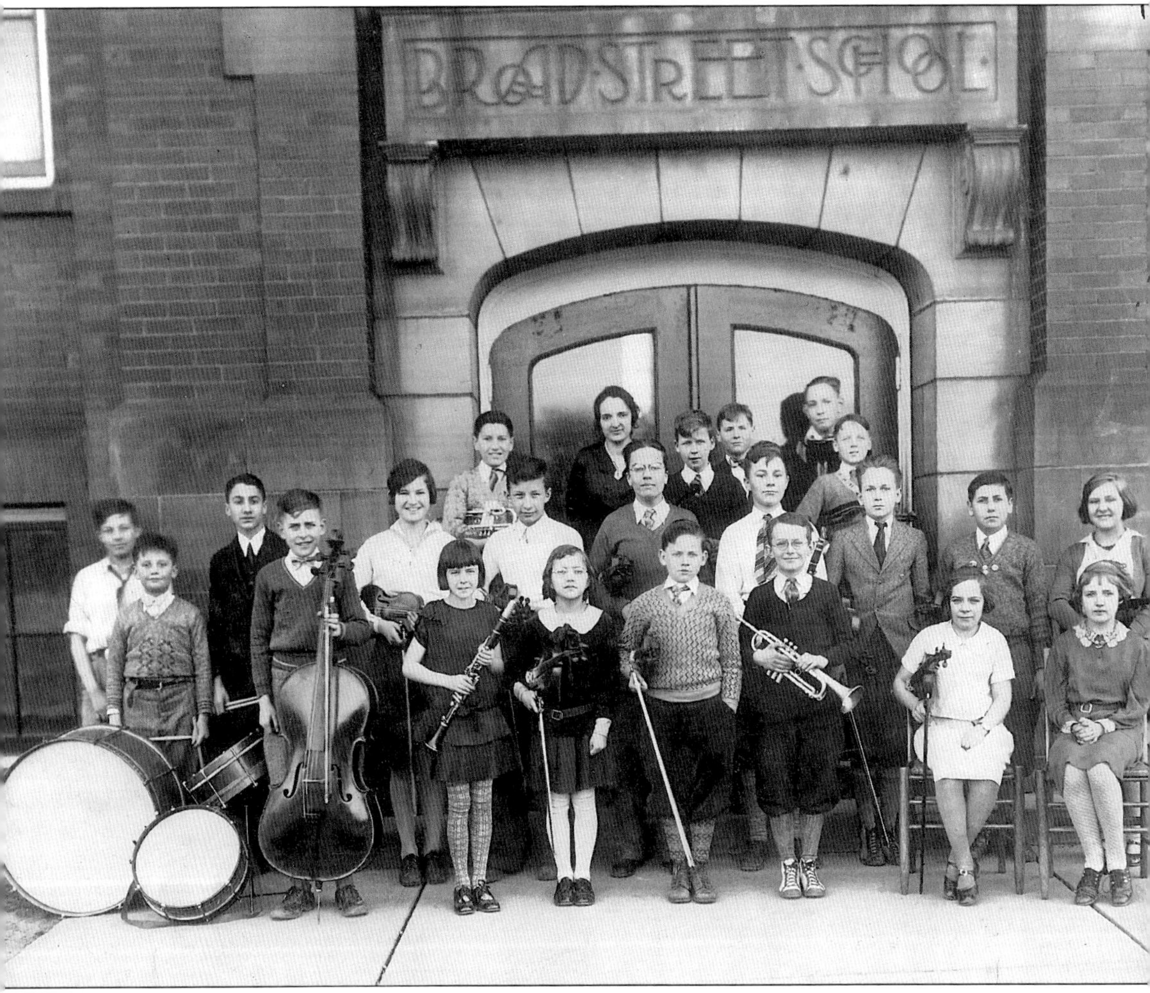

These students were members of the 1930 Broad Street School band. They are, from left to right: (front row) Burton Clapp (drums), Louis Dingledine (cello), Dorothy Bradley (clarinet), Carolyn Kemp (violin), Hubert Felton (violin), Robert Sterling (trumpet), Dorothy Brown (violin), Elaine Polstan (piano); (second row) Dale Sterling (drum), Gibson Tallentire (drum), Dorothy Season (violin), Raymond Long (violin) Kenneth ? (violin), Paul Endlich (clarinet), John Mansfield (violin), John Higgins (violin), Betty Jane Hazellet (violin); (third row) Jack Tartar (trumpet), Mrs. Mills (conductor), Carl Katzemeyer (violin), ? Beashem, Stuart Stoll (sax), and John Duke (violin).

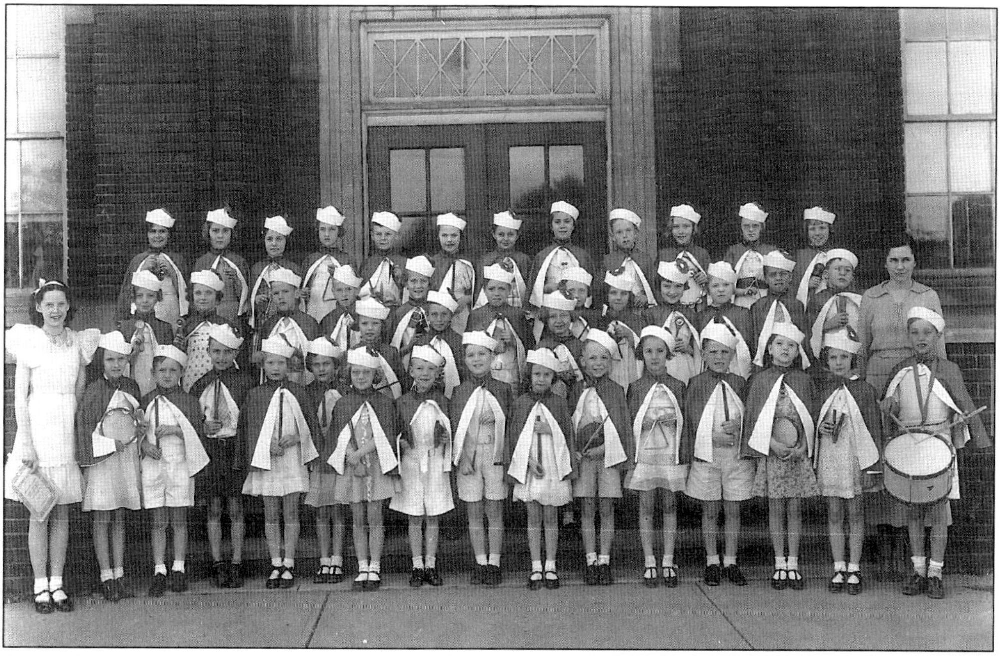

In 1935 the Grant School band, pictured above, performed at the high school. This picture was taken at the high school.

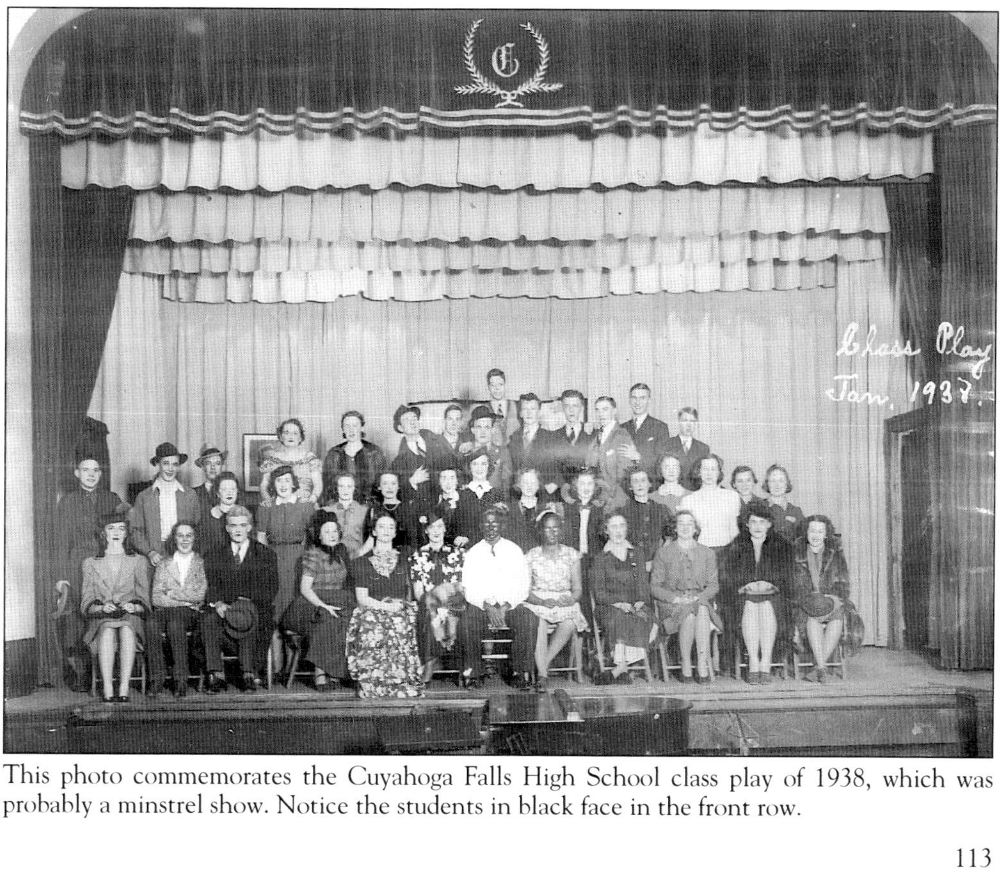

This photo commemorates the Cuyahoga Falls High School class play of 1938, which was probably a minstrel show. Notice the students in black face in the front row.

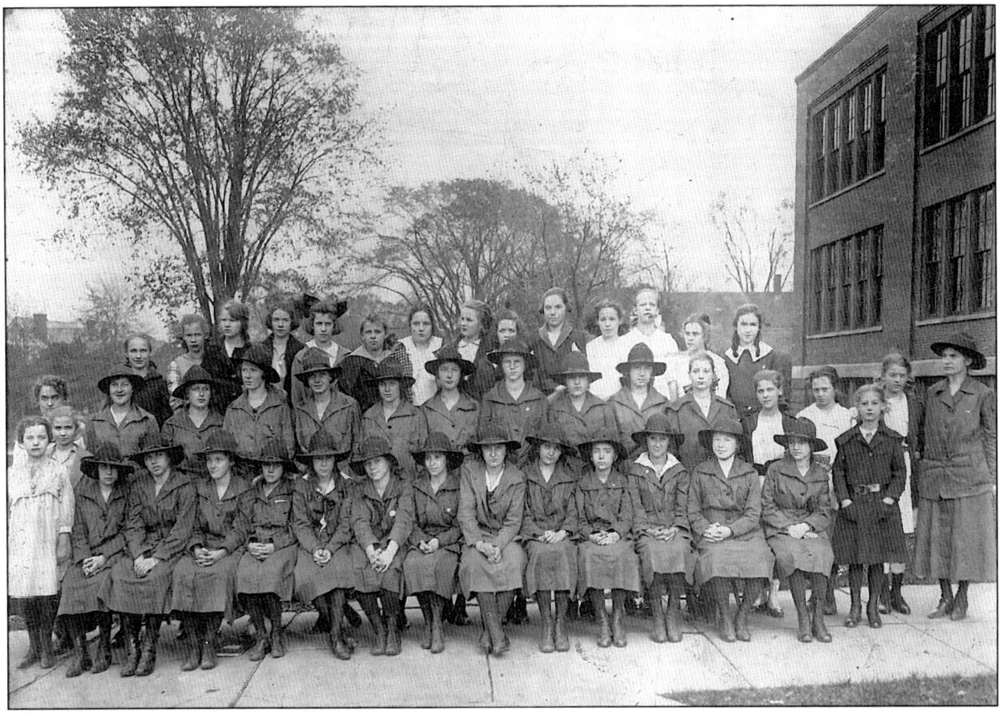

This undated photo taken at the Broad Street School depicts the members of Girl Scout Troop 2. No one is identified.

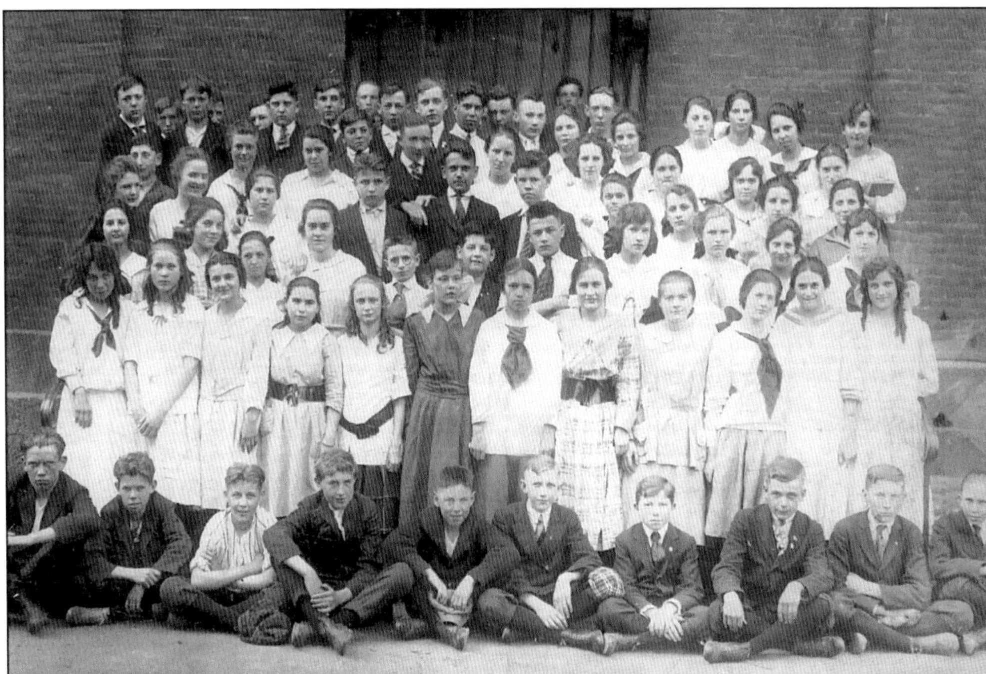

This photo is identified as Falls High in 1923; however, the students appear to be posing in front of East School.

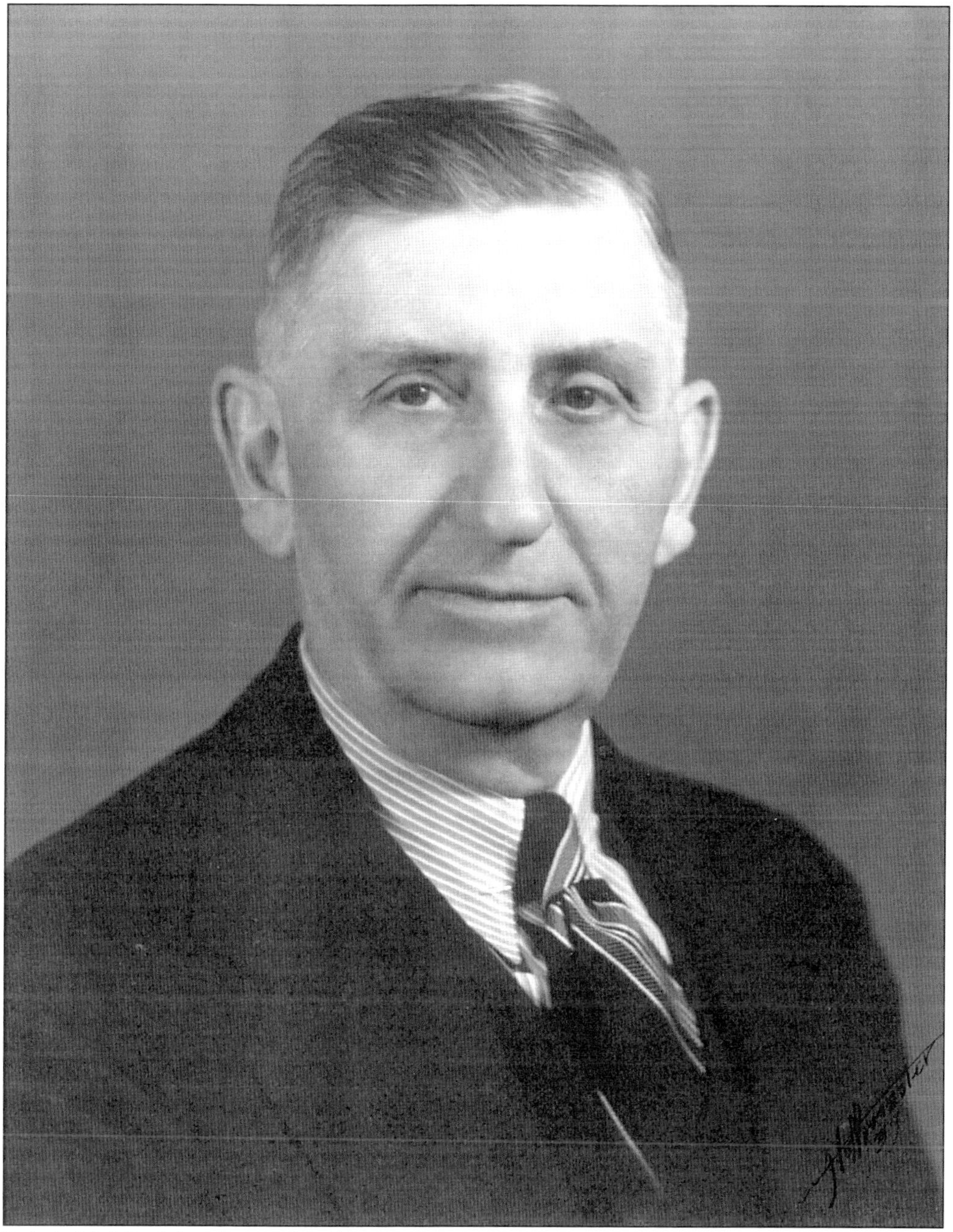

Bolich Middle School, completed in 1954, was named in honor of Harvey O. Bolich who was born in Wadsworth, Ohio. In 1902, Bolich came to Cuyahoga Falls after accepting a teaching job at the high school. He served as a teacher, a coach, and a principal. Although Bolich left the school system in 1920, he remained a prominent figure in the community. He became the Cuyahoga Falls village clerk in 1920, city auditor in 1922, and served as clerk of city council until his retirement in 1930.

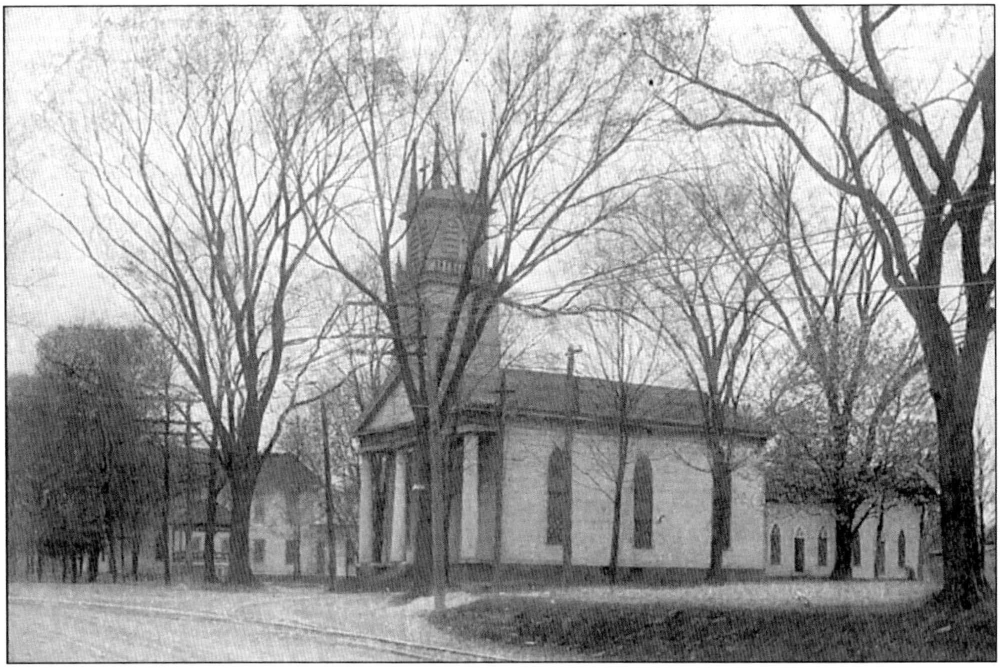

The first religious meetings in Cuyahoga Falls took place at the home of Cuyahoga Falls pioneer William Wetmore in 1818. In 1830, this group organized an Episcopal church, and continued to hold services at the Wetmore's home. Later, the block of land between Portage and Stow Streets and Second and Third Streets was dedicated as a church park. The Episcopal group built the first church on this land, St. John's Episcopal, which is pictured here.

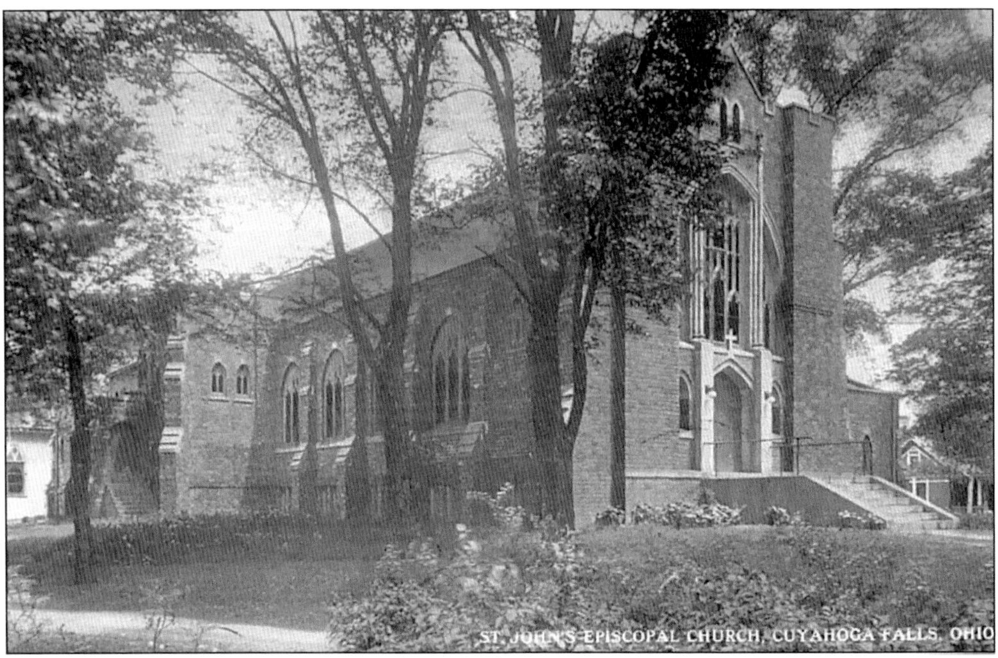

The present St. John's Episcopal Church was built on the site of the original wood building shown above. The structure was completed in 1909, and the first service was held February 14, 1909.

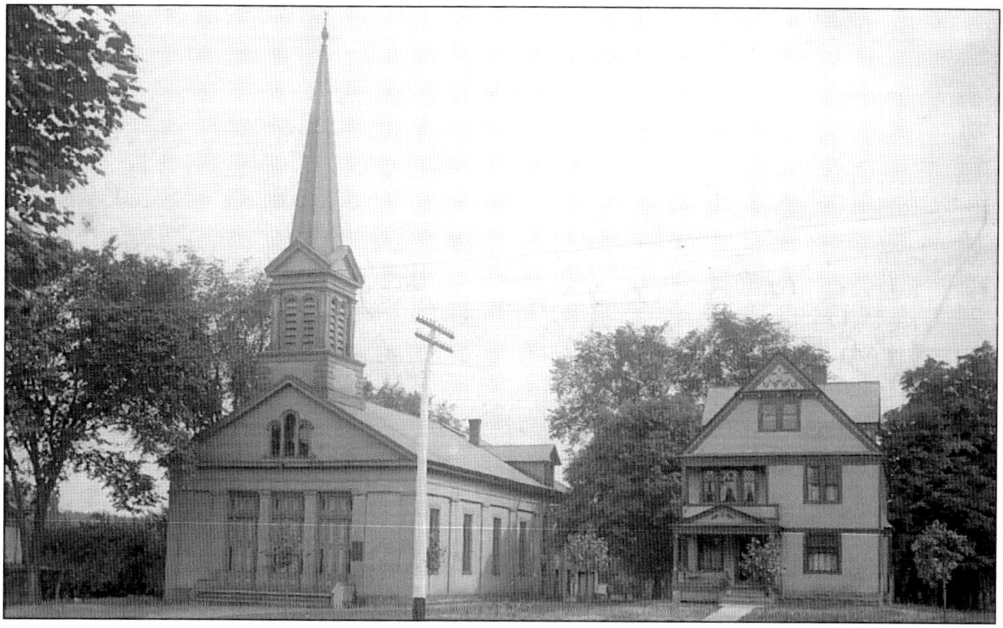

The Congregational Church began holding services in Cuyahoga Falls in 1834. Services were first held in a schoolhouse on the same site as the present Pilgrim United Church of Christ. As the church membership grew, services moved to the nearby Lyceum building. They continued there until the Congregational Church purchased the old schoolhouse where the church first began, and started construction on a new building. The church building seen here was completed in 1847, and a parsonage is on the right. Foundation stones for the church were quarried from the Gorge.

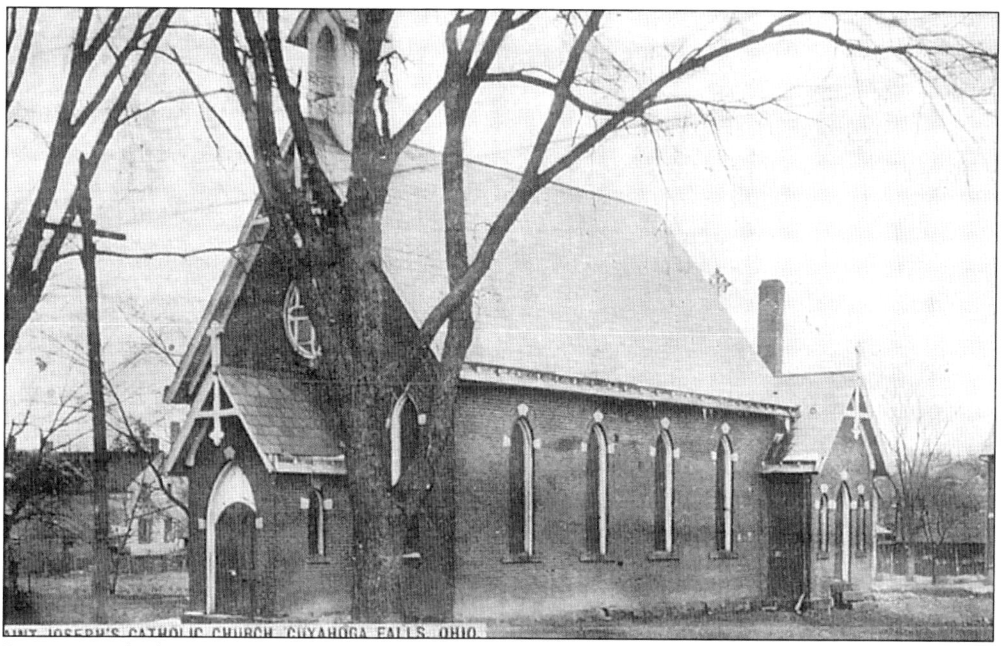

Roman Catholic services in Cuyahoga Falls began in 1834. St. Joseph's Catholic Church, the small brick building seen in this view, was erected at the corner of Second and Sackett Streets in 1885. Reverend F.P. Daugherty was the first to serve the congregation at this building.

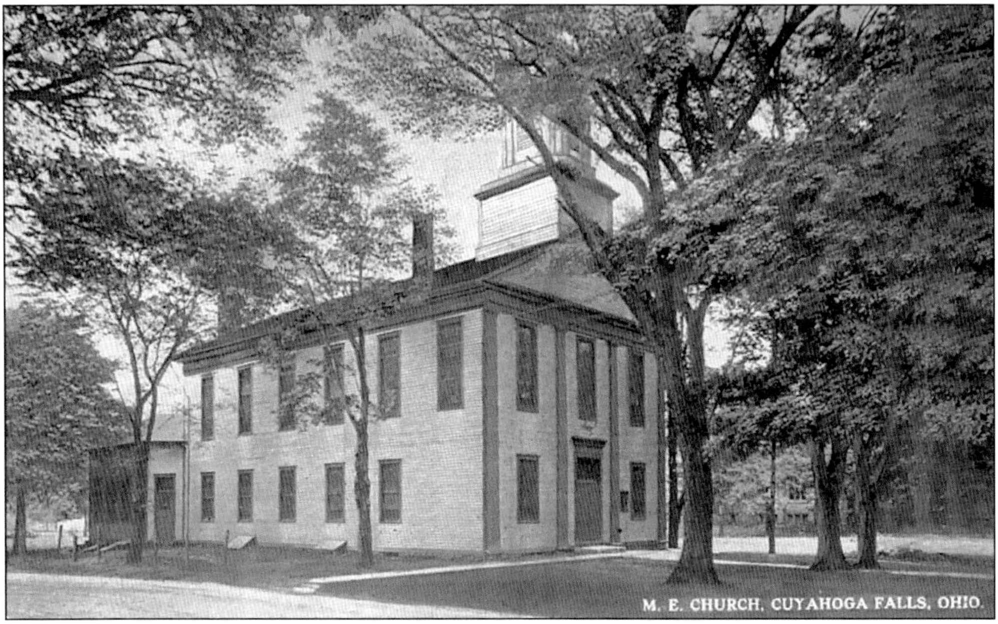

In 1830, the Reverend John McClain organized the Methodist Episcopal Church in Cuyahoga Falls. Services were held at a Northhampton Township schoolhouse and in members' homes until 1840, when a church was built on the southwest corner of the church park. The building pictured here was dedicated on December 31, 1840.

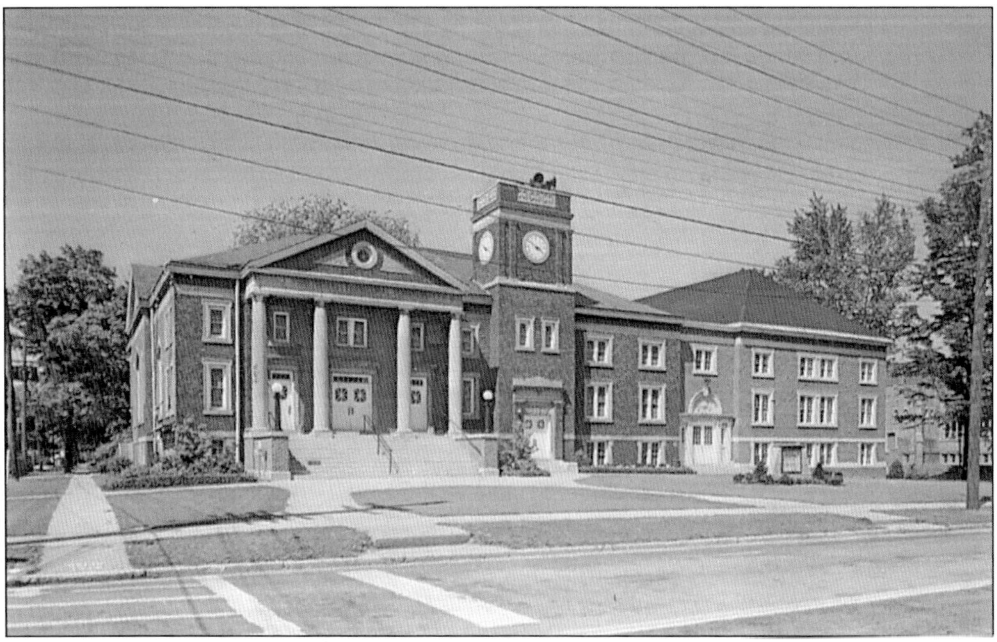

In 1920, the old Methodist church was torn down and construction began on the present building, which is one of the largest in Ohio Methodism.

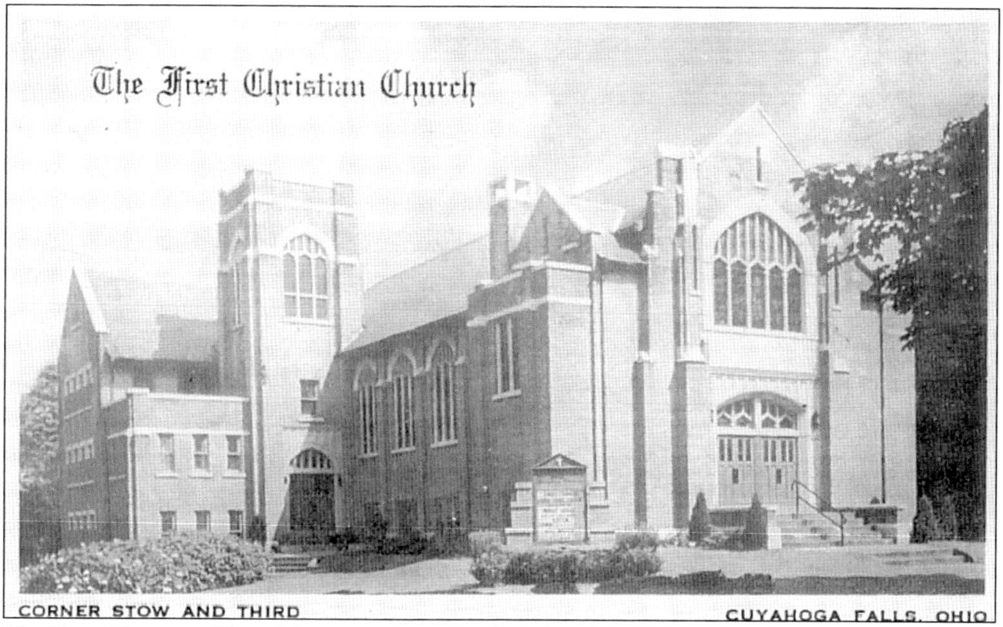

The First Christian Church began meeting as the Church of Christ in a second-floor storeroom in the Apollo Hall Building on Front Street. In 1881, the congregation organized and built their church on the northeast corner of Church Park. The building was abandoned due to heavy traffic on Second Street. The present building, pictured here, faces Third Street.

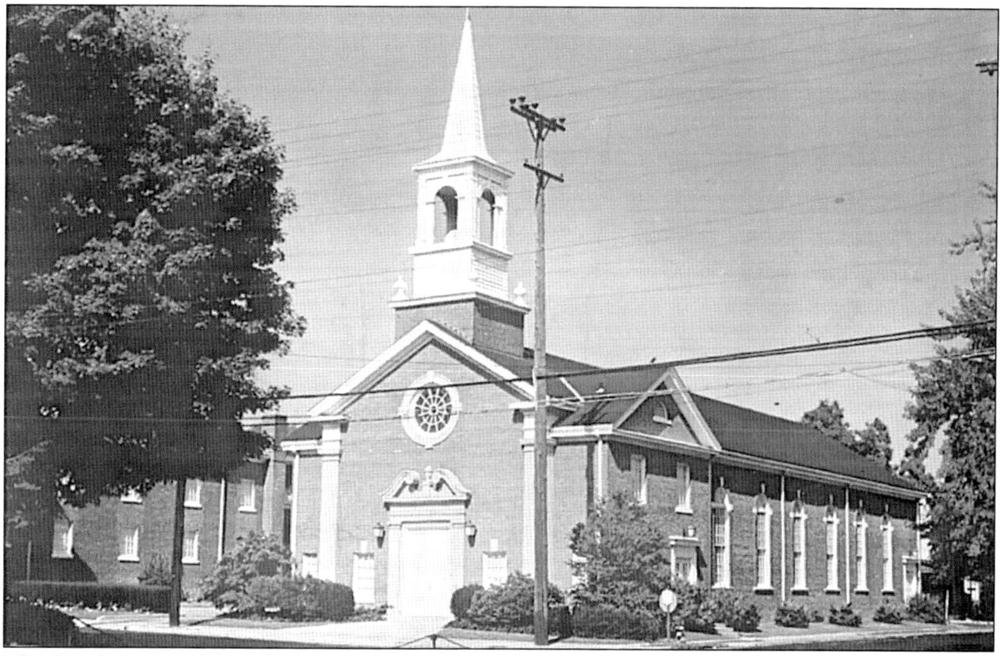

The Presbyterian Church in Cuyahoga Falls was first organized on December 17, 1916. The original sanctuary was built on a site to the left of the current brick building seen in this postcard view. The current sanctuary at Hudson Drive and Ashland Avenue was dedicated in 1957.

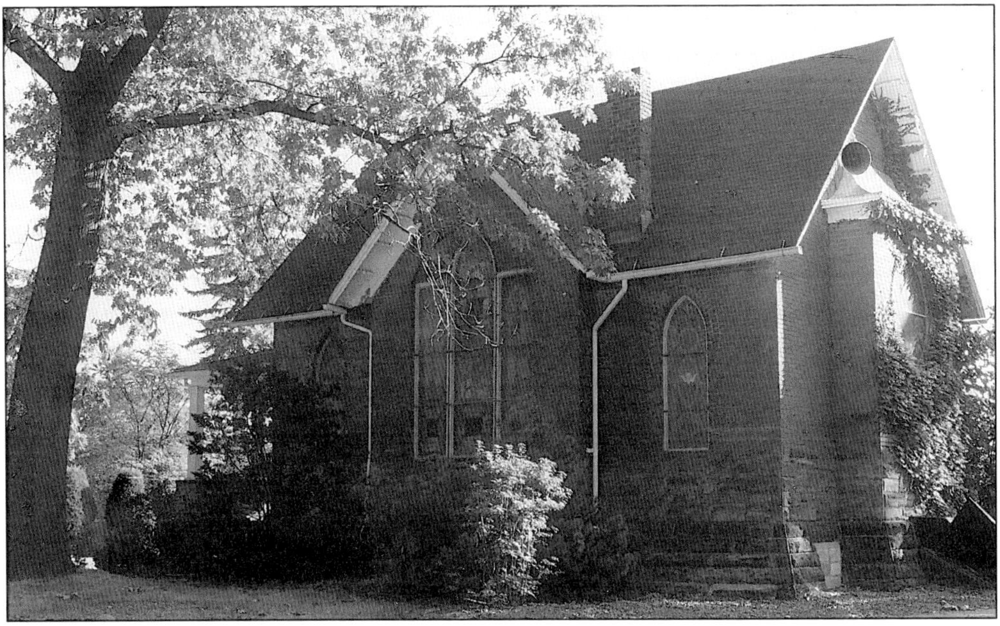

The chapel at Oakwood Cemetery was built and dedicated to all faiths in 1894. On the left side of the Sixth Street entrance are the graves of two of Cuyahoga Falls' pioneer families, the Sills and the Newberrys. The 12 stained-glass windows, some of which can be seen in these photographs, were donated in 1898 by some of the city's families and civic and fraternal organizations. The small round window above the entrance, for example, is inscribed with the name of Theodosia Grant and is a memorial to the infant daughter of Henry C. and Sarah Grant, for whom Grant School and Grant Avenue were named. Theodosia died in 1885. Other names memorialized in the glass include Turner, Heath, Wetmore, Tifft, and Willard. C. LeRoy Herrick of Akron designed the building. The porch was used as a stage for the annual Decoration Day memorial service and speeches for years.

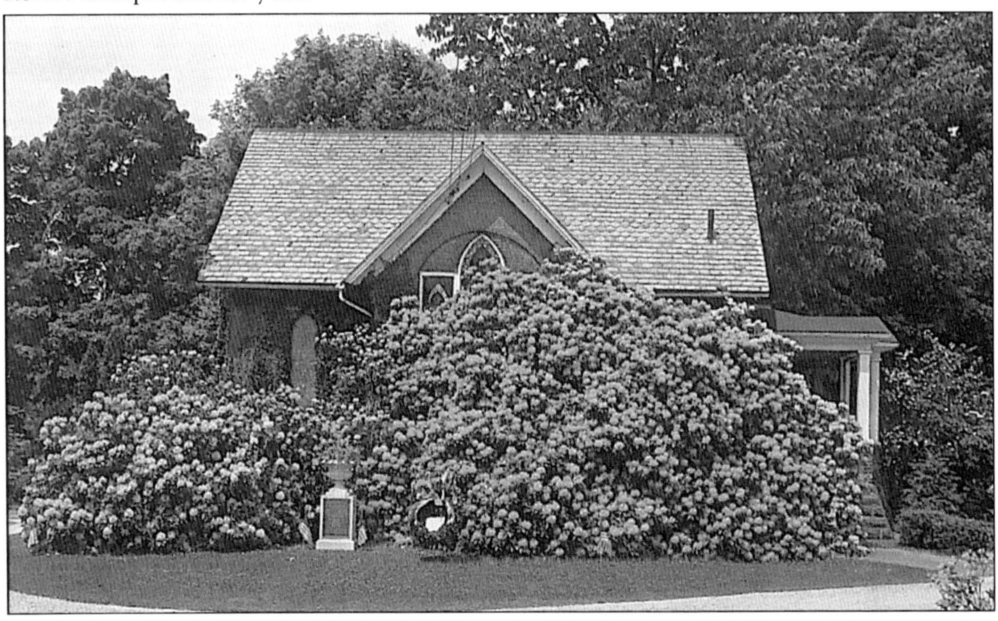

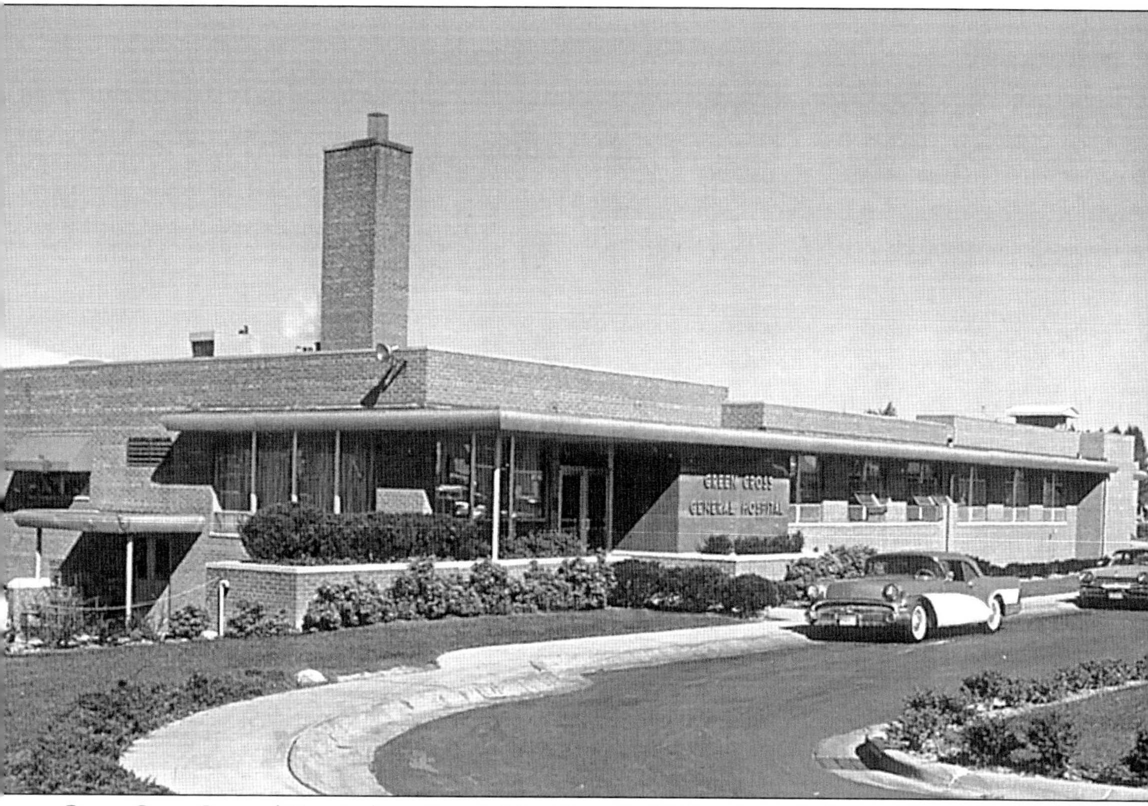

Green Cross General Hospital was founded in Akron in 1943 at East Market and Broad Streets. Originally, the hospital had 34 beds and four physicians on staff. The facility moved to 1900 23rd Street in Cuyahoga Falls in 1954. In 1970, Green Cross changed its name to Cuyahoga Falls General Hospital and began to grow and continually expand, and by 1954 the hospital had 78 beds. The facility expanded in 1958 and 1963, and now boasts 257 beds and 305 physicians on staff. It has the largest pain management department in northeast Ohio. Cuyahoga Falls General Hospital's rehabilitation center is one of only four in the state in its unique treatment program. Cuyahoga Falls General Hospital is independent and privately owned.

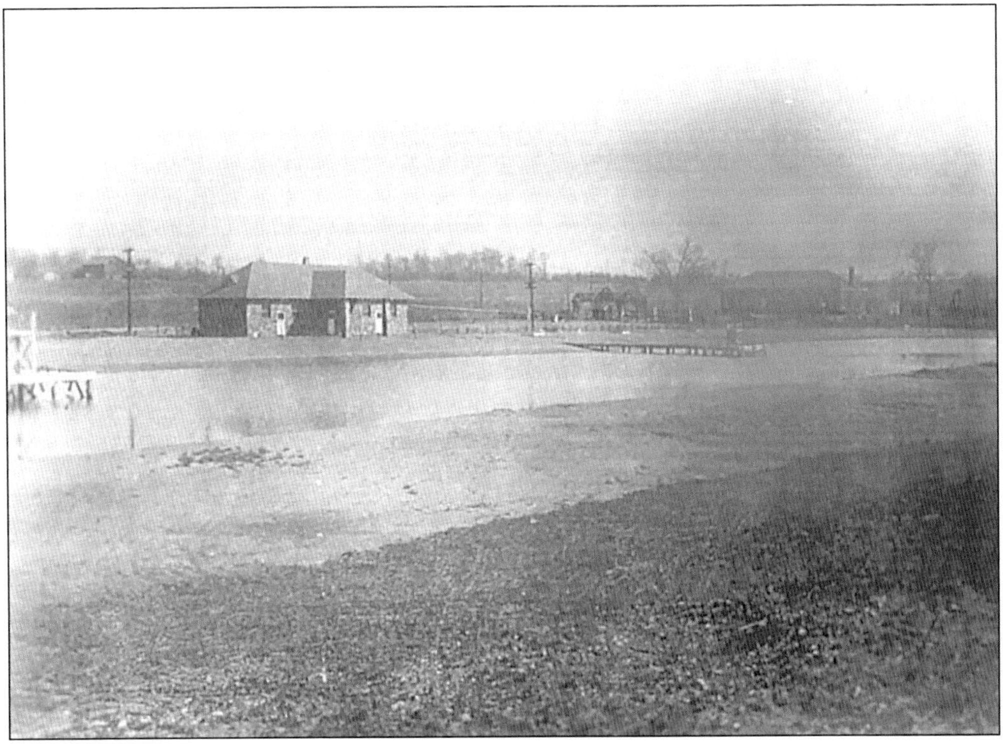

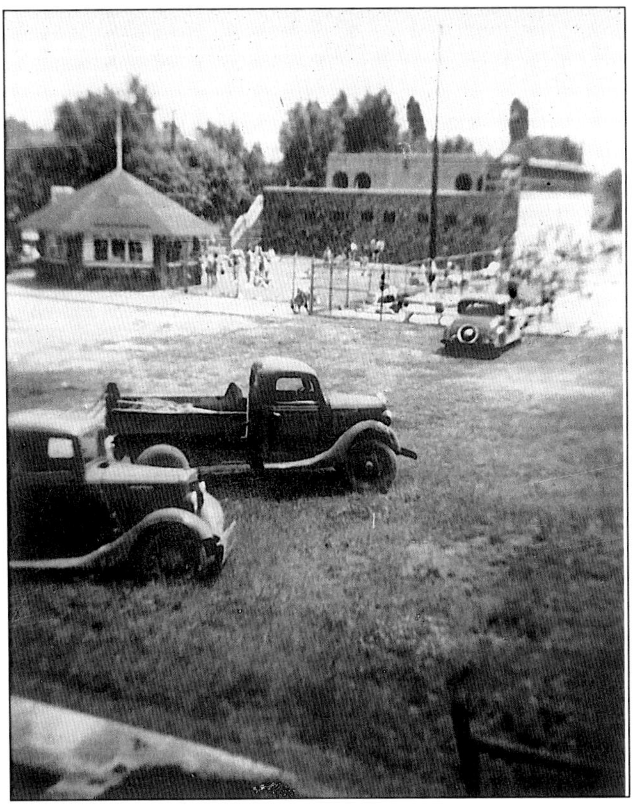

Denver Chatman's spot on the Cuyahoga River was once a favorite swimming hole for children all over the city. In 1914 the water department discovered wells in this area and acquired the land. A city park was developed on the land surrounding Denver Chatman's, and eventually the city added a cement swimming pool as its centerpiece. The park, shown in this early picture, was named Water Works. (Courtesy of Pete Mellinger.)

This photo of Water Works Park was taken in 1948 and shows the concession stand and bathhouse. (Courtesy of Earl and Alice Royer.)

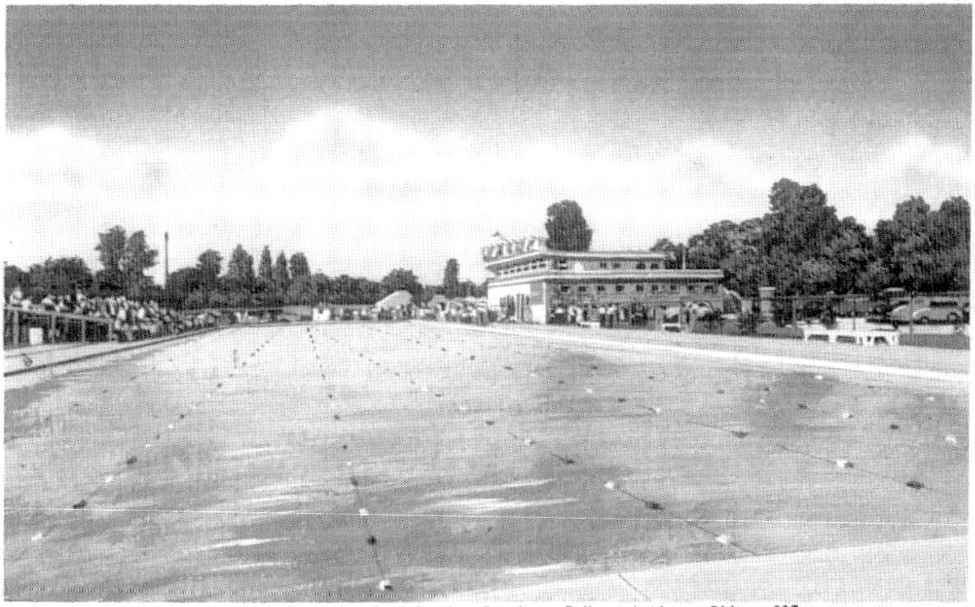

Water Works Swimming Pool Serving Cuyahoga Falls and Akron, Ohio — 837

The original Water Works pool was 100 meters long and met all specifications of the AAU. In 1945, Water Works hosted the national AAU meet. In later years, a walkway was added to the pool, thus dividing it in half so the park could no longer host swimming meets. Water Works has recently been renovated and expanded. The new Water Works Family Aquatic Center opened in 1997 and features a new pool, a lazy river ride and several water slides.

Waterworks Swimming Pool, Serving Cuyahoga Falls and Akron, Ohio

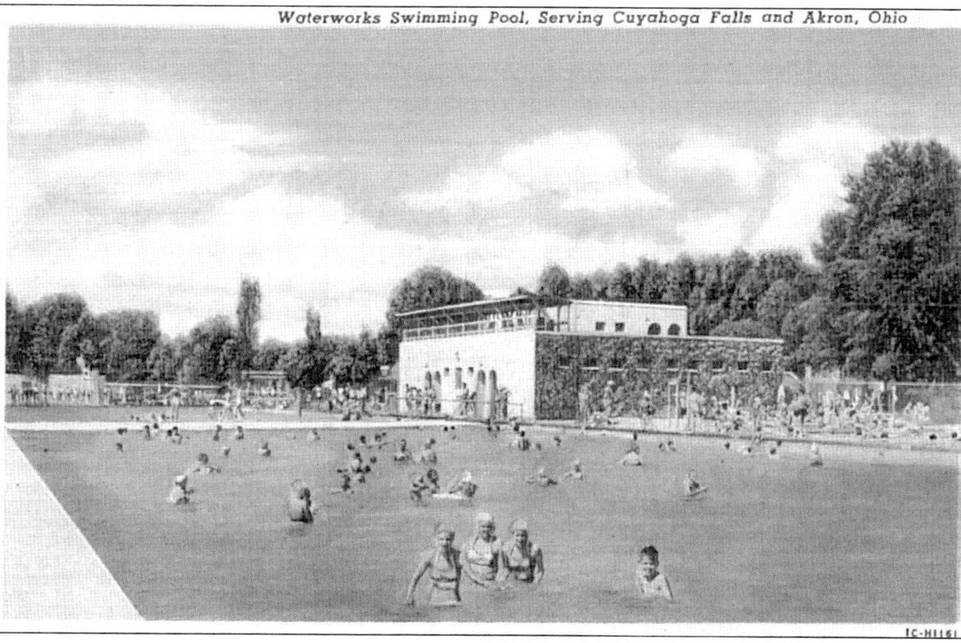

1C-H1161

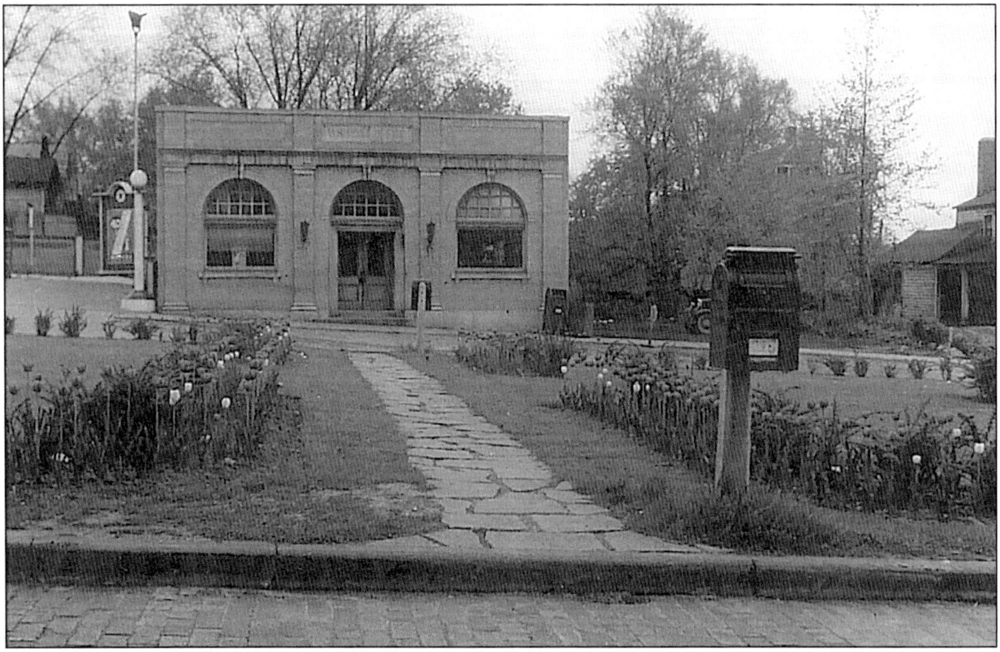

The first post office in the town was opened in 1826 after the town's name was changed from Manchester to Cuyahoga Falls. Henry Newberry was the first postmaster. From 1929 to 1939 the post office operated out of this building located at 125 Broad Boulevard.

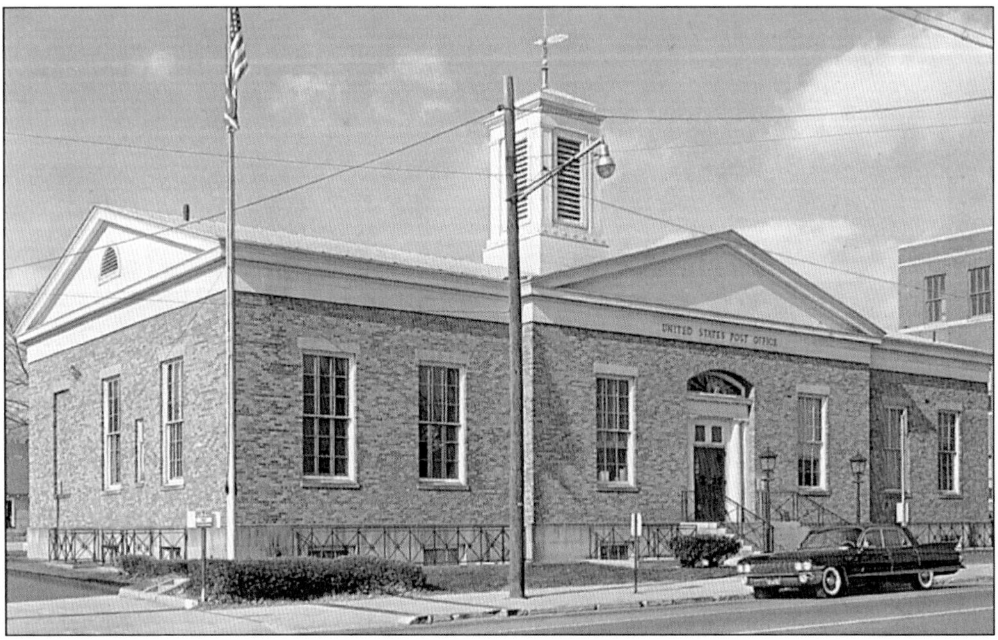

The United States government built the present post office, pictured here, at 2094 Second Street during the Depression of the 1930s. This was the first government-built post office in Cuyahoga Falls. A new Cuyahoga Falls Post Office recently opened on State Road.

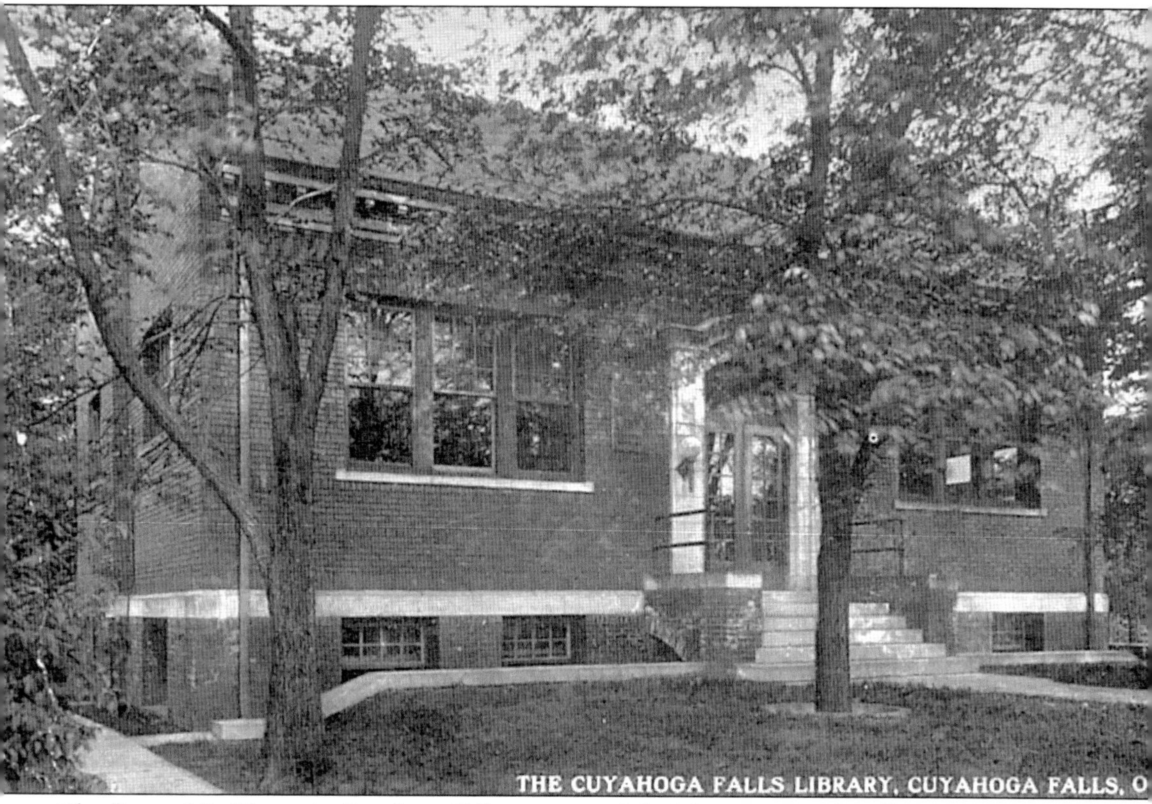

The first public library in Cuyahoga Falls was named for Margaretta and William A. Taylor. In 1909, Margaretta Taylor bequeathed $15,000 for a building and $3,000 for books. The red brick library pictured above was located on the east side of Second Street just south of Portage Trail. The library was officially dedicated on August 19, 1912, as "Taylor Memorial Library." Laura Vaughn, daughter of William Taylor's business partner, James Vaughn (Turner, Vaughn, and Taylor Machine Company), worked as a librarian for 27 years. Ms. Vaughn was considered an authority on art, and while serving as librarian she established an exceptional collection of books on arts and crafts. She also assembled an excellent collection of reference books that could be used in high school and college assignments. The library holdings eventually outgrew the available space, and in May of 1971, the present Taylor Memorial Public Library on 2015 Third Street was dedicated. An addition was dedicated on February 3, 1990.

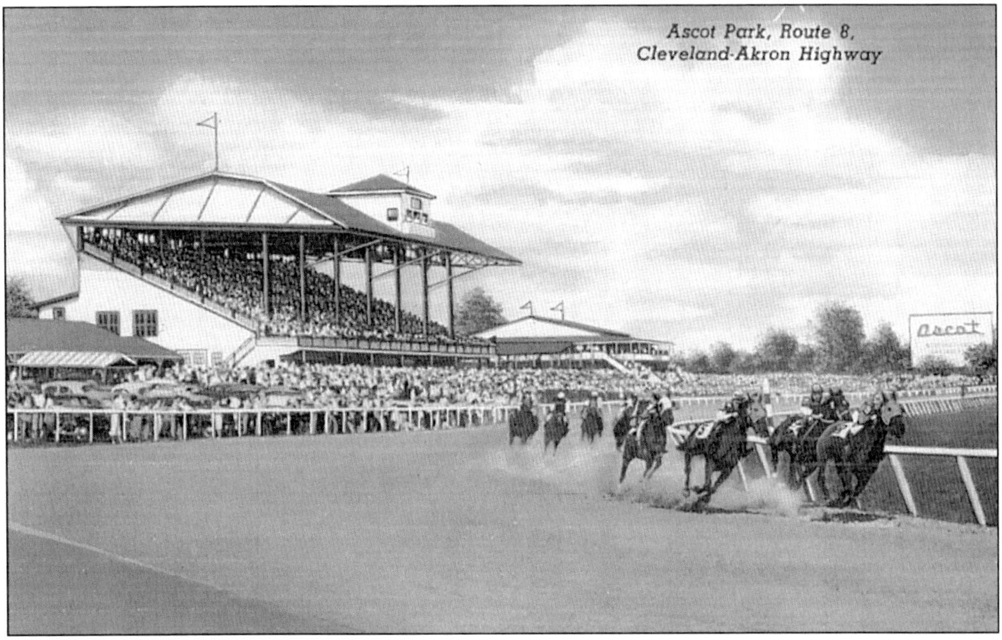

Horse racing has always been a popular spectator sport in Ohio. Cuyahoga Falls had its own horse race on Front Street in 1859. Two of the country's leading trotters—Flora Temple and Ike Cook—participated, but the race was discontinued during the Civil War. Later, a new racetrack was built on State Road. Ascot Park, pictured above, was a .75-mile racetrack with grandstand and clubhouse facilities. An industrial park is now located at this site.

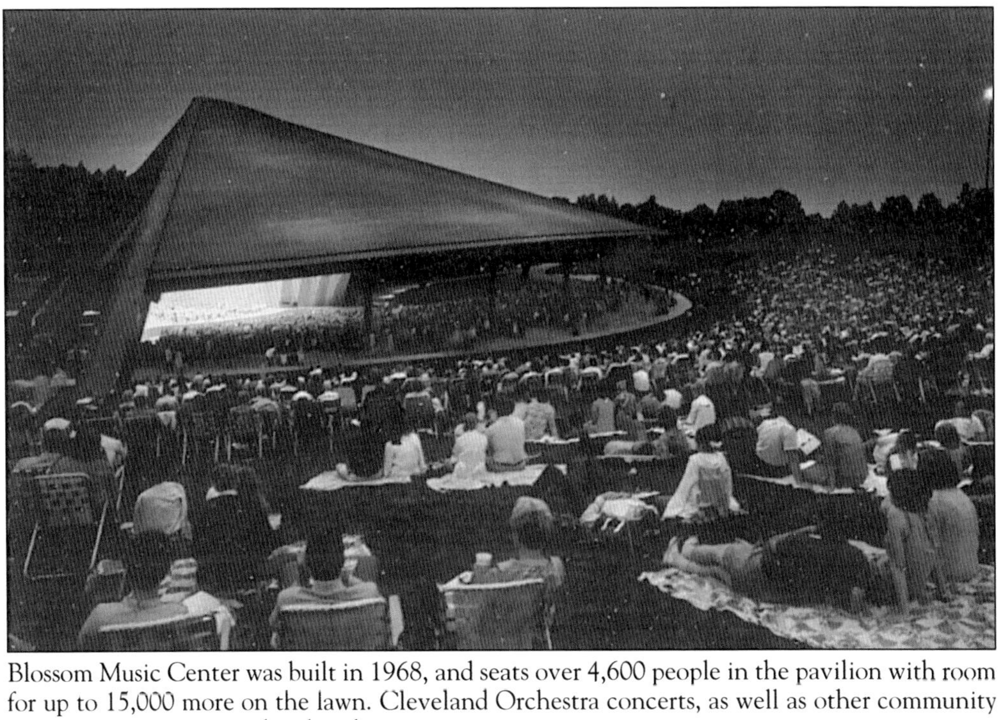

Blossom Music Center was built in 1968, and seats over 4,600 people in the pavilion with room for up to 15,000 more on the lawn. Cleveland Orchestra concerts, as well as other community entertainment events, take place here every year.

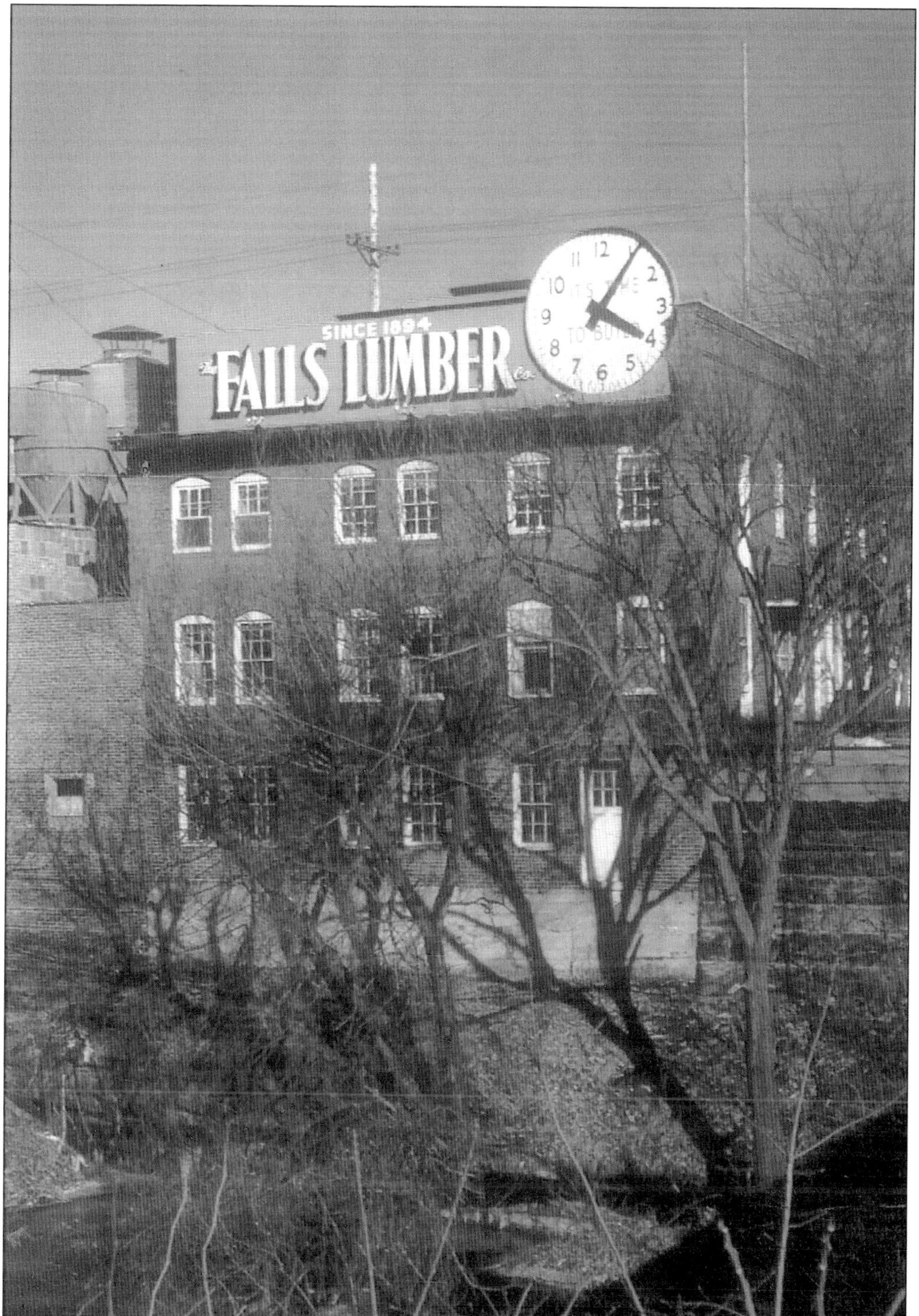

This clock that once towered over the Falls Lumber building was the largest in the district. The illuminated Telechrom featured a 10-foot dial with 12-inch numerals, and was installed in November of 1941. Those driving down Broad Boulevard could easily view the clock.

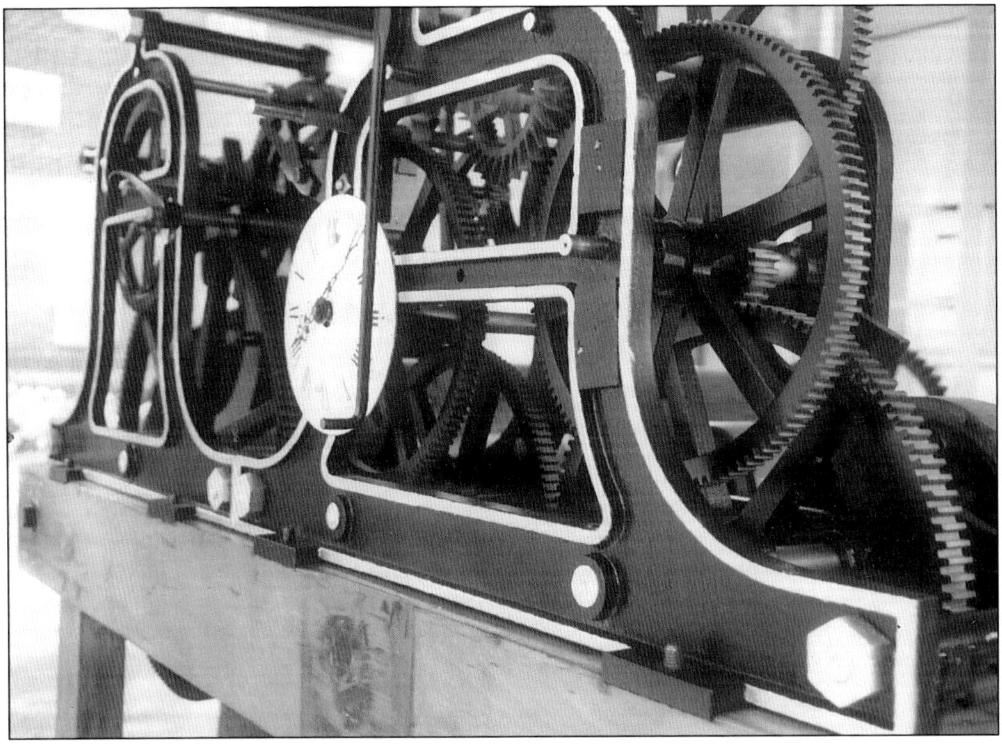

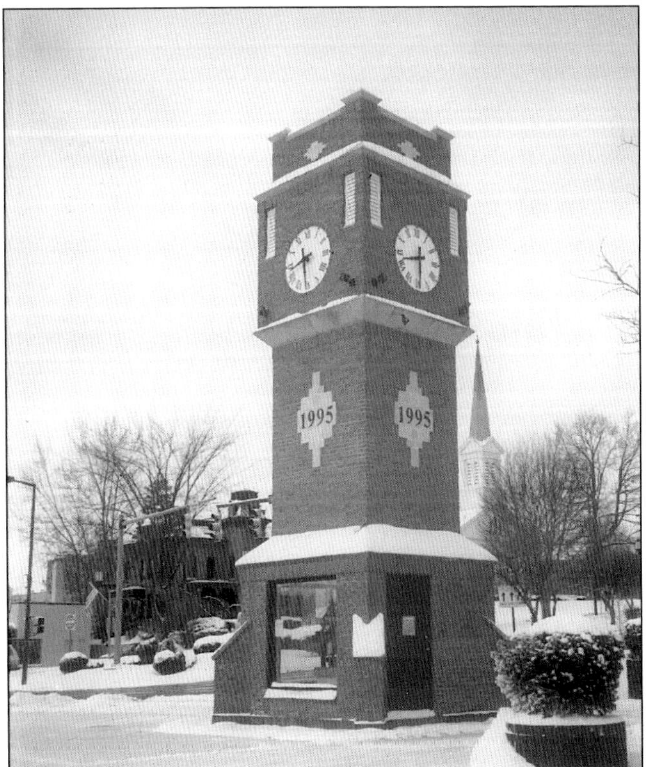

The clockworks pictured here were built in a machine shop in Cuyahoga Falls in 1865. The works were to be installed in the new city hall tower but were too large to fit. The clockworks were then donated to the Cuyahoga Falls First United Methodist Church and installed in their clock tower. In 1990 these clockworks were donated to the Cuyahoga Falls Historical Society.

This 35-foot clock tower was completed in 1995 and fitted with the refurbished clockworks from the old Methodist church. The red brick tower is located on the Riverfront Centre Mall near Broad Boulevard. The works are visible through three large street-level windows, thus bringing the past to the present.